The Book of

TIBETAN ELDERS

R I V E R H E A D

B O O K S

N E W   Y O R K

1 9 9 6

The
Book of
TIBETAN
ELDERS

LIFE STORIES AND
WISDOM FROM THE
GREAT SPIRITUAL
MASTERS OF TIBET

Sandy Johnson

RIVERHEAD BOOKS
a division of G. P. Putnam's Sons
Publishers Since 1838
200 Madison Avenue
New York, NY 10016

Library of Congress Cataloging-in-Publication Data

The book of Tibetan Elders : life stories and wisdom from
the great spiritual masters of Tibet / Sandy Johnson.
p.   cm.
ISBN 1-57322-023-X
1. Lamas—Biography.   2. Spiritual life—Buddhism.
I. Johnson, Sandy.
BQ7920.B66   1996
294.3'923'0922—dc20   96-5145 CIP
[B]

Printed in the United States of America
1   3   5   7   9   10   8   6   4   2
This book is printed on acid-free paper. ∞

BOOK DESIGN BY DEBORAH KERNER

This book is dedicated to

His Holiness the Fourteenth Dalai Lama,

and to the heroic people of Tibet.

ACKNOWLEDGMENTS

APART FROM THOSE whose words and wisdom grace these pages, I am indebted to my editor at Riverhead Books, Amy Hertz, for inviting me to take this journey; and to my friend and agent, Jill Kneerim, for encouraging me to believe I could. My thanks, too, to those who helped point the way: Nevada Wier, Lobsang Lhalungpa, Dechen Fitzhugh, and Peter and Jennifer Tadd.

I owe a special debt of gratitude and "Julley" to Bill and Adrienne Kite for their thoughtful and generous guidance in Ladakh; to Lama Rigzen for his dedicated translations; to Morup Namgyal and his family for their hospitality and advice; and to both Angdus (Big and Little) for many kindnesses. Thanks to Betty Fussell for joining me in Ladakh and for many of the splendid photographs that appear in this book. For Sogyal Rinpoche's photograph, I am indebted to Heinz Nowotny.

I wish to thank Tenzin Wandrak for his kind help in Dharamsala, and especially for introducing me to Tsering Choedon, whose excellent translations and continued assistance were invaluable. Tenzin Geyche Tethong, secretary to His Holiness the Dalai Lama, was most helpful in arranging my memorable audience with His Holiness and in suggesting elders to interview. Jampa Kelsang, of the Tibetan Institute of Medical and Astro Sciences, served as translator in those specialized fields.

I am grateful to Lee and Helen Maynard and to Margo Barr for taking on the difficult task of holding down the fort during my travel to India.

In California, a thousand thanks to Kimberley Snow for her painstaking transcriptions and editorial assistance, and to her husband, Barry Spacks, for his wise and caring suggestions. Countless teachings came with their help, as well as an enduring friendship. Both Lisa Leghorn and Chokyi, of the Chagdud Foundation, made valuable contributions; and Wangdu, a monk-student at UCLA, translated and transcribed some of the more difficult tapes.

Thanks to Adam Rodman for technical support, and to Anne for cheering me on; to Julia Adams for long walks and warm talks that kept me sane; and to Martin Wassell for his good counsel. Carol Moss led me to some precious elders, for which I am indebted; Jeff Cox, of Snow Lion Publications, offered generous factual assistance; and Nanci Ross shared valuable information with me. Warm thanks to the Paulus family for lobsters and love along the way.

Jorg Cantini was my wise and caring translator and advisor in Switzerland, and remained so throughout the writing and preparation of the book; Joanna Hess introduced me to Salome Hangartner in Zurich, who in turn kindly led me to Palmo Hafner and Jan Leiser, my hosts there. Palmo and Khando Netsang acted as guides and, when necessary, translators. I am grateful to Jaqueline Moulton for her eager interest and assistance during my stay in Switzerland.

I owe a special debt to the people at Lerab Ling in France: Patrick Gaffney, Susie Godfrey, Zanna Zuckerman, and to the staff, who made my visit so pleasant.

Many of the translations were difficult. I am grateful to Jeremy Russell, in Dharamsala, for permitting me to draw upon some of the same interviews previously published in "Cho-Yang."

And for Tashi Delek, the world's most enlightened puppy, who sits on my lap as I write this, my thanks to Bonnie Palmer, who let me have the best of her "angels."

As always, I am grateful to Mark Robinson; to Billy and Anthony Johnson for their enduring faith in me; to Bill Johnson for allowing me to put into print that which has always been in my heart; to Wendy Johnson for her unending inspiration and encouragement; and to my mother, who has grown with me during the writing of this book.

CONTENTS

FOREWORD

ALMOST ALL THE PEOPLE who tell their stories in this book were, like myself, born in Tibet. Many factors gave life in our homeland its particular character. The high altitude and harsh climate made life difficult. But on the other hand, food was plentiful and nutritious, and the water and air were clear. The soaring mountains and vast rolling plains gave people great feelings of peace and freedom. We shared this inspiring landscape with countless wild animals, who also lived freely, unafraid of human hunters. Ours was an environment that readily gave rise to contentment, with little cause for the anxiety and tension that afflict the lives of many of our more crowded neighbors.

Of course, there was more to life in Tibet than the pleasures of a beautiful landscape. Wherever we live in the world, whatever our beliefs, and whether we are rich or poor, as human beings we all want to be happy and free from misery. In Tibet, the teachings of the Buddha have been a strong and pervasive influence. From these we have learned that the key to happiness is inner peace. The greatest obstacles to inner peace are disturbing emotions such as anger and attachment, fear and suspicion, while love and compassion, a sense of universal responsibility are the sources of peace and happiness.

The Chinese invasion and occupation of Tibet has been one of the great tragedies of this century. More than a million Tibetans have died as a result. An ancient culture, with its buildings, literature, and artifacts, has been attacked and largely destroyed in its homeland, and the living holders of its traditions have been prevented there from passing them on. And yet in the face of such hardship, many of us who escaped into the freedom of exile have been able to save something. We have been able to preserve our religion and culture and reestablish our institutions. What is more, both in Tibet and in exile, our sense of Tibetan identity and our determination that our nation will be free once more are undiminished.

Throughout the last three and a half decades, much that Tibetans treasure has been lost. Nevertheless, there is a positive side even to such a disaster, for the values we hold dear have been put to the test. Even though I myself have spent more than half my life as a refugee, I feel I have personally benefited as a result.

The author refers to the people whose stories are told here as "elders," not because there is anything special about growing old, but because of the experiences they have acquired and the examples they set for those who follow. Because they are the link between old Tibet and new generations of Tibetans, they are our elders. Their accounts reveal many aspects of the traditional Tibetan way of life, both as it was practiced in Tibet and as it has been adapted to the changing circumstances.

I believe there is a great deal in Tibet's religious culture, its medical knowledge, peaceful outlook, and respectful attitude to the environment that can be of widespread benefit to others. I hope that readers of this book will find inspiration and hope in it to bring peace to their own lives, and that they also may be prompted to lend our cause their support.

HIS HOLINESS
THE DALAI LAMA

November 27, 1995

The Book of

TIBETAN ELDERS

INTRODUCTION

IN 1990 I HAD AN EXPERIENCE that to this day continues to baffle me. I'd been working on an historical biography of a Catholic missionary recently beatified for her work among the Native Americans in the late 1880s, and had come to a point where I stopped believing what I was

 writing. My resistance went beyond mere author's crisis when it burst into the visual form of a terrifying flash of light that blazed across the bedroom of my New York City apartment. Out of this strange light a face appeared. I was not to learn the reason for that incident for some time, although in the months that followed I would find the source of the apparition, the face. *How* it happened remains a mystery.

Soon afterward, I traveled to Native American reservations to speak to elders, who told me in their own words, from their own wounded hearts, the other side of the story: of the war the missionaries waged

against the native people of this country a hundred years ago. Among the elders I met was Pete Catches, holy man of the Oglala Sioux, the man I came to call Grandfather, the man whose face had appeared to me in the bedroom of my apartment.

The stories I heard so captivated my heart that they became the focus of *The Book of Elders: The Life Stories and Wisdom of Great American Indians.* By then I was living in Santa Fe, a place that attracts many people who are interested in native traditions.

In April 1991, while I was researching the elders book, the Dalai Lama came to New Mexico to meet with tribal leaders from the Hopi, Navajo, and Apache nations. His four-day visit, part of his North American tour, marked the fortieth anniversary of his nation's occupation by the People's Republic of China. The purpose of these historic meetings was to discuss religious freedom and the sovereignty rights of indigenous peoples.

Hopi spiritual leader Martin Gashweseoma had told me in an interview that if you dropped a plumb line down from Hopi through the center of the earth, it would come out at the holy city of Lhasa in Tibet. And curiously, he'd gone on, the words for sun and moon in Tibetan and Hopi are the same but reversed, and many of both peoples' chants and symbols are similar. Martin also talked about a prophecy Tibetans and Hopis share. The Hopi version, clearly a modern one, is: "When the iron bird flies, the red-robed people of the East who have lost their land will appear, and the two brothers from across the great ocean will be reunited." The Tibetan version was given by the eighth-century sage Padmasambhava, who had traveled from India to Tibet to establish Buddhism there: "When the iron eagle flies and horses run on wheels, the Tibetan people will be scattered over the earth and the *dharma* will go to the land of the red man."

Intrigued, I managed to gain an invitation to a meeting at the modern concrete gymnasium of the Santa Fe Indian School, where the Dalai

Lama would be speaking. A platform had been erected between basket-ball nets and scoreboards. A Tibetan national flag hung over the dais, and dozens of smaller prayer flags fluttered from the rafters. Students and Native American teachers filled the stands; elders and invited guests sat in front of them on folding chairs. Reporters set up their cameras and video gear along the walls, notebooks and jackets piled at their feet.

The Dalai Lama and his attendants filed in, identical in their burgundy-and-saffron monks' robes. The faces of the attendants were solemn, their arms held loosely in their robes, their sandaled feet moving silently down the aisle toward the dais, but the Dalai Lama wore an irrepressible smile. It was not that of one of the world's most venerated figures, but of a man who understood the absurdity of taking himself or his position too seriously. The smile and the laughing eyes swept over the crowd, inviting not awe but genuine, deep affection. The monks took their seats on the platform and watched a performance of a traditional dance by Native American children from Santa Clara Pueblo in full ceremonial dress. Then the young dancers presented the Dalai Lama with a teddy bear, an ear of corn (for planting when he returns to Tibet), a Navajo blanket, pottery, a bolo tie, and a bracelet. With a smile as childlike as theirs, he thanked the children. "As a monk, I do not normally wear ornaments, but today is an exception." Then, draping ceremonial white silk scarves around the necks of each of the gifters as a blessing, His Holiness presented the school with a hand-woven Tibetan rug.

In the speech that followed, the Dalai Lama, recipient of the Nobel Peace Prize in 1989 for his opposition to the use of violence as a means to free his homeland from its invaders, noted their common struggle for self-determination. He urged Native American leaders to develop long-term plans to preserve their identities and, most important, their language. "There are so many similarities between the Indian and the Tibetan peoples," the Dalai Lama said. "I believe we may have had common ancestors in prehistoric Central Asia."

The president of the Navajo Nation agreed. "What happened to us in this country is happening now in Tibet to our Tibetan brothers and sisters."

It was reported the next day that the Dalai Lama, a shawl covering his shaven head, was taken to the top of the Santa Fe Ski Basin on a chair lift. On the way up he smiled and waved to surprised skiers, and at the top he stood looking at the surrounding snowcapped peaks. According to the local paper, he said wistfully, "It reminds me of my own country."

I HAD JUST completed the final edits on my Native American manuscript when a call came from my editor. She asked if I would like to do a similar book on Tibetan elders. "But I don't know anything about Tibetan culture," I said. "What did you know about Native American culture five years ago?" said my editor.

I was flattered, but I had strong misgivings. Didn't it take a person a lifetime of study to understand the complexities of Tibetan Buddhism? Several lifetimes, in fact? How would I go about learning who the key elders are, and why would they talk to me? And since they are constantly reincarnating like perennials in a planetary garden, an elder could be four years old.

I hashed this over with my editor, who filled me with assurances that once I got started I would have no trouble. She had several ideas about the *lama*s and teachers I might speak with. They in turn would direct me to others.

From the time I had made Santa Fe my home, I was aware of the significant number of practicing Buddhists there, noticeable at first by the prayer flags that adorned so many houses. Over dinner one night with friends who were scholars of both Native American and Tibetan Buddhist traditions, I talked about how my years of exploring one culture seemed to be leading seamlessly into an exploration of the other. My friends were not surprised. They believed both traditions were rooted in the same spiritual earth and that I would find the parallels striking. They showed me photographs of their recent trips to India, Nepal, and Tibet. We marveled at the resemblances: the small stature of the people, their cheekbones, dark copper skin, and long shiny braids. Their ornaments of turquoise, coral, and silver evoked images of the Hopi and Navajo.

The next morning I found a large shopping bag on my doorstep, filled with books on Tibetan Buddhism, with a note attached: "Do it."

Fascinated, I read about a people who believe in the existence of a mystical kingdom of Shambala, a beautiful city where extraordinary beings live, cut off from the outside world by their own volition. It is a place of peace; its only weapons are bows and arrows that have the nature of exalted wisdom and are more powerful than all the destructive missiles in the outside world. Some Tibetans view Shambala as metaphor for one's own inner spiritual journey and dedicate their lives to finding it within themselves. The myth continues: As the forces outside Shambala get worse and worse, the warriors of Shambala call on their own strength, rise up against these negative forces, and defeat them. People who have taken the Kalachakra initiation—frequently given by His Holiness the Dalai Lama—are the ones who will meet again in Shambala.

I read of the devastation the Tibetans suffered at the hands of the Chinese Communists; the destruction of six thousand Buddhist monasteries; and the imprisonment of countless nuns and monks, among them many great masters. I wondered, Who will replace these teachers? If Tibet is lost, who will carry on the ancient traditions? I read the Dalai Lama's biography, *Kindness, Clarity, and Insight,* and marveled at his spiritual greatness: If a tradition could produce such an extraordinary being, it must be valuable; it must be preserved. I learned that those who survived fled to India; from there some went on to Europe, Canada, and America, where they continue to give teachings. But these might be the last people to have lived the tradition in their own sacred places, in the land where the tradition and teachings had existed for twelve hundred years. I felt then a sense of urgency to record their stories and their wisdom.

I sought the advice of scholars in New York, Washington, and California, and heard about a Tibetan elder, a much-loved and respected teacher, who lived just two miles away from me in Santa Fe. My journey, it seemed, would begin in my own backyard.

I FOUND LOBSANG LHALUNGPA in his lovely rustic house perched high on a hill just off the road that leads to the Santa Fe Ski Basin. A slight, slender man of indeterminable age—fine-featured, with brown almond-shaped eyes, buttery skin, and a captivating manner—he welcomed me with a smile whose warmth, I would learn, is universal among Tibetans, though I would never quite get used to it.

We sat in his large, airy living room, with its wide span of windows that overlooked the valley below. Books, many of them scriptures wrapped in bright yellow cloth, lined the walls. A hanging silk scroll, hand-painted and -embroidered in brilliant colors, hung next to the fireplace. A *thangka*, he explained, is a traditional Tibetan art form. The figures depicted on it represent various meditational deities.

He set a tray of tea and cookies on the table in front of us, and spoke softly and patiently in simple language my untutored ear could understand. A movement at the window caught my eye. I turned to see birds of every description lighting on the railing of his deck, drawn perhaps, as I was, to the magic of his words.

I told him I wanted to know something about the tradition that created such a peaceful people, a people who strive to attain the highest state, buddhahood, the state of perfect compassion. Where did such profound spirituality come from?

He explained:

"BUDDHISM IS NOT a religion in the sense that Christianity, Judaism, Islam, or Hinduism is. Buddhism does not subscribe to the belief in a creator and creation. Buddhism is not a philosophy, a pure intellectual criticism, or a love of knowledge. Called dharma, Buddhism is a class by itself, an alternate moral and spiritual discipline. It is a way of life—a complete process of human transformation. As such, Buddhism espouses individual responsibility and intellectual insight into life and reality. Its rational approach to overcoming existential trauma and interpersonal problems is guided by a combination of wisdom and compassion. Thus, cultivating and perfecting this wisdom and compassion make up the heart of Buddhist practice.

"Wisdom here does not mean intellectual power; that is not true wisdom. True wisdom is seeing where the problem of human misery is, what the solution is, and how we might perceive the true nature of things.

"The true nature of things is not easily perceptible to our senses. Our senses have limitations. Wisdom is the true, sensitive vision of mind that can penetrate ordinary appearances."

It would be months before I would begin to comprehend that one can actually—by means of meditation—perceive the world beyond what the senses show us and into the true nature of things. I continued to listen to his explanations, trying as best I could to absorb the meanings.

"The original dharma principles came from Buddha, who discovered them through his own compassion for suffering beings. His mission began from the moment he first saw these sufferings. You are born, you grow old every minute, then you get sick, and finally you die. This is the course of ordinary life. But there are other sufferings.

"Buddha gave up his royal position (he was a prince), left the kingdom, and wandered about as a mendicant in search of truth. What he discovered was, we don't need to look for the answer outside; it is right in our own existence."

IN THE SUMMER of 1994, I set out on a journey to a destination exactly halfway around the globe—as far as one can go without heading back—not as a mendicant, but as a journalist. I did not know if I would uncover any great truths or would come back with the knowledge that the answers to suffering do indeed lie in my own existence. In time, though, I would be led to extraordinary meetings with the men and women of Tibet, and to a glimpse of a lost world struggling to survive in each of the four corners of the earth.

As I had for my previous book, I gave careful thought to how I would define "elder." I had learned then that such a definition had less to do with age than it did with a state of attainment—of wisdom ancient and timeless; of knowledge of practices and powers held only by those who embody the teachings.

LITTLE TIBET

THOUGH SO MANY great teachers have left Tibet, I thought I had to begin there. Lobsang Lhalungpa had cautioned me not to try to get into Tibet as a writer; the Chinese would never grant me a visa. I could put "housewife" as my occupation on my application, but still I would not  be able to interview Tibetan people—even without a tape recorder—for fear of endangering them. "The Tibet I once knew," he'd said sadly, "is no more. It will never be the same. So what is Tibet really? Is it this extraordinarily beautiful piece of land, or is it the people and its culture? If it is the people, and I believe it is, then Tibet is wherever the people are."

He and others suggested that I first go to Ladakh, "Little Tibet," where many Tibetans have settled during the Chinese occupation, and which is similar to Tibet geographically and culturally. Situated high in the Himalayas on the Tibetan plateau, it is the last place where one can see something of what Tibet had been before the Chinese invaded. Almost as high as Tibet, Ladakh is reachable by a main route that is closed off by snow for nine months of the year, giving it the same "Shangri-la" mystique that Tibet once had. And, because of its strategic location on the border where India meets China and Pakistan, Ladakh had been closed to outsiders from the end of World War II until 1974. Only since 1979 have there been airline flights into Ladakh.

Buddhism came to Ladakh eight centuries before it ever reached Tibet—three hundred years before the birth of Christ—and these days, the country is probably more Tibetan than Tibet itself.

A writer friend and indefatigable world traveler, Betty Fussell, promised to join me for a time. It was decided: That summer 1994, I would begin my travels into the mysterious world of Tibetan culture and its particular form of Buddhism known as Vajrayana, literally the "quick path," by which the practitioner is reshaped through meditation and visualizion into a buddha. A symbol that is often used in Vajrayana is that of a lotus blossom, which grows out of the mud. Our mind, like the lotus, is innately pure, but this purity is obscured by poisonous emotions and habitual patterns. Our task is to rid ourselves of these defilements in order to uncover our true nature. Vajrayana abounds with methods and techniques for chipping away the mud and uncovering the crystal. The goal is to achieve not only enlightenment, but complete buddhahood. It is like imagining that we all could become Christ.

From Ladakh in northern India, I would go on to Dharamsala, the seat of the Tibetan government-in-exile, then fly to Nepal, where I might still be able to enter Tibet itself—as a tourist.

I flew from Albuquerque, where my youngest son, Anthony, lives. As we said good-bye, he handed me a notecard he'd written. It was addressed to "The JourneyMom" and carried a message of love and support, and prayers for a safe return. As we hugged, Anthony gave me a stern look and said, *"You come back."* I laughed and assured him I would. From there I flew to Los Angeles, where my middle son, Billy, lives. We spent the day shopping for last-minute gear, and after a farewell dinner he took me to the airport for my night flight. As we unloaded my bags, a lens suddenly flew out of my glasses, as if propelled by some awful force of its own, and landed at my feet. Billy looked at me in dismay. How could I possibly make this journey alone when I couldn't even leave Los Angeles in one piece?

I have three sons, all of whom are, of course, a good deal younger than I. But from the time I became single, and more important, I suppose, since my bout with breast cancer, they tend to treat me like a worrisome younger sister. Mark, the eldest, swears my gravestone ought to read, "We Think She's Here."

As I sped through the night to my destination, fragments of memories flickered like the stars that hung just off the wingtip. When I was in my teens, my grandfather used to say I was like the peregrine, the smallest and fastest bird in the upper sky, not known for its nesting skills. Reflecting on my peripatetic life, I wondered how I might have turned out if he had told me I was like the robin. Would my children be coming for Sunday dinner to the house where they had grown up, instead of seeing me off at airports and memorizing new phone numbers?

DURING THE FLIGHT, I dug into one of the several books on Tibetan Buddhism I had brought with me. The more I read, the more apparent the parallels between Native American and Tibetan cultures became. In their ceremonies, Native Americans call on ancestors in the spirit world; Tibetan Buddhists meditate on the Buddha in the form of different deities. Native Americans go to sacred places in the hills on vision quests; Tibetan holy men seal themselves off in caves to meditate. As Lobsang Lhalungpa had pointed out, both cultures revere the earth and all its creatures. The teachings—the Way, called Dharma by Buddhists—are what Native Americans refer to as the Red Road.

Back in Santa Fe, Lobsang Lhalungpa had told me:

"THERE ARE FUNDAMENTAL similarities between Tibetan Buddhist and Native American beliefs. Buddhism is intensely humane. It speaks of concern for others: community concern, and a universal concern that includes ecology.

"For instance, when the Buddha was alive, during the rainy season, he would hold the retreats for the monks inside a hut in the village, not outside, for fear of destroying the grasses and killing the insects. Even now, when monks go out into the forest, they are not supposed to break branches or pick flowers. This strong sense of respect for the natural world is shared by the American Indian.

"Both cultures are animistic: they view nature as not just a collection of trees, but a real living thing. Each tree, each body of water, each element exists as a habitat of a particular spiritual force. Thus, when you hurt a tree, you hurt not only that tree, but its spirit as well."

LOBSANG ALSO HAD mentioned the terrible similarities between the destruction of both peoples and their traditions. To this day, the Chinese are rounding up thousands of five- and six-year-olds, taking them away from their parents, and sending them to China, just as American missionaries forced native children into boarding schools in order to "Christianize" them. Tibetan children return to their families speaking Chinese and embracing Chinese mentalities.

In the process of colonizing Tibet, the Communists destroyed some six thousand monasteries and arrested and tortured nuns and monks. "If this is *karma*," Lobsang said, "it is very bad karma we are now experiencing."

I𝚃 SEEMED LIKE days after my plane took off—Did I see the sun rise twice?—that we landed in Delhi, where it was night again. I was met at the gate by a small man with a thin mustache, who bowed and introduced himself as Kushor, sent by the travel agency that had arranged my flight to Ladakh. I wondered how he managed to pick me out of the crowd, since all the faxes I'd been receiving from the travel agency were addressed to "Mr. Sandy." Kushor's instructions were to collect me and my luggage and take me in a chauffeur-driven car to a hotel an hour's ride from the airport.

I glanced up at the clock as I registered. "What time's my flight to Ladakh?" I asked Kushor.

"You must check in at the airport at six, madam," he said pleasantly.

I looked at him. "Six in the morning?"

"Yes, madam."

"Four hours from now?"

"Yes, madam. I will call for you at five." He bowed. "Have a good rest."

I had just enough time to shower, change clothes, and lie on the bed before the wake-up call that might or might not come. I thought back to another trip I had taken to the Far East. I was with friends; we were on vacation; we sat in first class and drank champagne and ate caviar sandwiches. I flirted with the captain. A Rolls Royce met us at the airport in Hong Kong and whisked us off to the Peninsula Hotel. As the red eye of the clock blinked the minutes, I wondered if it were possible to have all one's reincarnations in one lifetime. I was certainly living a different kind of life now. The money I save on a coach seat goes toward survival on the road.

FLYING FROM DELHI to Ladakh requires an act of surrender of all preconceived notions about travel. A ticket on India Airlines (otherwise known as Air Chance) does not guarantee a seat. Nor is it guaranteed there even will be a flight. (There are only three flights a week into Ladakh.) Taking just a short hop, only thirty minutes, the plane flies directly over the Himalayas and lands on a small airfield on a plateau that is one of the highest in the world. Since landings and takeoffs can be made in only one direction on the single runway, which runs steeply uphill, if the wind happens to be blowing the wrong way that day or if the airfield suddenly clouds over, the flight must be canceled.

So the bewildered traveler sits on the hard wooden benches of the windowless Delhi Airport waiting room in a jet-lagged stupor, no longer able to determine if the clock on the wall that reads eleven o'clock means A.M. or P.M. It was crowded; the air was stale. Babies swaddled in the folds of mothers' saris wailed. People dozed fitfully, heads draped over backs of benches, legs sprawled into narrow aisles. Periodically, the loudspeaker crackled unintelligible announcements.

Once or twice I approached the ticket counter to ask about the flight to Ladakh, and was met with the yes-no-I-don't-know gesture of the head accompanied by a helpless shrug of the shoulder that put an end to further questions.

A lovely Hindu woman wearing a sari the color of lime sherbet sat opposite me, a squirming infant in her arms. I smiled at the baby; the woman smiled back. "It's a girl, but they let me keep her anyway." My mouth went dry. I dared not ask.

Finally, a young British couple arrived and sat on the bench next to me. They had made this flight before and knew the ropes. Our flight was called at last, and we lined up for a final security check. Because Ladakh is a sensitive border area, my English friends explained, security is tight. Batteries were removed from flashlights, cameras, and computers and tagged for pickup at the other end. Checked-in baggage had to be identified outside on the tarmac prior to boarding or it wouldn't be loaded onto the plane.

The aircraft was a small old Boeing 737. I was lucky to get a window seat for what I had been told is the most spectacular flight in the world. It was my first view of the Himalayas. I stared, breathless, as we skimmed the jagged, dazzling white peaks of Nun and Kum that tore through the clouds and reached 23,300 feet. To the north was K2 (Mt. Godwin Austin), the second highest mountain in the world. I looked down as we began our approach to the Indus Valley below, and realized why so few pilots are qualified (or willing) to sign on for this particular flight. Sandwiched between two mountains and heading straight for a monastery, the plane banked sharply to the left and miraculously landed.

The first thing I noticed as I walked to the terminal was the light. The air is thin at that altitude, and the light so evanescent that objects seemed to shimmer. I looked up at the mountain we had just flown over. The peak had disappeared inside a cloud.

NO ONE WAS THERE to meet me. Taxi drivers asked me where I was going. I gave the name of my hotel, Hotel Stok. Frowning, they shook their heads. Frantically, I searched my bag to produce a letter with the hotel's name on it. My English friends had long disappeared, along with every other passenger on the flight. I was alone at the airport. Finally, I found the letter and showed it to the one remaining driver.

"Oh, *Stok*."

"But that's what I've been telling you, Stock."

"No, no," he said. "Not 'Stahk.' '*Stök*.' "

The small rural village where the hotel stands is fifteen miles from the town of Leh, past meadows of dizzying green and golden pastures of wheat and barley. During the journey, I leaned forward in my seat and asked the driver if they had had a lot of rain. The driver looked up at the sky and said, "No, I don't think so. It looks nice." I sat back in my seat. We came to a bridge strung with hundreds of prayer flags, which crossed a fast-flowing river. "What river is this?" I asked. "This is the Indus River." The Indus, I'd read, originates near the holy site of Mt. Kailash in Tibet and is responsible for nourishing these pastures and turning them this color that hardly seems possible on earth.

Whitewashed stucco farmhouses trimmed in bright red dotted the countryside, each with yards bordered by stone walls. I was excited by what I thought was a yak and pointed it out to the driver. He shook his head. "Not yak, dzo. Half yak, half cow." A little farther on he pointed to a massive animal with longer hair, a smaller version of the American buffalo, and said, "There is yak." The buffalo of old provided the Native American tribes with all their needs; the yak is similarly used: the milk and flesh for butter and meat; the hair for ropes, tents, and jewelry; the hide for boots and baskets; the horns for agricultural tools; and the dung for fuel. Both animals are themselves fully stocked supermarkets.

A herd of multicolored long-haired goats meandering unattended down the road brought us to a halt. The driver pounded his horn, leaned out of the window, and yelled at them, then nudged them with his bumper until they skipped out of the way.

Finally, we turned into the hotel driveway. The Hotel Stok is a larger version of the same architecture I had been seeing. Two boys rushed out to take my luggage; I followed them past a garden in brilliant bloom. Inside I found no lobby or reception desk, only a darkened hallway and a wooden staircase. My luggage was stacked against the wall, but the boys had gone. I stood looking at the closed doors, feeling what it means to be a stranger in a very strange land. When a tall, athletic-looking man with a blond ponytail appeared, smiling, holding out his hand, I wanted to cry with relief. "Tell me you're Bill Kite; you have to be Bill Kite."

He apologized for not meeting me. When the flight hadn't arrived in the morning, he explained, he was sure it had been canceled. He led me up the stairs to my large corner room. "You probably ought to take a nap," he said. "You'll need to get used to the altitude." Later, a knock at the door announcing dinner failed to rouse me, and I slept till the next morning.

AFTER BREAKFAST I set out for a walk. I passed a farmer herding his sheep, stick in one hand, prayer wheel in the other, which he spun 'round and 'round as he moved his lips in steady recitation of *mantras*. He wore the traditional Ladakhi thick brown woolen robe tied at the waist with a bright-colored sash. His broad smile creased his weathered, nut-brown face, and he cried, "Julley!"—a greeting that means Hello, Welcome, Blessings and is called out morning and evening like a song.

Bordering the road was a long *mani* wall, piled up stone by stone by those who wished to earn merit. Carved on many of the stones is "Om mani padme hum" ("Praise to the jewel in the lotus," the mantra of Tibet's patron saint, Chenrezig, the Buddha of Great Compassion). A garden with marigolds taller than I and sunflowers the size of a small tree astonished me. An oversized magpie, its tail streaming behind, landed on the stone wall and called loudly, fanning its green-black wings. I felt as if I were dreaming, walking through some otherworldly place where the stones and flowers and birds are symbols whose meanings are yet to be revealed to me, and where the air is so sweet I think it must be blessed by the prayers carried on the wind by prayer flags. They were everywhere, on every house, flying from rocks high on the mountainsides, faded and ragged and enduring.

IN THE AFTERNOON, Bill and his wife, Adrienne, took me into the town of Leh. We were driven by Little Angdu, nephew of the owner of the hotel. The uncle's name, Bill told me, is Sitting Angdu. "Sitting, as in Sitting Bull?" I asked. "No." He spelled it out: "T-s-e-r-i-n-g." I shook my head. We passed a golf course that is part of the military base. I noticed a sign near the eighth hole that reads, "Warning, Mine. Dangerous explosive," and I grabbed for my camera. My golfing sons had to see this. But Bill stopped me. "This is a sensitive military installation," he explained. "They'd take your camera if they caught you."

Leh has an ugly sort of charm, its one main street clogged with buses and trucks spewing noxious black fumes, all competing with cars and cows for right-of-way. Women sit on curbs, their fruits and vegetables laid out beside them on a dirty cloth, wilting in the fierce sun. Off the main drag run alleyways, warrens crowded with shops selling cheap sweaters, trinkets, backpacks, bottled water, cigarettes, batteries, alarm clocks.

Bill wanted me to meet Lama Rigzen, a Ladakhi monk working on his doctorate who, because he speaks English, Bill felt would be an excellent translator for my interviews. We walked down a narrow path just outside of town to a three-story house, where several monks live. Lama Rigzen, dark, curly haired, red-robed, a man in his thirties, offered to act as both guide and emissary for me. Next, back in town, we navigated the back alleys to the home of Morup Namgyal, composer and manager of All India Radio Station. Morup, gentle, soft-spoken, also offered his assistance locating and choosing elders to interview.

THAT EVENING WE were invited to Tsering Angdu's home to meet the royal family, friends of Angdu's wealthy father. At dusk, Bill, Adrienne, and I set out on foot to a house nestled in the park I had admired the day before on my morning walk. The house was large and seemed rich compared with the neighboring farmhouses. We removed our shoes and followed our host to a large parlor, where the queen of Ladakh, the queen mother, and the young king were seated. We were presented to each in turn (I had already been instructed how to bow, hands together). When I got to the king, a twenty-eight-year-old preppy who resembled my sons, he immediately stood and shook my hand, Western style.

Butter tea, a concoction of tea, yak butter, salt, and soda, was served in lovely china cups with lids. Bill stopped me as I raised the cup to my lips, and showed me the Tibetan custom of dipping one's finger in the tea first and flicking drops three times, as an offering to the deities.

The tea is a staple in Tibet and Ladakh, drunk morning, noon, and night by both old and young. As soon as I took a few sips, a young girl immediately refilled my cup, and continued to refill it each time I set it down on the table. "It's impolite to refuse," Bill whispered. "One drinks until the teapot is empty."

Jigmet, the young king, spoke perfect English with only a trace of an accent, while his mother and his grandmother sat silently, clearly not understanding a word of our conversation, content to observe in a manner that reminded me that this is a patriarchal society.

We took a shortcut through a field on our way home. Dusk, the grass silvery green and soft underfoot . . . Above us the sky turned mauve, a few orangey clouds catching the last of the sun's rays. Bill told me the royal family were dethroned in 1834, and although they are now only figureheads, they are still loved by the people. I could not imagine this place without its preppy king and shy queen mother.

SPACEMEN AND
CAVE DWELLERS

THERE WAS A FESTIVAL at the monastery in Phyang, a small hamlet twenty miles from Leh, which His Eminence Lama Duwang Rinpoche, a great master from the Drikung Kagyu lineage, would attend. Lama Rigzen told me that the old lama is a man of extraordinary powers.

 His name is Konchok Norbu; *Duwang* means Great Yogi (Meditator).

Lama Duwang came to India in 1992. Before that, he had been sealed off in a cave, meditating for fourteen years, his only sustenance a cup of water a day and a small amount of *tsampa* (ground and roasted barley). He remained in his mountainside cave all during the Chinese occupation and the Dalai Lama's exodus to India.

Lama Rigzen would meet me at the festival. He couldn't promise an introduction, but he'd do his best. Little Angdu picked me up just after a

Lama Duwang Rinpoche

breakfast of eggs, rice, potatoes, and dhal. I wondered if it was the altitude that made the yolks of the eggs white, but no one I asked seemed to know.

I dragged my mind away from the white-egg-yolk problem and pondered the sort of person who sits in a cave for fourteen years. What kind of powers would he emerge with? Did he discover the same keys to human suffering the Buddha saw? And what were those answers?

Lama Rigzen had told me that after the first eleven years, the *rinpoche* (precious teacher, or person of refuge) developed severe problems with his legs and his eyes. He got word to his master, Pachung Rinpoche, and said he feared he needed medical care. His master sent word back promising to say prayers for him, and added that if Lama Duwang's practices were strong enough, his ailments would disappear. Duwang Rinpoche stayed and continued his practice, and the promise proved true. When he finished his refuge, he went to a place in northern India to teach. In this place was a *stupa* with a very old, broken prayer wheel that no one had been able to use for years. As soon as Rinpoche arrived, the prayer wheel suddenly began to work again, considered a blessing. The old lama travels all over India, Lama Rigzen had explained, never settling in any one place.

A MILE OUT OF STOK, we passed another military base, a reminder of the political fragility of this peaceful country. Then suddenly we were in the middle of an immense lunarlike landscape of dry parched earth and sand dunes that stretched as far as the eye could see. But for the towering Himalayas I might have been in the middle of the Sahara or, for that matter, New Mexico. An occasional cluster of small, brave, purple desert flowers defied the sand; overhead was the cloudless, impossibly blue sky.

We turned onto another dirt road that led past a series of *chortens* to the monastery. Built in the sixteenth century, the multitiered white-washed complex sits high on a hilltop of blue slate and resembles a medieval palace. We climbed endless flights of steep concrete steps to the main prayer hall, where we were greeted by two young monks. Then, removing our shoes, we entered the darkened hall, so dark that for a moment I could see only the huge gold Buddha statue glowing in the flickering light of votive candles. At the far end of the hall were more enormous gold-painted Buddha statues behind a glass, standing and sitting, surrounded by candles and vessels of yak butter and water.

On another wall hundreds of small statues of deities rested in orderly rows on wooden shelves. Ancient wall paintings of the wrathful and peaceful deities were in remarkably good condition, as was the collection of thangkas displayed only on festival days.

We climbed more steps to another smaller chapel with more wall paintings of the five Dhiyana Buddhas—representing the five branches of buddha-nature—and statues of the wrathful four-armed Mahakala, one of the major protectors, in its many manifestations. On entering each of the chapels we removed our shoes and remembered to walk clockwise around the altars. Offerings of a few rupees were gratefully accepted, to be used for the upkeep of the monastery.

Down on the festival grounds, crowds of villagers in full ceremonial dress and dozens of tourists with cameras and camcorders waited for the Duwang Rinpoche. The air shimmered with excitement. Children jostled one another to stand in front of cameras, and smiled eagerly. Adults too were pleased to be photographed. I searched the sea of burgundy-robed monks for Lama Rigzen and spotted him talking and laughing in the middle of a group of Europeans. Everyone seemed to know him, monks and villagers alike. He jumped over a stone wall to greet me, making me laugh. "You see, I'm a monkey-monk!"

He took me to the visitors' section, which had a good view of the throne from which His Eminence would observe the dancing. The area was carpeted with a large Tibetan rug and shaded by a yellow-and-red canopy. I took my place and sat cross-legged behind a long, low table. The visitors were mainly well-to-do European travelers, but also a number of hippies turned up, frozen in time from the sixties, in sandals, amulets at their necks. Village women wore elaborate turquoise-studded winged hats, *peraks*, perched precariously atop long rich braids joined at the ends midway down their backs. Their ankle-length dresses were heavily brocaded and worn under a vest of contrasting color, with several strands of turquoise and coral beads. They served us butter tea from exquisite copper and brass teapots, and tsampa.

Finally, horns sounded and His Eminence Lama Duwang Rinpoche appeared in the distance, leading a procession of chanting monks. Their path was lined with villagers and visitors who strained for a look. Tourists darted back and forth with their cameras to find good vantage points. The large ancient-looking man approached in a heavy, wobbly walk, his great girth enfolded in yards and yards of burgundy and saffron. On his head was what I assumed to be a rather unusual sort of hat, shaped like a beehive and the color of his woolly gray hair. He was escorted to his throne of brilliant patterned cushions, and sat protected from the now blazing sun by a canopy, under which another beautiful Tibetan carpet had been laid.

The dancing began as soon as His Eminence was seated. The dancers moved slowly, trancelike, to the beat of a hundred drums. Lama Rigzen came to get me. "Hurry," he said, handing me a carefully folded white silk scarf. "He will see you now."

"What do I do?" I asked, realizing I did not know the protocol.

"Take off your hat," he whispered as we drew near. Lama Rigzen prostrated himself to the old lama, then presented me. I bent low, offering the white *katak*, which the rinpoche took and placed around my neck. He smiled a broad, toothless smile and took my face in his hands. Then he motioned me to sit on one of the cushions at his feet, and listened, nodding, as Lama Rigzen explained my mission. I stared, fascinated, at the long wiry strands of chin whiskers that hung to the middle of his chest and at the hat, which I suddenly realized was not a hat at all; it was his hair, wound loosely on the top of his head and wrapped with a leather thong. Certain holy men, Lama Rigzin later explained, do not cut their hair. Lama Duwang agreed to an interview later in the afternoon, after the archery contest.

RINPOCHE SAT, LEGS tucked beneath his robe, on a bed draped with brightly patterned fabric, sipping tea. Behind him hung a gold-painted silk-and-brocade thangka. Once again Lama Rigzen prostrated himself, and the rinpoche motioned for me to sit. He watched with interest as I, somewhat nervously, set up the tape recorder and tiny microphone on the table in front of him. I had written out my questions in my spiral notebook. Smiling at him, pen in hand, I prepared to begin the interview.

But the rinpoche, through Lama Rigzen, took the lead, asking me where I come from.

"America."

"I heard an American traveled to the moon. Is that true?"

"Yes." I was thinking that the rinpoche must have been quite surprised to learn that a man had been to the moon and back while he was sealed inside a cave in Tibet.

"What was his name?"

"Neil Armstrong," I said, amused. I started to ask my question. He interrupted me.

"What does it look like?"

"The moon?"

"Yes."

I pointed out the window to the moonscape outside. "Like that."

"Ooh." He nodded his head. "And how big is it?"

Was I really having this conversation? How big *is* the moon? "Well, not as big as the Earth," I said, hoping that would do.

"You Americans are very powerful. They tell me your president was in China recently."

"Yes." There had been a summit meeting earlier that spring in China.

"And will your president do something to help us get our country back from the Chinese?"

I had heard that the issue of human rights had come up at the meeting but was shelved, lost in the conversations concerning trade agreements. Hard put to try to explain that to a holy man and feeling ashamed for my country, I told him I didn't know but that I sincerely hoped something would be done.

I got halfway through my first question when the rinpoche, peering at me from under grizzly eyebrows, asked, "What do you understand about the philosophy of Buddhism?"

I looked at him. Remembering what I'd been reading, I answered, "I understand that it is based on compassion and love. And on living a good life, so one can have a good death and be born again into a good life."

"And how do you identify love?"

Oh no, a trick question. "A feeling from the heart for all other people and all animals and birds and insects. And a desire to protect them and treat them with kindness and compassion."

"Very right," he said, nodding his head. "Whom did you learn this love and compassion from?"

Feeling a sense of confidence that I was getting the answers right, I began to tell him about the Native Americans in our country who share a similar philosophy, and about the holy man who taught me and made me his granddaughter.

"So they are not Buddhist?"

"No, they are not Buddhist."

His eyes were so penetrating, I felt as if I was beginning to fade under the force of his gaze, like a photograph left out in the sun.

"How do you define compassion?"

"Compassion is caring for all other people without judging them, and accepting them unconditionally," I answered miserably, knowing these were only words.

"Okay, if you know very clearly love and compassion, what more do you need to add to this?"

"Wisdom, I suppose." He saw into the very depths of my ignorance.

"So, whatever I want to say to you about wisdom and compassion and love, this you already know. So I have nothing more to tell you."

I looked to Lama Rigzen, who sat silently watching me. No clue from him. I had passed the test but flunked the interview. The rinpoche's eyes were closed, but his lips were moving, reciting mantras. After a moment I began to gather my things.

"What else did you want to know?" he asked just as I reached the door.

Words came tumbling out, ringing with frustration. "I need to understand how to get to that." I was surprised by the intensity of my reaction. What was this sudden leap from objective journalist to spiritual seeker? How did I go from interviewer to subject? "I think I understand these concepts, but I'm not clear how to take the steps to get there. I don't know how to become compassionate and loving and wise—"

He raised his hand to silence me. "Then sit down."

I took my place on the cushion on the floor and looked up at him, embarrassed by my outburst. But in his eyes, which rested softly on me, I thought I saw the tiniest flicker of amusement.

"Now we are in *samsara,* in this world, in this wheel of life. So what is the main cause of rebirth in this wheel of life?" He was not finished with me after all.

"To learn what we didn't learn in the last life?"

"Yes. In this life, sometimes we find happiness, and this is a result of the positive things we have done in previous lives, when we have done very good things in another life. If we have unhappiness in this life, it is the result of negative things—bad deeds, bad thoughts—that we've done before.

"The main cause of being born into this wheel of life is desire and attachment. We must avert all the desire and attachment. With attachment, we think: This is my mother; This is my father; These are my children; This is my property; This is my country; This is—" he pointed to the tape recorder—"my recording machine. All of this comes from attachment. Me, my, I. This 'I' is everywhere. But when we go to analyze this *I*, when you remove, one by one, our outer body—the hair, the eyes, the arms—do any of these contain the *I*? No. You analyze each part and find there is only emptiness."

For some reason I chose that moment to take his picture.

"What is that?" he asked sharply.

"This? This is my camera," I answered, wondering if I should have asked his permission first.

The rinpoche threw his head back and laughed, a huge rumbling laugh that shook his entire body. Lama Rigzen joined in. I looked from one to the other, bewildered. Rinpoche pointed to the camera again, about to say something, but was overcome with another fit of laughter. Tears streamed from his eyes. He dabbed at them with a corner of his robe, then blew his nose. With each wave of laughter, Lama Rigzen was equally stricken, and the two began anew. Finally Lama Rigzen explained.

"Rinpoche is laughing because you called it *your* camera."

I looked at him blankly.

"Just as he is speaking about attachments. I, me, my. Don't you see?" And a fresh round of laughter set in.

"Because he is saying that attachment is the main cause of rebirth in samsara. He says we may think that we know about compassion and love and desire and attachment, but this is not enough, it has to become part of our lives on a practical level. We know everything from books, not empirically. There are so many books. It has all been written about. These things have to be practiced. You just happened to illustrate that at the perfect moment."

The rinpoche had regained his composure. "So according to Buddhism," he explained, "we don't just accept that we know compassion and love and not act on it. We must activate all the compassion and love in our minds. And how can we know compassion and love in the activity of our minds? Say another person has a lot of problems. We must think: 'All of his problems I will take; I have some happiness, so I will give my happiness to him; I can take his problems to myself.' We must think like this. This is the application for our mind.

"Buddhism is difficult; it is a very deep philosophy. But if people strive to perfect their practice, then they will get it. It is very useful not just for us, but for all human beings. It will bring benefit for all sentient beings, but it is very difficult to uphold this compassion and this love."

Moments passed in silence. Rinpoche addressed Lama Rigzen, who said to me, "Rinpoche wants to know what you're thinking about so hard."

I knew I was receiving a teaching of greater magnitude than I could comprehend; I found it dizzying. "I might wish for enlightenment, but I wonder if I would have the courage."

The rinpoche said:

"WHEN YOU SEE a person who is, as you say, enlightened, and you wish you would be able to attain these qualities, it is very important that you put this wish into action. Everything is practice. It is not enough just to think or to wish, we must put it into practice from now on. It will get very, very difficult. Many obstacles arise in our minds. When we run into these obstacles, we begin to doubt. We think to ourselves: I'm having more difficulties, more obstacles; Why should I do this?; Should I leave this path and find another? So many doubts and difficulties come into our mind.

"At that time, we must forget everything that we think is true in samsara, in this cyclic existence—things like, my country, my this or that. We must forget clinging. And just practice the dharma. Then you will begin to achieve something."

"I guess my biggest obstacle is fear," I said.

"Do you know what those fears are?"

"Fear of giving up what I have, of being sick, of being poor, of being alone."

"So what you are actually asking is, How can someone who is just beginning on the path remove such fears from her own mind? Regarding the fears and the problems that we encounter in life—and who doesn't encounter those, they are part of living—we need to develop a strong renunciation for the ordinary cycle of existence as we experience it. The word renunciation here means, literally, a certainty that arises in your mind that you want to be, and will become, free of that cycle. So it is not renunciation in a pessimistic sense, so much as recognizing the shortcomings of where we are and the certainty that we want to, and will, rise beyond that, be freed or released from that. That's what I mean by renunciation."

He leaned forward, looked at me with piercing eyes, and waited for an indication from me that I was following him. I realized that Lama Rigzen was trying very hard to translate word for word what the rinpoche was saying, without any interpretation of his own. I nodded, and Rinpoche continued.

"Further, we must turn our backs on our grasping or fixation on cyclic existence, on the things of cyclic existence, and on our ordinary state of being. When fears and problems arise, the worst, the most problematic thing we do is to become attached to the fear that is arising. This is what gives clinging its power: We have this sense that something really there causes us fear, causes us a problem; we invest the existence of events, things, and emotions with solidity. And because we cling to that notion, we fuel our own love-hatred of being either very attached or very averse to something. We are constantly pushed or pulled.

"Overcoming this grasping is not something that is easy for beginning practitioners. For someone who has reached a very advanced level, it is more straightforward, but still it often requires years or even eons of practice to get to the point where they stand above all of that. For the average unenlightened being, it is very difficult to move beyond grasping, the fundamental factor that gives rise to fear and problems in the first place."

This below-average, very unenlightened being wondered what kind of practice he was talking about. Lifetimes? Eons?

"Without such extensive practice, then, it is difficult in the short term to deal with fear in any effective way. It is not something that you're going to be able to figure out immediately. We begin by contemplating this cycle of ordinary existence that we are caught in at this point. We develop a sense of disenchantment, even disgust, a kind of revulsion at cyclic existence, that it no longer fascinates us, that we have a certainty we are going to be released from it, that we have the intention of being liberated from this, that we view this cycle of existence as we would a fiery pit into which we have fallen."

I felt turned upside down. Part of me did not understand a word; yet, strangely, there was another part of me that caught a glimpse now and then, like the quick reflection of the sun on the wing of a bird as it soars off.

"It is useful to regard cyclic existence as this fiery pit, a stinking swamp, as a land inhabited by cannibal demons who are threatening us at all sides. As long as we think that samsara is nice, samsara is sweet, samsara is delicious, samsara is fine, we are not going to be released. And as long as we have the attitude that samsara is sufficient or satisfactory in itself, we will never be liberated from it. We have to have that dissatisfaction and disenchantment."

"Are you saying it is *life* we want to be liberated from? I thought Buddhists believe human life is precious."

He turned to the window. Sunlight etched the myriad lines deeper in his face and caught the pewter of his hair.

"The principal means by which we put our renunciation and disenchantment with cyclic existence into practice is to meditate on impermanence, again and again, until our awareness of impermanence is ingrained in us, so that we are, as a matter of course, aware of impermanence in meditation, regarding everything that has gone before, everything that is happening now, from the point of view of how everything is subject to impermanence and change.

"Another important factor is to cultivate a 'noble attitude,' that is, an attitude of lovingkindness and compassion toward others. Again, this is something that for you as a beginner will not come easy. You won't be able to develop love and compassion just off the bat, so to speak, just because you want to. But you need to cultivate it, and this comes about through developing an altruistic approach, one of really taking the welfare of others into account."

I was not sure if he had answered my question, but he was already on to another subject. It occurred to me that perhaps this master was giving me the information I needed rather than the information I thought I wanted.

"You begin by appreciating that there is not any being that has not been your mother or father in some lifetime, that all beings are alike—from beginningless time, in the cycle of existence, through countless lifetimes. This applies to beings throughout the six classes or six states of conditioned existence, not just humans, but all of these beings—all of us—have been one another's parents.

"Understanding this, that there is no distinction that we can make between one being or another, is very valuable. It would benefit you to have this understanding.

"While there are more abstract, elaborate techniques or processes of contemplation that traditionally are explained, for now, just try to focus on love and compassion and not become too caught up in the details. First, we appreciate what our parents in this lifetime have done for us, and contemplate the basic kindness that we have received from them. Then we extend that kindness to all beings. Thus, it is through an understanding of the role that our parents have played in this life that we gain an understanding of our connection to other beings."

He closed his eyes and began moving his lips. After several moments he looked at me, smiled, and said, "That's it."

I got more than I had bargained for. Renunciation, the nonexistence of the self, eons of practice, the idea of every being having once been our parents . . . Are bad parents anathema to Tibetans?

ON THE WAY back to Stok, I looked out the window at the lunar landscape and suddenly wondered: The old lama showed no interest in *how* an American got to the moon. Was it because he already knows? I remembered reading somewhere that in Shambala they've been going to the moon for twelve hundred years.

THE MOUNTAIN

I WOKE THE NEXT MORNING, quaking with cold. I tugged at the thin blanket and tried to curl myself into it, but I could not get warm. My throat felt raw, and my head throbbed. The previous night's intense dream lingered. I had been reading by candlelight—power in Stok is out more of-

ten than not—and my eyes had soon tired. But then I lay awake, my mind a maelstrom, swirling with questions that only led to more imponderable questions.

I kept seeing the image of the old lama sitting cross-legged, laughing, rocking back and forth on his stack of cushions like a giant red buoy in a stormy sea. His laughter followed me into a dream, except that in the dream it was me he was laughing at. "Where is your 'I'?" he taunted, pointing to my head. "There?"—my arms; "There?"—my feet. "Not there." His laughter echoed, filling my head with a terrible roar. I felt myself recede and grow smaller as his face, disembodied now, grew larger. The toothless mouth widened, came closer and closer, as if to devour me. I knew it would be useless to scream; there was no one to hear me. Drenched with perspiration, my skin burned cold, like dry ice.

It was the kind of dream I have if I am feverish. I realized I did have a flu of some sort. When Kansa, the cook, knocked at the door, I asked for a thermos of hot water and more blankets. Neither Kansa nor Jai, the houseboy, spoke more than kitchen English. Bill and Adrienne Kite had left for Khatmandu; I was alone in a hotel, twenty miles from town, with no phone—and no one to call if I had one.

I fumbled in my toilet kit for a thermometer and took my temperature: It read 103°. I drifted in and out of a terrible sleep, dreaming scenes from my life. People appeared, characters in a play, and spoke out.

WHEN I HAD MARRIED my second husband, Bill, his daughters were ten, eight, and four. We spent weekends, holidays, and summers with them, and became extremely close. As Bill was more than a decade older than I, the girls were younger sisters as much as stepdaughters. Wendy, the eldest, to whom I was "Wick" (for Wicked Stepmother), became a Buddhist and made her home at Green Gulch Zen Center in northern California.

Two years before my trip to India, Bill, who was now my second ex-husband, had a heart attack and a bypass operation. Then, just before I left for India, my sons told me their father was ending a marriage that had been troubled from the first. I had never fully forgiven myself for breaking up the family; worse, I had gone on to make two more hasty marriages that mystified friends and distressed my parents.

Still, Bill and I had remained close through those years and somehow managed to sustain an outline, albeit blurred, of a family. We had developed a philosophy, values, soil in which to grow our sons and his daughters, which lasted until he married a woman who resented the children and insisted on shutting them out, and communication between us ended.

Wendy appeared onstage in my dream and, in an un-buddhalike way, accused me: "It's because of you that Dad is stuck in an awful marriage that never should have been. And it's because of you he had the heart attack. You broke his heart, you know. Why? Why did you have to do it?"

I searched for an answer, but I could not account for the person I was then. I wanted to tell her that, but she disappeared, and my closest friend, Gerry, whose young life was stolen by cancer years ago, stood in her place. She shook her head at me. "You can't keep wreaking havoc in everyone's lives you touch. Things cost, you know. Actions cost."

I woke from this dream sobbing, my heart pounding. I turned to look at the window. The mountain was so near I could almost reach out and touch it. I stared until shapes began to form in the light and shadows and became faces. I saw Pete Catches, whom I loved and revered. He had died six months before, leaving me desolate. I saw his face, with its arched nose and sweeping forehead, distinctly carved in the mountain. I could make out the hollows underneath the cheekbones, and the crevices around the mouth. Over and over I called his name, then finally I drifted off again.

I saw my mother. She looked at me with the same expression I remembered from my brother's funeral. I had just given the eulogy. From the dais where I had stood, I saw her sitting there in the front row, looking at me with angry blue eyes that told me she had lost the wrong child. I confronted her now; I asked her if that were true. Without answering, she turned from me and walked away.

Scenes and faces continued to parade through my dreams. Awake, I saw that the faces were still there in the mountain, changing with the shifting shadows as daylight faded to dusk. Friends lost, friends dead, friends betrayed in moments of rash selfishness. I had descended into one of the Buddhist hells I had read about. If this was not my death, only how my death will be, then I prayed it would be quickly finished with me.

THE FEVER AND its demons raged on for two more days. Then, on the third night, I suddenly remembered the antibiotics I had brought. Why hadn't I thought of them earlier, or of the sleeping pills right there in my case? I took them and fell into a heavy, dreamless sleep that lasted until late the next morning. Then, cautiously, I stood up, went to the window, and opened it wide. The mountain shone bright and innocent, dazzling in the morning sun. At the peak, snowy clouds encircled it: a white silk offering scarf.

A LIFE OF LUXURY

It was only two days since my demons had come to visit. My recovery was quick after I had taken the antibiotics. Too quick, I thought, for the medication to have had an effect on the supposed flu. I was convinced that whatever illness I'd had was at least partly psychic, a purification, an ego cleansing.

 My friend Betty was due to arrive that morning; I got up early to meet her at the airport. Tsering Angdu materialized again and wanted to come along. I anticipated Betty's arrival with relief, realizing how very alone I had been feeling. I had thought I would approach Buddhism as a journalist, with a journalist's objectivity; instead my whole system of thinking was under attack, and I was eager to talk about it.

The flight was of course delayed, but when it finally arrived, Betty got off the plane in great good humor and we greeted each other like schoolgirls. Hardy soul that she is, she needed only a short rest and time to unpack. Then we sat in my room and had a beer and talked.

I recalled what Lobsang Lhalungpa had said about the self before I left Santa Fe:

"WE BEGIN LIFE with a strong sense of selfishness, a selfishness that comes from ignorance. Ignorance is not being able to understand the true nature of one's own life, one's own mind, reality. Therefore, we create this central kind of entity called self.

"This central self is so very precious to each person that it becomes the center of one's world. 'Everything else is different from me and connected to me. Therefore I must exist. I am concerned only with that which improves my security, my well-being, to the exclusion of the rest of humanity.'

"The answer, then, is very clear at that point: Work with your own inner conditionings. Find out where you went wrong. You might not even remember so clearly. But still you carry the impact of your ignorance, and you make a lot of mistakes. You perceive things in a distorted way because your fundamental notion is that you are an exclusive entity. You can look at connection in many different ways: physically, mentally, spiritually, environmentally. There is a very strong interconnection. Recognize that the way we look at it, things seem to be very real; we look and say, Okay, what I see is real. But is it *really* real, what you see? What you see over there is only image; it's real for you, for your mind. But we lose sight of the true nature of things. We don't look at things as they are, but as we perceive them to be, as we assume them to be. Buddha said, let's clear this root of ignorance and tackle the problem of selfishness. Open up your own closed world and understand the connection. Then you'll begin to understand why we are interconnected, this whole universe. We are part of that great thing. So we don't need to feel totally isolated; we don't need to feel antagonized. Then we begin to accept our personal responsibility. Whatever I do, say, think, has an impact—not only on my own life, but on my environment, my family, my wife, my children, my friends, my society, everybody who comes into contact with me. Having a certain responsibility to this understanding makes a person much more sensible. And that is the beginning of a responsible life; that is what Buddhism teaches."

But how does one go about finding out what one really is? What does that mean exactly? "Find out where you went wrong," Lobsang had said. Isn't that what we in the West spend years on the couch doing? "And defining our ego," I said to Betty. "If I'm not my 'self,' what am I?"

Betty and I talked long into the night on the pros and cons of the couch versus the cushion. I was more confused than ever.

I HAD BEEN TOLD about a crone who lives in a cavelike dwelling at the bottom of the mountain in a medieval village a day's drive from Leh. Betty wanted to see something of the country; and I, with all the talk about renunciation, was drawn to see how this woman, who is exactly my mother's age, lives. In this same village lived an oracle, whom I hoped we could see. I hadn't thought about the concept of an oracle existing since the days I'd read about them in Greek mythology.

It was a harrowing drive on an upaved razorback trail that climbs to 13,000 feet and falls away to a gorge 3,000 feet below. The next day was my birthday. *Never mind,* I thought, *I'll not live to see it.*

But suddenly the river valley broadened and miles of golden wheat and barley fields stretched before us. Then the tiny, remote, eleventh-century village of Wanla appeared, unchanged by time. We climbed down a mountain, slipping and sliding—to the intense delight of the local children, who by then had decided to join us. We seemed to have collected curious villagers as well, who followed us to Skalzang Dolma's. We bent low, almost crouching, to enter the doorway. The only source of illumination came from an opening in the wall, a window of sorts through which shafts of afternoon light cast a dusky glow. A small fire burned in the crude clay oven. A series of platforms and shelves fashioned from stone held her pots and utensils.

The old woman sat on her knees on the bare earthen floor and looked curiously at us, bewildered by the sudden attention. She had seen few Westerners in her life, and certainly had never had a conversation with one. Villagers and children were crowded in as well. With the cameras and tape recorder and microphone I had set on the floor next to her, we caused a small event. I asked her if she would talk to us about her life. Dolma's eyes lit up; she drew up her knee and leaned on her clasped hands.

"I WAS BORN into a family whose house name was Gyagarpa. My father arranged a marriage for both my sister and me to a man from another house. He was our *mag-pa* [husband]. He is dead now. I lived happily with the mag-pa. I had no children with him, but my sister did. She had two sons and one daughter. The son is a sculptor; the daughter married into a family with the house name of Solpan-Pa-Wanla. Both my sister and I worked very hard. We grazed our cattle and collected fodder for winter, and sometimes we also had to work in other houses.

"I had a very difficult childhood. We had no rice, wheat, flour, or sugar. I used to go begging for my meal of the day. Sometimes I worked in the houses of my relatives in exchange for food. In olden days, children had to labor to earn their own livelihood.

"A lot of changes have taken place in my village. Even the sky has changed. It is more cloudy now. And people also have changed. Back then, people showed more concern for one another; they were more religious-minded and performed more religious deeds. I too fasted often and made offerings of a complete set of my clothing to the monastery and, on two occasions, a set of a hundred butter lamps and butter to fill the silver chalice before the statue of Chenrezig [the patron saint or Buddha of Tibet]. I didn't have the good fortune to build stupas, or statues of gold and silver for the temples, but I used to invite all the people of Wanla to gatherings, where I served *chang* [Tibetan beer] to everyone. In my younger days, I used to wear my perak and my fleece hat, and my fur apron on my back. I still have my perak with three rows of turquoise, which I wear when I go to the *gonpa* [temple] to see a lama.

"When I was able-bodied, I went on many pilgrimages. I saw His Holiness the Dalai Lama three times in Ladakh, and I saw the Karmapa Rinpoche once. I remember he had to hold on to his hat so that it wouldn't fly off his head. Now the farthest I can go is to Lamayura Gonpa."

"Do you live here alone?" I asked, wondering how she could possibly manage.

"I am eighty-five years old, and I can still do all my chores myself, except during Losar [New Year] and the winter months. Then I go and stay with my nieces and nephews in the family house, which is quite far from here. But in spring I return here to my own small house. I water my fields, I fetch my own water, and cook with the firewood my nieces and nephews bring me. They also bring me barley flour, tea, butter, and chang. My eyesight has become weak now, so I can't always recognize people."

We were curious to know if she remembered any folk stories or legends that might have been handed down from her elders.

"I used to sing all the different traditional songs and do all the folk dances. There are many songs and love stories, but at this advanced age I cannot remember many of them. I would spend whole nights singing and

Skalzang Dolma

telling stories. They say I was like a parrot in my younger days, very quick
at learning. In those days we did not have a schoolhouse, we never even
heard of such a thing as a school. There were no shops, either, and no ra-
tion depot. People had to grind their own flour from dried fermented
grains."

"Don't you ever get lonely, living here without your family?" I asked,
thinking how dependent the elderly are in my country.

"I don't feel lonely. I spend most of my time saying, 'Om mani
padme hum,' and another short prayer to Chenrezig. As I get old, I get my
various lives mixed up and recite only the prayers I know by heart. My bed
is near a window. Before I go to sleep I prostrate to the Buddha and pray
that all my wrong actions from the past be pardoned. On auspicious days
like the tenth, fifteenth, and the thirtieth of each month, I offer a hun-

dred butter lamps. Then I say all the mantras I know, and the prayer of refuge to the Buddha, the Dharma, and the Sangha. These I used to recite with the monks as a part of the fasting ritual. My fingers developed sores from counting the beads on my *mala*.

"I hear that people in the outside world live comfortable lives with tables and chairs and carpets in their homes, and have everything needed to be happy—sugar and rice and all that. I have only tsampa and *tukpa* [soup] to eat, but I am happy; I have no teeth in my mouth anyway. I see you in your fine clothes, and I am in rags. Yet I hear there is much unhappiness in the outside world. Can you tell me why that is?"

"No, I can't," I admitted. "Do you have some thoughts about why that is so?"

She shrugged. "Maybe your fine clothes and all your furniture and riches take up too much of your time and leave you no time for prayer. Maybe your riches have taken more away from you than they have given. But I don't know about these things. . . ." She yawned, bringing the conversation to a close.

As we got up to leave, I gave her a folded-up hundred-rupee note (about four dollars), which she opened and stared at. She took it to the window to make sure, then smiled happily.

"Wait," she said excitedly, "I will show you!" She disappeared into a black opening in the wall, where she sleeps, and came out carrying her headdress, with its seven rows of turquoise, and her moth-eaten goat-skin shawl. We followed her outside, and she donned them for us, swirling around and around like a girl. Then she took a bow.

It was nearly dark. As we made the climb back up the mountain, I realized what I had just seen had less to do with a life frozen in time than it did with a life lived according to a tradition fervently believed in. Have our riches indeed taken more from us than they have given? I struggled to find my footing, grabbing for bush branches along the unmarked path, and I thought about the busy-ness of my own "rich" years a little more. . . .

Lama Rigzen and Little Angdu were ahead; they stopped to wait and reached out to help us.

No, I doubt I ever would have found the time to climb a mountain to see the oracle of Wanla; nor the state oracle, who advises the Dalai Lama on important matters of state, whom I would see later in Dharamsala.

These local spirit protectors, it was explained, are part of a tradition that goes back thirteen hundred years, to the time of Padmasambhava. They are more concerned with the personal lives of the townspeople than with politics.

THE ORACLE
OF WANLA

IT WAS DUSK in Wanla when we were taken to the house of the oracle. We were led to an inner room lit by oil lamps. Once again children and adults crowded in to watch. The oracle sat against the wall on a bench that was covered with a rug. He greeted us shyly.

Lama Rigzen explained to him that we had come from America and had never met an oracle. Would he tell us about himself?

"DURING THE PERIOD of King Senge Namgyal of Ladakh [late sixteenth century], there were seventeen very powerful ministers. Lama Lhompo was one of them. He was the reincarnation of some great hero, and his power was special, maybe magic.

"One day Lama Lhompo came from Leh to Wanla on foot. When he died, many lamas and other oracles said that he couldn't get into heaven or hell, but had to stay in a kind of in-between state, the *bardo*. So his spirit wandered the village.

"Seven years ago he began to speak through me with his power to tell our present, past, future, everything. This spirit speaks through me to tend the people of Wanla, even the people of Ladakh, who benefit from the oracles. When they have problems in their lives, or if they have to make a decision, they come to the oracle. The spirit also gives them advice about how to have success in their lives. But he does not have the power to heal.

"The first time the spirit came to me, I felt very uncomfortable in my mind and my body. There came a sound, like a knocking at the door, and I was afraid. 'Who is that coming?' I asked, and became very suspicious. The people in the village took me to Leh to talk to some lamas. They advised me to do certain things, make offerings to the monastery, and pray. I did as the lamas advised. There was a seven-day period, like a baptism.

"The lamas made a special *puja* [prayer ritual] and invited the Lhompo to speak. A lama asked him, 'Are you the Lhompo?' And the spirit answered, 'I am the Lhompo, living in this area right now.' I never remember anything that is said afterward. But sometimes there are sharp pains, very strong.

"Actually, before that, eight or nine years ago, the head lama of Lamayuru came to this village and saw Lhompo get down from his horse and give some directions to the people of Wanla."

We asked if we could speak with the spirit of the oracle. The man nodded. A woman brought a thermos of butter tea and set it on the table in front of him. He drank rapidly, draining the cup three times as the woman refilled it. The room was quiet; the villagers waited silently, respectfully.

After a time his eyes closed. His head twitched sideways, then the whole upper half of his body jerked spasmodically. Like an epileptic in the throes of a seizure, his head fell forward, then was tossed backward. He opened his eyes, but only the whites were visible. With trembling hands he lifted his cup and gulped more tea. It dribbled down his chin and onto his shirt.

Suddenly he shouted, "*Heh!*" startling us. Then in a gruff voice quite different from his own, commanded, "Stand up!"

We rose to our feet. I looked at Betty. We both were taking this very seriously. "You," he said, pointing to me, eyes rolled back behind fluttering eyelids. "You must study very hard. *Heh!* And you will need to consult scholars to teach you what you must know for this work. *Heh!* And this work will teach you how to live your own life in peace and liberation." He paused a moment. "But first you must find your teacher—for your *true* work."

The room was so still I could hear the quick beat of my heart. My true work? When I'd had my brush with mortality, I'd decided I would devote my writing to books that would be of some benefit. Wasn't I doing that?

"And what is that, can you tell me?"

"Your true work is to become as enlightened as you can in this lifetime. But to do that you must first know yourself. For that you will need a teacher."

Seemed I had been hearing this at every turn. Was this what I was being led to?

"Your life is going to change again. You are going to move to another place."

Oh, no.

"Near a great ocean."

The Oracle of Wanla

I looked at Betty and grimaced. California? I'm afraid of earthquakes. "You ask him something," I whispered.

Betty tried to explain the rift between the various members of her family, which Lama Rigzen had difficulty translating. Finally, she asked simply, "Will-my-broken-family-be-mended?"

The oracle answered: "Let them all go."

THAT NIGHT WE spread our sleeping bags on the floor of a hut at the edge of the pasture where we had seen the yaks. Nearby in another hut, the children of the village slept, a Tibetan version of a kibbutz. Lama

Rigzen and Little Angdu brought us a pot of soup, a donation from one of the houses, which we set on a cot, a makeshift dining table. The children giggled and giggled until all at once they wound down and fell asleep.

Later, when the moon was nearly full, flooding the pastures with a silvery light, I stood looking at this dreamlike place I had come to. I thought about the oracle's predictions. Are our lives already written somewhere; are we held fast like marionettes by the strings of destiny? Was I always going to be standing here underneath this moon on my birthday eve, while at this very moment the sun shines on all the people of my own world?

I wanted to make a birthday wish on the near-full moon. I used to wish for health, happiness, and the way to support myself doing what I loved best, but now I no longer knew what to wish for.

TIBET IN INDIA

TODAY BETTY AND I would brave "Air Chance" once more for a flight to Delhi. She had to get back to the States; I would hire a car and driver for an eleven-hour trip from Delhi to Dharamsala, where I would meet lamas and wait for my audience with the Dalai Lama. I had written

to His Holiness's private offices some months before, as soon as I knew I would be in India, to request a meeting.

We arrived early, as instructed, for security checks, and waited for our airplane to appear. Suddenly there was a commotion at the entrance. An entourage of red-robed monks came bustling through the terminal doors; at the center was Lama Duwang Rinpoche, my laughing lama who had wanted to know what the moon looked like.

"That looks like someone important," Betty said. "Have you interviewed him?"

DHARAMSALA, IN NORTHERN INDIA, in the state of Himachal Pradesh, is nestled in the Dhauladar Range of the lower Himalayas. It is the seat of the government-in-exile and the present home of His Holiness the Fourteenth Dalai Lama. A hill resort from the days of the British viceroys, it was to this place in the Kangra valley that the Dalai Lama and ten thousand of his followers settled in 1960 following the Chinese invasion of Tibet.

We were driving along a ridge that leads to Dharamsala, when we passed a colony of gray monkeys at the side of the road. I asked the driver to stop so I could take a picture, and I rolled down my window. The monkeys turned to stare with bold, curious expressions, and I clicked away. I tossed a lemon drop wrapped in paper to them. The one who picked it up unwrapped it and popped it into his mouth, and the others started toward us.

"Quick, close the window!" the driver said, and started the engine.

I did as he asked, wondering if he saw them as emanations of the Hindu monkey god, Hanuman, and feared them.

As soon as I was settled in my hotel, I telephoned Tenzin Geyche Tethong, secretary to His Holiness, and left a message. Because I was neither a student of Buddhism nor a devotee, I wondered if I would get the Dalai Lama's blessing for my project. Tenzin Geyche told me they would call me back with the time of my audience.

DHARAMSALA IS DIVIDED into two sections. The Tibetan community, with its monasteries, schools, libraries, and the headquarters and residence of the Dalai Lama, is in McLeod Ganj, elevation 6,500 feet, just at the edge of the snow line. Known as "Little Lhasa," the area is a cultural potpourri: an assortment of spiritual seekers in raggedy shorts, sleeveless vests, Timberland boots, and backpacks mingled with swarms of burgundy-robed monks and Tibetan women in their kimonolike *chubas* and striped aprons. The main road was lined with stalls selling everything from batik skirts and mohair sweaters to prayer wheels and malas. Wafts of incense mixed with the sweet, pungent aroma of marijuana filled the air; a beggar sat contented in the shade of a tree by the side of the road, playing a toy sitar, a hauntingly lyrical sound one could hear a mile or two away. Attached to the strings of the makeshift instrument were two marionettes dressed as an Indian prince and princess, which danced as he strummed. It was the best show in town.

ON THE FIRST MORNING, I had breakfast on the patio of my hilltop hotel and watched two hawks glide just above the tips of the pines. They caught a thermal and soared a bit higher until they were exactly eye level to where I sat sipping morning tea—at the hawk line.

Lobsang Lhalungpa, who is the son of the Nechung oracle, had given me a letter of introduction to Tenzin Wandrak, the second state oracle. Unlike the Wanla oracle, the second state oracle is concerned only with affairs of state. I set off down the hill to the Gadong monastery, of which Wandrak is the founder, to find him.

WHEN PADMASAMBHAVA FIRST brought Buddhism into the land of the "cannibal demons" in the eighth century A.D., the local deities, by nature extremely wrathful, resisted the peaceful aspects of the new religion. Padmasambhava, however, gradually subdued each of them in a series of supernatural battles, and placed the local spirits in a hierarchy according to their powers, establishing a network of spirit protectors in Tibet to watch over the dharma.

The last and most powerful of the deities vanquished by Padmasambhava came to him in the form of an eight-year-old novice monk. Padmasambhava touched his head with a *dorje* (a ritual object representing a thunderbolt, symbolic of the path of compassion), placed nectar on his tongue, and named him and his brother spirits Pehar Gyalpo—the Five Ferocious Kings.

In time, a system—also hierarchical—of mediums who have access to these spirits grew. The two state oracles, the Nechung and the Gadong, are the most important because they have access to the spirit of Pehar Gyalpo. Even today, one of the signs of the true Nechung oracle is that his breath has no odor before he becomes entranced with the spirit of Pehar Gyalpo, but during the trance it will develop a strong odor. And the imprint of a dorje will appear on his forehead.

When the Fifth Dalai Lama consolidated temporal power in Tibet in 1642, he named Pehar Gyalpo protector of the now central government, and had the Nechung monastery built as a dwelling for his medium. Eventually the monastery became the official seat of the state oracle of Tibet, who was called upon to "channel" the power and prophetic ability of the protectors. Frequently Dorje Drakden, the minister of the Western King of Speech, is the spirit who occupies the body of the medium while he is in a trance, acting for Pehar Gyalpo. It was Dorje Drakden who warned the Thirteenth Dalai Lama of an assassination plot against his life by his regent and, as early as 1945, alerted Tibet to the coming danger from China. He also urged the Dalai Lama to go to India in 1956 to establish lines of communication with Nehru, which proved invaluable to the Tibetan refugees who flooded the country in 1959.

THE GADONG MONASTERY lies on a hillside near the temple and residence of the Dalai Lama. Tenzin Wandrak, in slacks and shirt and European-style haircut, resembled more a casually dressed businessman than the second state oracle. He received me graciously, and after a friendly chat, he placed a phone call to Tsering Choedon. She is a young Tibetan woman who speaks excellent English, Mr. Wandrak told me, and might be available as a translator. She arrived soon after, smiling brightly, eager to be of help. She wore the traditional striped apron and crisp cotton blouse; raven-black hair pulled tight in a long ponytail. I asked Choedon if we might begin with a brief introduction.

"MY FULL NAME is Tenzin Wandrak Gadong. I was born in Gadong, Tibet. I am fifty-eight years old. There were five sons and four daughters in our family. My father had two wives. After giving birth to one son and one daughter, his first wife died. I am the eldest of the second wife."

"And how was it that you became state oracle?"

"My father was the state oracle of Gadong, as was his father before him. I used to watch my father in trance. Because I have seen it since childhood, I never thought of it as anything special. It was traditional. The mediumship is our lineage, passed down from father to son. Our lineage is said to have started seven generations back, during the time of great Fifth Dalai Lama. One son must become the medium of Gadong. Others are free to do public service or whatever else they like.

"Since the age of sixteen, I had served the Tibetan government in Tibet. In those days, Tibet was an independent country. In 1955 when His Holiness the Dalai Lama visited China, I traveled with him in his entourage of more than seventy as part of his lower division staff. When we returned, the situation inside Tibet wasn't good. I had seen the conditions in China, and I felt that sooner or later China would invade. I made an excuse to my mother; I told her I wanted to go on a pilgrimage to India. This is how I escaped, in 1957.

Tenzin Wandrak

"At that time, although my father knew that I was going to India forever, we did not tell my mother because we knew she would be against it. But on that fateful day as I was leaving Tibet, my mother called me back. She gave me some tsampa to squeeze in my palm to make my imprint. Then she took it and put it in her cupboard. I think she knew in her heart that she would not see me again.

"I worked at Kharshang Radio Station in Darjeeling until 1963, when my father sent me a message to come to Dharamsala to join the exiled government. So I went there to work in the office of Tibetan Children's Village for a few months. Then I was moved to the Tibetan Library. In 1964 at a meeting, His Holiness gave a speech about the difficulties in Tibetan settlements in India and expressed the need for some volunteers. So I went to the Tibetan settlement in Orissa.

"During that year, I traveled back to Dharamsala for a Yamantaka re-treat [Yamantaka is a meditational deity—the wrathful form of the Bud-dha of Wisdom]. One evening as we were having dinner, a very unusual cold feeling came over me, and my body suddenly experienced other strange sensations. I was very scared; I thought I was going to die. That was the first sign of the onset of mediumship. After that, for the next few years, nothing more happened.

"Then in 1967, I started getting sick often, and sometimes while asleep, I would become so scared I would jump out of bed. It felt as if someone had thrown fire inside my body. I was told these happenings were the sign of the spirit.

"Because I wasn't feeling well, I took two months off and came again to Dharamsala. I told my father about my experiences. I saw several dif-ferent doctors, but none of them could help me. Medication didn't work. I was losing weight, getting very skinny; my complexion darkened.

"One day I consulted the oracle about my health. The answer was, 'Just keep yourself clean [spiritually], and accordingly the radiance of five lights will be revealed.' I did not understand the meaning of that answer, so one day I went to see my teacher and asked the meaning of 'the radi-ance of five lights will be revealed.' He explained that the spirit of the pro-tector deity is the emanation of five Buddha families, and the message meant that I was going to be the oracle.

"By the time my father died, in 1975, I was the only son residing in the Tibetan settlements in India and serving in the Tibetan government-in-exile: one of my brothers was living in Bhutan, and another in Canada; the others were back inside Tibet. I was asked to take over the responsibil-ities of this monastery, and in 1976, I was appointed oracle.

"It is difficult to explain exactly how I first experienced being a medium, because although I sense some uneasiness in my nerves before the onset of the trance, I don't remember anything when I am fully in trance. It's quite complicated. When the spirit is about to enter my body, I start to shake. It seems as if all the channels, the veins of my body are being filled up. There is a considerable measure of discomfort.

"Since this is not prevalent in Western countries, some people ask if mediumship can be learned. But it is not something that can be either taught or learned. It is more like the relationship between a landlord and a tenant. That is, your body becomes a house for the spirit, and you become totally unconscious. You don't know anything about what has taken place during the trance.

"On the tenth day of the first month of every Tibetan lunar calendar year, the two state oracles, Nechung and Gadong, go into trance together and hold a ceremony. (We also go into trance individually at times.) The ceremony takes place in the big temple hall. During official ceremonies, outsiders are not permitted to attend, but there are other ceremonies where outsiders can observe. For instance, Drepung monastery could request a ceremony, and for this people would be permitted to attend. If someone wants to hold a trance ceremony with the state oracles, one has to get authorization from His Holiness."

I HAD SEEN pictures of the state oracle's ceremonial dress. It looked like an ancient warrior's costume. Before a ceremony, the oracle dons red brocade trousers with six-foot-wide legs, which fit over his normal pants and are folded and tied at his ankles; and knee-high white leather boots with curled toes, appliquéd with the fiery red eyes of wrathful deities. Over a red silk shirt, he wears two heavy robes, tied loosely, since during trance it is not unusual for the oracle's body to swell up two inches. On top of all of this, he puts on an ancient Tibetan mail jerkin of gold-leafed ringlets. Something resembling a backpack, which holds four flags and three victory banners, is then secured around his waist. In addition to strips of red cloth that bind his sleeves—the left padded as for archery and stitched with three scarlet eyes—he wears a red, yellow, and gold silk front-piece with a golden mirror in its center. As the oracle begins to hyperventilate in trance, the mirror will quiver and shake.

A three-foot-long silver sword and buckle is attached to his left side, a golden quiver filled with arrows to his right. Each article is decorated with elaborate embroidery and encrusted with turquoise, amethyst, and other jewels.

Tenzin Wandrak told me that when he is not in trance, he often strains his muscles from the enormous weight of the full regalia. The huge headdress would snap the neck of a normal man. But once in trance, the oracle leaps about, bowing easily to the Dalai Lama, swinging the sword, tossing scarves twelve feet in the air, and dancing the ritual steps that are part of the ceremony. Since the oracle loses consciousness during the trance, he must rely on attendants.

"A SPECIALLY TRAINED person must tie the headdress underneath the chin of the oracle. If tied too early it could kill the oracle, too late and it can't be tied on at all because the spirit becomes so active. It all happens in a few seconds. It is equally important to untie the knot the moment the spirit leaves the oracle.

"While the oracle waits for the spirit to enter, the headdress rests on his head, held by the attendants. Once the spirit is in trance, the knot will then be tied. As far as I know, no one has ever weighed it, but when I am not in trance I can't move with the headdress on.

"We were unable to bring the original costume to India; it was lost to the Chinese during the invasion. A new headdress and costume were made here in India under the sponsorship of His Holiness the Dalai Lama.

"Many Western people think that since I am the main oracle, whatever I say is the prophecy, but that is not so. Only when I am in trace and consulting, whatever the deities say, that's the oracle's prophecy. Otherwise, I am only a layperson, whatever I believe may or may not be true."

"And who exactly are these spirits?" I asked, wondering if they were who people in the West call spirit guides, and who Native Americans refer to as the Grandfathers.

"There are different kinds of spirits. We are talking here about the spirit which emanates from buddhas and *bodhisattvas*, whose main purpose is to help beings develop spiritually and to lead them to the path of the truth.

"People think that the spirits are the advisors only to His Holiness. It isn't that simple. The spirits are, in effect, the dharma protectors. We humans need to communicate with them; and they in turn need to speak to us and advise us, and protect our minds from hindrances and obstacles, not just offer prophecies and tell the future.

"In the case of His Holiness the Dalai Lama, the dharma protectors are like his employees, who do what he tells them to do. For example, an employer might ask his employees to find information about certain things. The employee goes and discovers the specific information, then reports back to the employer. After gathering all the information, the employer then makes his final decision. So the relationship between His Holiness and the spirit works like that. Therefore, the dharma protectors work under him, rather then above him.

"To do such a job, the spirit has to be very powerful. Some spirits are capable of telling events within one month's time, some one year's, five year's, a century's, and so on. The one that we are talking about can fore-tell an infinite amount of time."

I told Mr. Wandrak about the Wanla oracle and asked if he knew of him.

"No, but besides the state oracles there are others who are accessible to the general public."

"Do people generally find the information to be accurate?" I asked.

"If you ask a question that falls within the perimeter of the spirit's clairvoyance, he will give you the right advice. If your question is beyond the reach of the spirit's ability, he will tell you. I personally believe that spirits' prophecies are accurate, since the spirit in question can tell both past and future. That is why we consult with the spirit to find reincarnations of late, great lamas and teachers.

"I would like to add something here. It is important for us to know how much understanding you people have about our tradition. Because if we don't understand how much you know about our culture, we might say things which need not be said. And sometimes we don't say enough so that you will understand. For example, the Nechung spirit plays a big role in safeguarding the welfare of our country's religious and political system. Whether we use the information or not is totally up to us. It is the nature of karma that happiness comes as a result of our own good deeds, and suffering results from our bad deeds. The fulfillment of the prophecy, then, depends a great deal on our actions. It is certain that if karma and all the conditions are right, the prophecy will come true; otherwise, not. This is just a very basic explanation of how this system works.

"The Tibetan people's lives are inextricably interwoven with Buddhist belief and philosophy. To know more about our tradition and how it works, one has to view it in the light of the Buddhist belief system. Therefore, it is important to have some knowledge of Buddhism in order to understand Tibetan culture and rituals."

I WAS BEGINNING to see how much the Tibetans had lost as a result of the Chinese occupation. The traditions they managed to bring with them into exile had been torn from a fabric as ornate and intricate as the oracle's ceremonial dress. Was it realistic to think it could be stitched into life outside of Shangri-la?

PALACE INTRIGUES

Tenzin Wandrak had arranged for me to meet a monk who is the son of Gyalten Namgyal, tailor to both the Thirteenth and Fourteenth Dalai Lamas. The son would take Tsering Choeden and me to his home.

We walked past the kindergarten complex to a ground-floor apartment, where his father the tailor lay on his bed, propped up on pillows. He had been ill; the skin on his face was thin, translucent, the eyes sunken. His head seemed to float above the bedcovers, a disembodied skull. Yet he seemed eager to talk, and recalled his life in astonishing detail. I promised to keep the interview short so as not to tire him, but he insisted on telling his story.

We arranged ourselves on chairs and stools around the bed, and I set up the tape recorder and microphone. My eye was drawn to the bookcase on the opposite side of the room, to the odd assortment of objects set among the religious articles and scriptures: a Garfield cup that read, "What do you mean we're out of Coke?"; two books, *Gone with the Wind*, and *Scarlett*; an *ET* doll; an autographed photo of Richard Gere; a statue of Goofy. Sounds of children playing outside and dogs barking did not drown out the old man's determined voice.

"I WAS BORN in 1912, the Year of the Water Mouse. My grandfather was a *ngagpa*, a lay Tantric practitioner, and came from a village near Lhasa called Dechen. The people in that village owed allegiance to the estates of Demo Rinpoche, the Thirteenth Dalai Lama's regent. Demo Rinpoche asked my grandfather to come to Lhasa to administer the estate. He gave my grandfather and his family a house. Since we had no schools at that time, my grandfather taught my father to read and write.

"But a few years later, in 1898, my grandfather died. A few months after that, the regent was imprisoned. He had joined a plot to kill the [previous] Dalai Lama by means of black magic. They had written spells on a piece of paper to be put inside His Holiness's beautiful new boots, but the Nechung oracle, while in one of his trances, learned of it, and Demo Rinpoche was arrested and thrown in jail. He died there shortly after.

"My mother came from the largest house in Nyamo Tsang. Her father, who was chief administrator to the Sixth Panchen Lama [secondhighest lama in Tibet], brought his family to Lhasa and rented a wing of our house. Later, our families arranged a marriage between my mother and my father. My father was master of robes to the Dalai Lama's family, and secretary in the Sokhang, the head office of the tailor's guild.

"He taught me to sew when I was eight. When I was ten, my father was asked to make appliqué thangkas of the Sixteen Arhats, and allowed me to work on them. He also took me on his tent-making jobs for the no-

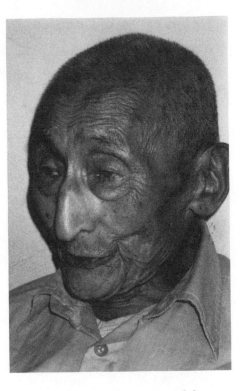

Gyalten Namgyal

ble families, who used them for picnics. The tents were very elaborate, round, in Mongolian style, and had carpets on the floor and thangkas on the walls.

"I became skilled enough to be entered into the tailor's guild for further training. The tailor's guild had been established by the Fifth Dalai Lama in the seventeenth century, and was an institution of high prestige with a special area in the temple. We all wore round yellow hats that indicated we were in government service. Novices could be severely disciplined by the ones on top, who were allowed to slap them in the face for being slow.

"The Thirteenth Dalai Lama [the current Dalai Lama is the Fourteenth] was particularly interested in fine arts, which is why there were so many great painters and artists during his time. I had always wished to enter the Dalai Lama's service, even though everyone was afraid of his temper. When he felt in an angry mood, he wore red, and everyone around him was very careful. Even English government representatives who had audiences with His Holiness were afraid of him when he wore red.

"I remember the first time I saw His Holiness. He had come to the workshop to distribute his annual gift of silver coins to the tailors. He was imposing in his golden brocade robe. After that, he would often tour the sewing rooms, scrutinizing the tailors as they sat cross-legged on their cushions, cutting and sewing. If he saw something he didn't like, he scolded us. Once, when we had finished a piece of work and presented it to His Holiness, he asked if we had washed our hands. "These brocades belong to the government; they're not for you to make dirty."

"The Thirteenth Dalai Lama changed his brocaded robes every day. The brocades came from the Norbulinka treasury, many of them from the Manchu emperors, and had been offered to successive Dalai Lamas over centuries. When I was fourteen, the Dalai Lama decided he wanted a Tibetan national flag made, and designed it himself. When a prototype was approved and the first flag commissioned, I was the one to execute the work.

"My father died suddenly when I was seventeen. My mother, whose youngest was barely walking, became desolate. She decided I should take over the household and look after the family. By then I was getting private work in addition to the money I earned from the government; a marriage to a girl from a good family was arranged.

"One night as I was doing my sewing in my house, I heard shouting outside, calling for mourning and ordering that all prayer flags be lowered. Men must unwind their hair, and women should remove their ornaments.

The Thirteenth Dalai Lama had died. It had happened quite suddenly. Only a few days before, he had come into the workroom to ask me if the white brocade robe I was working on would be ready for the Kalachakra initiation. I assured him it would. He was never to wear it; it was worn by our present Dalai Lama when he gave the Kalachakra initiation in Lhasa.

"He had also asked that the house in Shol, below the Potala, be fixed up, because soon someone would be coming to stay there. I didn't think much of it then, but after he passed away, I realized that His Holiness had known that the regent would soon be enthroned. The house in Shol always served as the regent's residence; the Thirteenth Dalai Lama was announcing his forthcoming departure for the Pure Lands.

"Eighty of the 130 tailors of the Sokhang were selected to make the brocade decorations for the new stupa, which was to be placed in the Potala with the mausoleums of the other Dalai Lamas. We completed it in thirteen days.

"The construction of the stupa and the preserving of His Holiness's remains took about a year. The mummifying process was done in the Potala in the traditional manner: the body fluids were extracted with salt; then, after the drying was completed, the remains were covered in gold. I was among the fourteen people to go inside the golden stupa and arrange the robes. Just before the remains were dressed, a protrusion in the shape of the Chenrezig statue had emerged from His Holiness's shoulder. Reting Rinpoche, Ling Rinpoche, and Gyalwang Tulku were among the others who saw this. Reting Rinpoche told me I had served His Holiness well, and that when the new incarnation came to Lhasa, I would be serving him.

"My wife died giving birth when I was twenty-four, and the baby was stillborn. My mother saw this as a sign that we should give up all worldly things, our lovely house, and all our possessions, and dedicate ourselves strictly to the dharma. Everyone in the family became a monk or nun. I took my vows from Phabongka Rinpoche and received my new name, Gyalten Namgyal. My mother removed her ear ornaments and set out for Bhari Labrang, where she spent many years in seclusion. She wanted me to resign my post as Chenmo, but I had already been appointed to lead the restoration of the temple decorations at Samye. I promised I would resign when the work was completed.

"While at Samye I became friends with the oracle of Tsuimar, Samye's main protector deity. During the ceremony, I watched him go into a trance. He began by eating a raw animal heart, then danced wildly, brandishing a weapon. He blessed me to ensure the protector's support in the renovations. Then, on the third day of the trance, the blind oracle ran along the edges of the roof. When the trance ended, he was the same old man with no eyeballs, feeling his way around with his stick.

"When work at Samye was nearly finished, we heard that the Fourteenth incarnation of the Dalai Lama had been found and recognized in Amdo [eastern Tibet], and that his arrival in Lhasa was imminent. All government officials, lamas, and abbots would be part of the elaborate welcoming celebrations. I was ordered to remain at Samye to make tents, the most important being the 'Great Peacock Tent,' in which the young Dalai Lama would hold his first audiences before the final procession to Lhasa. When I saw him, he looked very small yet composed on his throne; I was overjoyed to receive our new Holiness's blessing."

It had been explained to me that the Dalai Lama is seen as an emanation of Chenrezig—a living buddha.

"When the celebrations were over, I handed in my resignation according to my promise to my mother. The cabinet, unwilling to accept my resignation, made me a monk official instead, so that I could continue to serve His Holiness. At the age of twenty-seven, I was appointed Namsa

Gelong, personal tailor to the Dalai Lama, and a workshop was set up under my direction. New decorations were ordered for the three monasteries of Drepung, Sera, and Ganden in time for the enthronement. I was also responsible for all the statues and new sets of robes for the Nechung and Gadong oracles. I chose sixty of the best tailors in Lhasa. We were given a large space at the foot of the Potala.

"On the appointed day, the thirtieth of the second month, all the monks and lay government officials lined up in front of the Potala. The Dalai Lama watched the procession, which took several hours, from the window of the palace. The Nechung oracle came out in trance with his retinue. The day before, there was a throwing of ritual cakes and the sending off of the scapegoat, a man dressed in a goatskin with one side of his face painted black and the other white. He would go around the Barkor, begging for money, knowing that people would never want to displease such an inauspicious character as himself. His expulsion began with a game of dice with the abbot of a nearby monastery. This game was supposed to determine who would be the scapegoat, but many say the dice were fixed because the same person always would be chosen. Two monks would drag him out of Lhasa by the collar, all the way to Samye. This ceremony was said to originate in the days of the Early Kings, and was meant to appease negative forces in the political sphere.

"Many preparations needed to be made for Gyalwa Rinpoche's [the Dalai Lama's] entrance into the Drepung and Sera monasteries. We worked for six months with materials from the Namsa treasury high up in the Potala. Very few people were allowed into this storehouse of brocades, and those few had to take off their chubas first so nothing could be concealed in their robes. An official at the curtained door checked everything that went in or out. The Namsa treasury—named after the Buddha of Wealth, whose statue was inside—was only one of many storehouses within the Potala. Once, I went into one that had been dug right into the mountain, while torches lit our way through the total darkness among the massive foundation walls.

"As I worked to restore the hermitage and to make new ceiling friezes and pillar hangings for the Sera and Drepung monasteries, great political intrigue swirled around my head, but I didn't pay much attention. I won't go into it now, but many things happened then and later, including the destruction of the Reting monastery, which I think helped to use up Tibet's merit, therefore making it possible for the Chinese to invade."

The tailor then recounted how he had been personally affected by the Chinese occupation—horror stories that I would hear again and again (so much so that I have dedicated an entire section of this book to those experiences, which begins on page 129). Finally he was able to leave Tibet and fulfill his dream: to make a new hat for the Fourteenth Dalai Lama.

GLIMPSES OF
ANOTHER WORLD

HAVING GLIMPSED A LITTLE more of the gilded world of ancient Tibet, with its rich brocades and palace politics, I was curious now to learn something of the monastic system. I had heard almost nothing about the role of women in Tibet, so I asked Choedon if we might visit the nuns in  the abbey we passed on the way back from the tailor's.

I noticed that the nuns wear the same burgundy-and-saffron robes as the monks, and with their shaved heads, they are virtually indistinguishable from their male counterparts.

Although Tibet is a patriarchal society, the ancient texts tell of the origin of Tara, one of the female buddhas. Her name was Princess Yeshe Dawa, Wisdom Moon, and she lived many eons ago. Her practices were so great and her offerings so numerous that she was told by the lamas, "If you pray to come back in a man's body, you will become enlightened in the next lifetime."

Yeshe Dawa refused, and made a vow instead to remain in a woman's form. She would work for the benefit of all sentient beings until the cycle of samsara ends and there is no more suffering in the world. Then, after many more eons of practices and meditation, she herself was finally liberated from samsara.

According to legend, Yeshe Dawa would not eat her breakfast until she had freed a million beings from suffering; lunch until another million were freed; and dinner until she had freed still another million. In time she became known as Drolma, the Mother Who Rescues, the Tibetan name for Tara. Yet I had heard of very few female *tulku*s, recognized reincarnations of enlightened beings.

THE GEDEN CHOELING Buddhist Abbey in Dharamsala was founded in 1973 by twenty-one exiled nuns under the care of the Tibetan Nuns Project. This population has grown to more than two hundred, with more nuns arriving from Tibet each day, many of whom have endured suffering beyond comprehension.

Before the Chinese invasion, there were eight hundred abbeys in Tibet, housing up to twenty-seven thousand nuns, the largest group of Buddhist nuns in the world. Monasteries and abbeys were an early target of the Chinese Communists. In the words of Chairman Mao Zedong, "Religion is poison. It has two great defects: It undermines the race and retards the progress of the country. Tibet and Mongolia both have been poisoned by it."

In occupied Tibet, nuns and monks are regarded with deep distrust. Their resilience in the face of interrogation and torture in prison is viewed by their captors as provocation. After each crackdown on demonstrations, it has been the nuns who have initiated new marches. It is their duty, they feel, to confront China and to fight for Tibet's freedom.

Newang Choezin, age sixty-nine and born in Lhasa, is the retired head nun. She led us up the stairs to her small room, with its neatly arranged desk and book. She motioned for us to sit on the bed as she took a seat in the straight-backed wooden desk chair.

"I WAS THE UMZE, prayer master, of this abbey for a long time, but now I am retired. The umze's primary responsibility is to see that everyone is in prayer position; she then leads the prayers. The umze also teaches the younger nuns.

"My mother died when I was a child, and I felt so alone. Since I already was interested in learning the dharma and becoming a nun, it was not hard for me to enter the abbey. My dharma teacher, who was a relative, was very kind. I was never lonely after that."

I told the umze that it was difficult for me to imagine what life in an abbey must be like for a little girl. I had heard about the rigors of a monk's life in a monastery, and wondered if they were the same in an abbey.

"Discipline in an abbey may seem strict, considering we were allowed to visit our family only twice a year. And we had to rise early in the morning, at five. Then we would have prayer sessions, then lessons, and after that, lunch.

"In addition to learning to read religious scriptures, we became skilled at embroidery and appliqué work. We made colorful things out of dyed yak hair, handicrafts which we used and which also brought in money to supplement our abbey's funds.

"There were nunneries at the top of the hill, where nuns who had studied in Lhasa taught Tibetan poetry, grammar, astrology, and so on. I went there to study. History I learned from some Christians I had met in the village.

"My childhood in the abbey was a happy time. My room was only a little smaller than this one we're sitting in. The house was constructed of stone and mud, and quite comfortable."

"And did all of you get along well?" I asked, wondering if nuns are immune to petty jealousies and tensions other young women are subject to.

"All of the women got along quite well. Since we all were dharma students, we were taught to watch our minds. Jealousy is human nature, so occasionally there might be some tension, but not so that everybody would get involved. Also, I think that generally nuns tend to be pretty adaptable women.

"Buddhist philosophy says that everyone wants happiness. So if you want happiness, help others be happy; then there is no conflict. His Holiness is always reminding us of this."

"Is there confession? And to whom do you make confession?"

"Confession is not like it is in Christianity, when you say, 'I have done this and this and this.' But within the scriptures, there is a place where you visualize, admit what you have done wrong, regret having done unfortunate actions, vow to yourself not to repeat them, and do prostrations and other things to purify any bad acts within the past fifteen days. You think this to yourself, not out loud."

"Was it a difficult adjustment—to leave Tibet and live in exile in India? Is it very different here?"

"In Tibet, we could do anything we liked, but now in exile we have to depend on others. Also, I have a problem with the water here. The water in Tibet was so clean, so pure. I miss it.

"I left Tibet in 1961. When the Chinese came and there was the unsuccessful uprising, everyone felt fear. It was either flee Tibet or be killed."

I would learn more about the invasion and the uprising in the months to come, and of the extraordinary spiritual heroism of the Tibetan people.

Newang Choezin

I LEFT CHOEDON and headed toward the hotel. She would meet me for tea in the morning, and we would go together to see Locho Rinpoche, a master whose name had come up frequently in my reading, and Ani Gomchen, the eighty-seven-year-old nun whom Newang Choezin had told me about.

Later on that night I was suddenly felled by what the desk clerk called—euphemistically and with a certain proprietary fondness, it seemed—a "Delhi-belly." He prescribed a foul-smelling potion, which actually provided enough relief to buy me a few hours' sleep.

THE NEXT MORNING Tsering Choedon called for me as arranged, and we went to find Ani Gomchen. On the way we met an old man sit-

ting by the side of the road under a makeshift tent. His few belongings—
a cup, a bowl, some candles, sticks of incense, bottles of water—were
neatly arranged to one side. On the other, stacks of scriptures lovingly
wrapped in cloth sat next to piles of smooth stones. A fire was kept going for his tea; beside it a bag of tsampa. We stopped to watch as he
carved a mantra onto a stone, so deep in concentration he did not notice us for some time.

When he looked up, I asked him, through Choedon, where he got
all the stones.

"I BUY THE smooth stones from the Indian traders, who bring
them on the backs of horses from the riverbank. Before I carve the stone,
I paint the words first, because I believe that if you start carving on the
bare surface, then you will be creating life on the naked body. We believe
that the stone has feeling. After I paint it in red, I compare it with the
scripture to make sure it is right."

Pleased that we showed interest in his stones, he went on tell us
about his life as well.

"I lived on a farm in central Tibet. In my family were four sons, including me, and four daughters. I became a monk at the Sera monastery,
but I left at the age of twenty-five, during the Regency, because of a conflict involving a ceremony. I didn't know then that the Chinese were coming. For twelve years I worked as a cook in a school in Delahousie. After
that I worked on road construction, like all of the Tibetan refugees. But
then, when there was no more work, I started stone carving. For four years
I watched and studied how people did it, then I started doing it every day.

"I come here every morning at eight-thirty, and stay until five or six
o'clock in the evening. Sometimes I go to the river to wash my clothes.
Otherwise I am always here, all year round. My daughter is a pharmacist at

the medical center. I get red powder from her and mix it with water to paint the rocks."

"What gave you the idea to carve the stones?"

"I didn't want to be a beggar. It is enough that I have something to eat and something to wear. People sometimes give me offerings for my stones, but if no one buys them I put them in that stupa up there near the river. The water that touches the stones spreads the blessings carved on them. Also the wind that blows across the stones saves insects and other living things from a bad rebirth. I believe this work is holy work. I pray as I carve for all those in the six realms of samsara. In the morning I burn three incense sticks and pray that whatever accumulation of merit I make out of carving the stones be for the benefit of all sentient beings. This is my prayer every morning."

WE WALKED ON in silence. I was lost in thought, moved by what I had just seen. Not all holy men wear robes, it seems.

When we reached the other side of town, we turned down a dusty lane well off McLeod Ganj's main road and came to stone steps, which lead down to a row of apartments. I stepped around slugs the size of cigars that clung to the stone, and reminded myself that these too are sentient beings and that repulsion is only a personal view. In my next life they might be a litter of puppies, albeit ugly ones.

Choedon knocked at the door, and the nun's face appeared, smiling a wide, toothless smile. Hands together in front of her face, Ani Gomchen bowed to us in welcome to her tiny one-room hut, and beckoned us to sit. We settled on the edge of the only piece of furniture, her bed. Ani Gomchen sat cross-legged on a cushion on the floor.

The walls were filled with photographs of the Dalai Lama, prints of the deities, altar cups; a prayer wheel hung by a string above the bed. Ani

Gomchen's skin was smooth and unlined, her head shaven. Her burgundy robes were frayed and stained and looked as if they had not been washed in years.

A large mouse jumped from an open cupboard onto the slab of grease-coated concrete that served as a countertop. A film of dust and grease covered everything in the room: the teacups, the boxes of food, the iron pot on the stove. My hostess asked if we would take tea; at the risk of seeming impolite, I declined. Then, reaching behind a soiled curtain, Ani-la brought out a basket of biscuits. I shook my head and put my hand to my stomach to indicate my "problem," and the nun immediately handed me a small brown pellet wrapped in paper. Choedon explained it was a Tibetan pill, but I thanked her and smiled and demurred.

Once more I reminded myself that it is the condition of one's consciousness that is important, not the externals. At the moment it was all I could do to keep my mind off the condition of my very upset stomach and concentrate instead on the clarity in her eyes and the pure joy of her smile.

"My ORIGINAL NAME was Yeshe Toma, but when I was in an abbey in Delahousie, I was given the name Ani Gomchen, which means Grand Meditator. If someone came here asking for Yeshe Toma, no one would know who that is. This is how I got my name: His Holiness the Dalai Lama had come to the abbey in Delahousie to give teachings; afterward he went in to see our temple. We nuns waited a long time at the door to get a glimpse of him. Finally, one of the nuns went to see where he was. She came running back and said His Holiness wanted to see me. I was very nervous. When I got there, he asked, 'Is this your seat?' I said yes. 'What prayers are you doing?' Then he asked to see my prayer book, which was very old and worn. His Holiness took it and touched it to his forehead, then handed it to me and said, 'Thank you.'

"After that, the head nun honored me with the name Ani Gomchen.

"I am eighty-seven-and-a-half years old now. I was the youngest of nine children in our family. My father's family comes from lamas, from a big family in Kham. My mother comes from northern Tibet. When I was very young, I would recite mantras in my dreams. When other girls would take skins of mutton and exchange them for fancy things, I would take whatever I had and offer them to the lamas. Since childhood, I knew I wanted to be a nun. Even in my next life, my wish is to practice the dharma, whether I am male or female. If I am male, I'd like to be a monk; if female, I'd like to be a nun—if I have a choice. But I don't think we're given a choice.

"When I was thirteen, my parents were going to arrange a marriage for me into a noble family, but I begged them to let me go on a pilgrimage to Mount Kailash with a friend of my sister's. They tried to discourage me, telling me that the journey was very hard, that we would have to support ourselves by begging and might be attacked by robbers. I pleaded and pleaded, and finally they let me go. I did pilgrimages all over Tibet, visiting the holy places. When I'd reach a monastery I'd do a full prostration. At that time, it was easy because I was young, not like now. At Mount Kailash I did many full prostrations.

"When I was seventeen my mother passed away. My father went into closed retreat, and I would deliver food to him through a small hole. I did a 'dark retreat,' where you sit in a room with only a pinpoint of light. I requested to do this with my friend. The lama said that it would be harder to do it with another person because we wouldn't be able to lie down to sleep; the hut was big enough only for one person. But my friend and I wanted to do it together.

"After one month, we made circumambulations with prostrations all around a hill, which took a whole day. Suddenly a hailstorm came up, with

Ani Gomchen

much thunder and lightning. We prayed and the hailstorm went back. I was watching the sky. All of a sudden a vision of Guru Rinpoche [Padmasambhava] appeared, so big it filled the sky. Then it turned into a rainbow. After a while the rainbow turned to green. While it was green, I saw Green Tara. At one point, she was smiling. We both saw that. Rinpoche was very pleased when I told him what I had seen. He said it was the blessing of the guru.

"When I was twenty I took some jewelry and valuable objects from our house, went to a high lama, offered him my hair, and asked him to ordain me as a nun. When I entered the abbey, I felt as if I had been freed from prison.

"Later on, I did a long retreat. I didn't have a clock, but I used to start the Tara rituals at about four in the morning. During those years, I vowed to recite ten million Vajra Guru mantras of Padmasambhava: 'Om ah hung vajra guru padme siddhi hum.' When I came out of retreat, I heard about the invasion.

"I received a letter from my lama saying the Chinese had invaded Tibet and it would be better to leave: 'No one knows what will happen in the future, but if you want to join us, please come.' Two thousand of us left for India. I was fifty-one then.

"Word came to me that my brother's son, who had been recognized as a tulku belonging to the Drikung monastery, had been arrested. The Chinese tried to get him to abandon his faith and to denounce the Dalai Lama. He refused, saying they might as well kill him, he would never denounce the Dalai Lama. Eventually he died at the hands of the Chinese and has been reborn abroad.

"We came directly to Dharamsala. The Indian government had given us tents to live in, and jobs building roads. The Dalai Lama was living in the Old Palace at Swarag Ashram then. Twice a week he would give audiences, and we all would go to see him, which made us very happy.

"Two years later, I was invited to join an abbey in Delahousie that belonged to the Karmapa. I hadn't finished the ten million Vajra Guru mantras in Tibet, so I spent another three years completing that. I had the same routine: silence for seven days, then one day to get food. Otherwise my door was firmly shut. During the retreat, a very good neighbor would buy things—food, other things—for me."

"You brought nothing with you?" I asked, trying hard to imagine the life of a renunciate.

"I don't have any other belongings, just what people have given me. They ask me to do pujas for them, and give me offerings. This house was an old kitchen of an Indian family. It used to be smaller, but during my three-year meditation retreat, I cut out a wall to have more space."

"What would you do if you became ill?"

"I never got sick during all the years in retreat, but once, here in Dharamsala, I became ill for a month. I thought my image of Guru Rinpoche and my copy of a scripture should be given to His Holiness, so I sent a message to his residence. The next day, two members of his staff came to get me to take me to him, but I wasn't even able to get up. So the two men picked me up and carried me to the Dalai Lama's residence. When they put me down I could hardly see. His Holiness came over and stroked my head and asked, 'What has happened to you?' He recited some mantras and blew three times on me. I got well right after that. Now if ever I get sick, I visualize that His Holiness is blessing me and I get cured."

"Have you had other opportunities to see His Holiness?"

"This year there was a big prayer going on in the Palace. His Holiness invited me to stay the whole time. In Tibet, nuns were not allowed to participate in many of the big prayer festivals, but His Holiness specifically said during one of his teachings that the Buddha had taught his discipline for both male and female ordained beings."

FROM THE TIME I was a small girl, I used to write my wishes in my diary. My cousin and I would make lists on our birthdays and again on the New Year—we allowed ourselves exactly twelve wishes. When Ani Gomchen was thirteen, she wished for a pilgrimage; at thirteen, I wished for a bra (and bosoms to put into it), a horse (not like Heartaches, who always complained and had a habit of rolling in the mud—with me in the saddle), and to skip the next three birthdays and get to the magic sixteenth. Later, as an adult, I wished for a home in the country if I lived in the city; and when I lived in the country, I wished for an apartment in the city. But all Ani Gomchen needs is the blessing from His Holiness and the holy words she performs.

Denma Locho Rinpoche is the retired abbot of Namgyal monastery, the Dalai Lama's monastery. He lives in an apartment on the top floor of the Green Hotel in Dharamsala. A monk attendant showed us to a reception room off a large patio filled with well-cared-for plants. I admired Rinpoche's Lhasa Apso dog, whose name, I learned, is Champa (Compassion, in Tibetan). After some moments, we were escorted to Rinpoche's private quarters. Immediately upon entering, Tsering Choedon raised her clasped hands over her head, and instantly she was on the floor, her ponytail tossed overhead like a cat pouncing on a ball of string. She performed these prostrations three times with such simple reverence that I was moved almost to tears. I had never seen such pure devotion.

Denma Locho Rinpoche's face was clear and smiling, as open as a child's. His gaze was direct and peaceful. I presented my katak, which the rinpoche draped around my bowed head, and he invited us to sit.

I explained that I was still trying to get a picture of Tibet before the occupation, and I asked him if he would talk about his early life.

"I WAS BORN in eastern Tibet, in Kham. I am sixty-four years old. My mother married when she was eighteen, but did not have a child for many years. This worried the family a great deal, so they did many prayers and rituals, even read the whole Kangyur. After seven years, I was born.

"The hamlet where I grew up fell between nomad territory and farming land. From the nomads we'd get yogurt, cheese, and meat, then barley and turnips from the farmers. My father was a trader, and my mother looked after the fields. We kept mostly dzos and dzomos, a cross between a yak and a cow. We'd get milk from the dzomo and use the dzo to plough the fields.

"I remember the pastures full of wildflowers in the summer, and watching my boots turn yellow as I ran through a meadow blanketed with saffron flowers.

"Another memory I have is of seeing many butter lamps coming from one of the big houses nearby and hearing my family all speaking in sad, hushed voices. I experienced a sense of gloom and distress. The Thirteenth Dalai Lama had just passed away.

"I also remember that when the weather got very cold, the water would freeze in the offering bowls on the altar inside the house. I would take them out, dislodge the ice, which was exactly the shape of the bowl, then stick two of these back to back to make a small *dhamaru* [ritual drum] to play with."

In Tibet, when a child shows highly developed spiritual gifts or feels drawn to ritual objects, this indicates a deep connection with the dharma from a previous life. Called a tulku, that child is then recognized as the reincarnated lama of a specific monastery and will be raised there, eventually to become its abbot. Thus, when Denma Locho created a ritual drum out of ice, he revealed himself as a possible tulku.

"When I was about six, people began to say that I was a reincarnation of Gen Locho, a well-known scholar from a nearby monastery called Selkhar. This did not please my uncle, who wanted me to become the leader of the family. Anyway, when they came from the monastery to give me Gen Locho's robes, I refused to wear them. I went outside and curled up beside our huge mastiff watchdog. Eventually I was initiated as a monk, but not in Selkhar. I was sent to Bamchu monastery, where I spent a good deal of time memorizing prayers. When I was eleven, my uncle told me I could study in Lhasa. We set off with a caravan of two hundred yaks, carrying trade goods and whatever else we needed for our two-month-long journey.

"At last I was able to settle in Drepung monastery and begin studying

Denma Locho

for the Geshe degree. Most of the student monks in the college followed basically the same curriculum: introductory topics for one year, the perfection of wisdom for five years, then the philosophy of the Middle Way for the next two. I lived in a room in Denma House with an elderly monk who had come with me from Kham. As soon as we got to Lhasa, he turned into a real tyrant, making me memorize my lessons thoroughly and never allowing me to miss any classes or debates. He would beat me at the slightest provocation, always believing he was doing it for my own good. After he died of pleurisy, I continued to persevere at my studies, eventually taking in students of my own. I tried to find dedicated, serious students who would not waste their time or mine.

"In the monastery, many monks encountered beings that were non-human, and I had one such experience. It was during a retreat on the deity Yamantaka in the room of my principal teacher, Gen Nyima. I had settled down to sleep in the large room, with the skull cup containing inner offerings in front of me. I heard footsteps, but since it was pitch black, I just lay still and listened. Then I heard the clink of the skull cup cover being lifted off and, a minute or two later, replaced. When I looked the next day, only a little of the tea that we used for the inner offerings was left in the cup. I never found out who took it—maybe a hungry ghost—but I can still remember vividly the sounds and the footsteps as I lay there in the dark.

"Once, in Lhasa, Gen Nyima and I had gone to a house to perform a ritual to insure prosperity. Gen Nyima left as soon as it was over, but I was slow about going. Just as I had gotten on my boots, a woman came in, supported on either side. I was told that she was possessed and asked if I could do anything to help her. Usually when someone is possessed, they will scream or rage, but she was quiet. I asked the spirit who was possessing her who it was, but the spirit refused to answer. I'd heard that spirits can enter and leave a person's body by way of their ring finger, and that tying a string on the finger prevents the spirits from escaping. In this way, you can trap a spirit in someone's body and get it to promise to leave the person alone.

"After I tied a piece of string to the woman's finger, I took some white mustard from my pocket, which, if blessed in Tantric rituals, is a powerful substance. I burned it, blowing the smoke in the woman's face. She began to shriek, saying that she was standing in a thornbush. When I asked the spirit who she was, she answered that she was a woman from a village near Drepung. When she'd gone to market that morning, she'd met this neighbor who wouldn't speak to her. Out of anger, she entered the woman's body."

I glanced over at Choedon, who was relaying all this without expression. Witchery and possession were utterly unremarkable to her. It seems these people of Shambala go flying in and out of each other's bodies by way of ring fingers as easily as we cross the street.

Rinpoche explained how this was a witch who went around harming others. "I suppose that her body slept while she inhabited someone, or perhaps she had the power to emit a double. In any case, when I trapped her spirit, it frightened her very badly, and I made her promise by the Palden Lhamo (female dharma protector) of Drepung Podrang that she would leave this neighbor woman alone."

Rinpoche left me to ponder the power of the witch who could emit a double, and returned to his own story.

"AFTER RECEIVING MY Geshe degree, I went on to Gyume Tantric College until 1958. The discipline there was very harsh. In summer, we weren't allowed to wear shoes, although the streets of Lhasa were very poorly paved. I had to walk to my debating sessions, and soon my feet blistered. Even the better-paved streets were very cold in the early morning, and after a time my feet developed a thick skin. Finally, I thought of a solution: I bought some flesh-colored cloth and stuck it to the bottoms of my feet without anyone knowing. I considered getting flesh-colored socks, but they were ribbed, and I was afraid someone would notice."

He laughed, remembering. His attendant came in and spoke quietly to him. Rinpoche apologized and explained he had to leave for an appointment. He would be glad to continue our talk on another day.

THE SHAMBALA
TOUR GUIDE

OVER A LUNCH of *momo* [Tibetan dumplings] and rice at the Hotel Tibet, I asked Choedon, who had lived outside Tibet half her life, if she had ever seen any of these phenomena herself. She smiled brightly. "Oh, yes. In fact, I can take you to meet the rinpoche who has been to Shambala."

WE WENT TO the home of Khamtrul Rinpoche, who, Choedon explained, is the fourth incarnation of a scholar and saint from eastern Tibet. Scholar, meditation teacher, and ritual master of the oldest Buddhist lineage in Tibet, Khamtrul Rinpoche is the only holder of the Fifth Dalai Lama's complete words in direct transmission in India today. He lives with his wife and daughter in a house near the temple in Dharamsala. His daughter, who had been educated in the States and seemed remarkably Westernized, explained this as she showed us to Rinpoche's room. Seated behind a large desk in front of a window, his head encircled by the light behind him, he reminded me of a Buddhist painting.

"MY REAL NAME, my personal name, is Jamyang Dontrup; my title as a lama is Khamtrul Rinpoche. The *kham* there refers to my monastery, which has kham in its name. The *trul* is for tulku, or incarnation, for I'm recognized as an incarnation of a lama of this monastery.

"I was born in an area of eastern Tibet known as Litang on December 19, 1927, into a middle-class family of merchants. Most of the families in the area made their living through trading rather than farming. At the age of four, I entered a monastery known as Litang Gonchen, which means the great monastery of Litang. It was founded by the Third Dalai Lama, and this is a monastery of the Gelugpa school. I remained there until the age of eight.

"In the prophecy of my birth, a place named Ba was mentioned, but because my parents moved from Ba to Litang when I was very young, the people who searched for the incarnation in Ba couldn't find me. Since the prophecy said the search would take a long time, they kept looking. The abbot of a different monastery made a similar prophecy about my rebirth, and said not to look in Ba, but in Litang. So the committee went there and asked to see all the children born in the Year of the Dragon. There were five of us born that year. A list was submitted to the search party. When they met me for the first time, I was so happy that they had come, I went around singing. They told me, all right, we're glad you're so happy, but before we take you away, you have to tell us who we are and what are the names of our horses. I identified each of them, the men and their horses, and they were satisfied. They took me with them.

"As a small child, no matter where I lived, I tried to go someplace else. Always at sunrise and sunset, I would have a very clear memory of my previous monastery and relations in that life. So it was no problem to recognize the men who came looking for me.

"I would discover later that Tibetans believe the strongest past-life memories occur between the ages of three and five. After that, the picture begins to fade.

"From the age of eight up to the age of twenty-five, I studied in the Nyingmapa tradition, learning their religious rituals, astrology, and philosophy. But when I was sixteen, my mind would frequently become upset and unbalanced. I consulted many people, but no one seemed able to help me. Finally, I consulted my spiritual guide, Jamyang Khyentse Chokyi Lodro, who did a divination. It was suggested that I make a pilgrimage to a sacred site in Minyak, eastern Tibet, and recite 400,000 prayers to Padmasambhava.

"I made the pilgrimage, but being young and lazy, I recited only half the prescribed amount of prayers. But while I was there meditating in a sacred cave, I had an amazing dream.

"In this dream, a girl of about fifteen or sixteen—more beautiful than any girl I had ever seen—appeared to me. She was dressed in clothes and ornaments very different from those of a traditional Tibetan girl. She behaved so seductively toward me that all the atoms in my body began to dance. I probably told her all sorts of things, although I can't remember exactly the words, I was so excited. When I calmed down a little, she said to me, 'Brother, we should visit the kingdom of Shambala.' "

I leaned forward in rapt attention. At last I was hearing firsthand about the kingdom in the north of Tibet, known in English as Shangri-la. I searched my memory for what I had read: After the Buddha Sakyamuni gave the Kalachakra *tantra* to King Suchandra, he took it to the kingdom of Shambala in the north and built an inconceivable mansion for the Kalachakra Buddha. The king was followed by seven dharma kings and twenty-one lineage-holders, all of whom guarded these teachings. As with all the tantras, the purpose of the Kalachakra practice is to purify the body, speech, and mind, as well as gradually to release the imprint of the karmic patterns in our mindstreams. The story states that in the future, when things look very dark, the warriors of Shambala—the dharma practitioners—are to rise up as an army and fight the negative forces. Khamtrul Rinpoche told me his reaction to the girl's invitation:

"When this beautiful girl in my dream said that we could visit there, my first thought was, 'Wow!' Then I realized that she had called me Brother, hardly what my excited atoms expected. As her brother, I couldn't tell her how I really felt about her, so instead of calling her Sister in return, I said, 'My friend, I very much want to go to Shambala with you, but I have to tell you that I have no idea how to get there.'

"Again she called me Brother, and said that I didn't have anything to worry about, that she was there to guide me. Gathering up my courage, I asked her how she knew who I was. Laughing, she said, 'You fool, don't you recognize me? Just look straight into my eyes.'

"She showed me her seven eyes: two in the ordinary places, one between her brows, two each on the soles of her feet and on her palms. In this way, she revealed to me that she was, in fact, White Tara. She said that if I looked straight into her eyes, this would create conditions for my longevity. Since I'm now sixty-five, and my predecessors didn't make it past fifty or fifty-five, it must have worked. She also told me that I wouldn't remain a monk, but that I'd benefit many beings and marry a woman named Dolma or Dolka. None of my previous incarnations had married, but when I had to leave Tibet because of the Chinese presence,

Khamtrul Rinpoche

everything changed. It became necessary for a number of tulkus to marry in order to maintain their family lines. I gave back my monk's vows and married, but I remained a lama. My wife's name is Dolka.

"I sat on a white cloth next to this beautiful girl, and we flashed away. Being close to her created so much bliss that I had no questions, no doubts, no conceptions in my mind. What I felt was beyond any kind of ordinary experience. And we went so fast! If I could go that quickly in an airplane, I could visit New York from India three times a day.

"We flew over a mountain that looked like it had a snow lion on it. 'Look, there's the Dergey Printing Press. At the time of your predecessor, Pema Lundrup, I was your auntie Tsewang Lhamo and I carved some of the woodblocks, which are still there.'

"As we sailed through the air in my dream-vision, we saw Mount

Kailash, then a magnificent range of snow mountains, and an area that looked like a snake about to catch a frog. We also passed a desert that looked like a tiger's skin laid out flat, as well as too many other places to mention, including a vast barren area that didn't seem to support any form of life at all.

"We continued to fly north until we came to a great circle of mountains that looked like a gigantic open lotus with thirty-two petals. She told me that each petal had thirty-two cities, each the size of New York. Furthermore, each city was itself surrounded by nine hundred smaller cities; altogether, there were almost a million little towns and more than a thousand great cities. The houses themselves were splendid golden-roofed palaces decorated with brilliant jewels, tinkling bells, and lovely rainbows. Just looking at these dwellings gave me a great feeling of ecstasy.

"The families in Shambala each owned large parks, with ponds filled with scented water, and great wealth, which came from their wish-fulfilling jewels and cows. No one had to work, for whatever a person desired would spontaneously appear. Since everyone was rich and healthy, free from sickness and war, I had a feeling that they were not born from their mothers' wombs like we are, but appeared miraculously. Most extraordinary of all was that in the kingdom of Shambala, there was no sense of you and I, no competition or discord, only perfect peace and harmony.

"Some of the houses were built of light. From this I concluded that not all of the inhabitants of this great place were humans, but perhaps celestial beings or maybe *nagas* [water gods]. Right in the center, in the heart of the kingdom of Shambala, ringed by all of the grand cities, lay the mansion of the deity Kalachakra, built by King Suchandra. In the tantras it states that the inhabitants of Shambala will subdue the evil in the universe with bows and arrows, and I wondered about that because of all the destructive modern weapons that were developed in World War II. When

I asked my companion about this, she said that I should not worry because whatever destructive methods are created in our world, the counter-agents will come automatically and appear in the kingdom of Shambala. The weapons in our world, she explained, are created out of various types of materials, but the antimissile systems of Shambala have the more powerful nature of exalted wisdom.

"When we were presented to the king, he was in deep meditation and shone with such radiance that I was unable to look directly at him. He dissolved first into light, then into a lama, who gave me a number of empowerments. After that, everything disappeared like a rainbow except the girl and myself. We began to express our love for each other.

"Then suddenly, in my dream, I found myself back in my cave. I woke up, and it was dawn. I don't know if dreams are true or real, but this dream of my visit to the kingdom of Shambala with White Tara as my guide was very vivid indeed."

I asked Rinpoche if knowing such a place exists, in dream or in fact, helps him in times of difficulties. He thought a moment; his expression grew serious.

"The most difficult period of my life was when the Chinese invaded Tibet, making their unwanted reforms. I was twenty-five. I went to live in Lhasa in 1956, but I kept hoping that the situation would change for the better. I couldn't go back to Kham or the monastery because the Chinese were there. The inevitable came with the unsuccessful uprising in 1959. Just after His Holiness left, I decided to leave Tibet. Fleeing the country was hard not just for me, but for all Tibetans. But instead of challenging my faith, these experiences have made it stronger.

"I have no specific feeling about the Chinese today. The people were under orders to invade our country. It wasn't their fault; it was their leaders' ignorance. They thought it was good for the future of the Chinese, but that is wrong thinking. For such ignorance I feel bad for the Chinese people.

"Throughout the world, anger, desire, and ignorance are the roots of all suffering, whether among Chinese or Tibetans. I wish that these poisons could be banished from the world. A person who has anger for his enemies and love only for his neighbors will ultimately suffer. We all should understand the importance of this, whether we believe in religion or not."

THE INTERVIEW HAD come to an end. Just as I was unplugging the microphone and putting away the earphones, Choedon asked Rinpoche if he would do a divination on behalf of a friend. She asked matter-of-factly, as if she were requesting nothing more unusual than a cup of tea, and Rinpoche complied as easily. My mind automatically flashed to all the high-priced psychics in the States.

I watched with fascination as Rinpoche took three dice out of a silver box and, first concentrating a few moments, threw them onto the table. He gave Choedon the answer, and she thanked him.

I asked Rinpoche if he would mind explaining the art of divination. He nodded, and I hurriedly took out the tape recorder again.

"Both the diviner and the person seeking advice must have pure motivation. Together they both must pray to the Buddha, the Dharma, and the spiritual community; their Root Lamas; their deities; and dharma protectors, especially Palden Lhamo, for a clear answer. I personally visualize myself as my personal deity, Dorje Shonu, or Vajra Kilaya, then call on Palden Lhamo. Then I throw the dice. If the answer is not clear, I throw it again until I am certain of the answer."

Rinpoche said something to Choedon, who turned to me. "Would you like Rinpoche to do a divination for you?" she asked. I felt my face redden, flustered by my eagerness. "Yes. Thank you."

"On what subject?" she asked.

"Primarily on the state of my health—now and in the forseeable future."

Rinpoche nodded, listening. I held my breath as he closed his eyes and mentally asked the question. He then threw the dice and studied them. "The illness you were stricken with a few years ago will not return," he said. "You are fine."

I smiled, so pleased with the answer that I forgot for a moment to wonder how he knew I'd had an illness. Then he added, "But you must take care of your things properly or you may suffer a loss."

I stared at him. I had spent the better part of the afternoon frantically searching for my notebook, which contained my entire journal of the trip, lists of interviews, addresses. I'd had lunch at the Hotel Tibet with Father Bob, an Episcopal priest from Chicago, who had come to Dharamsala for an audience with the Dalai Lama. We were staying at the same hotel and had walked back together, stopping at the bus station to confirm my reservation for the following day.

It was not until I was about to leave to meet Choedon that I realized my notebook was missing. I ran to find Father Bob. For the next hour we retraced our steps; with each passing minute I grew more frantic. We had all but given up, when I decided to look a second time in the restaurant. I questioned the waiter again. Then, just as I was about to leave, I decided to have another look at the table where we had been sitting. There was the notebook, on a chair! Impossible. I had already searched there, and so had Father Bob.

Khamtrul Rinpoche suggested I go to the temple and make an offering to Mahakali and ask for her protection. Choedon said she'd take me there. I thanked Khamtrul Rinpoche.

"And you will marry again," he said when I was almost out the door.

"What?"

He laughed and said, "Go make your offering now."

CHOEDON AND I walked up the hill past a stream of people, mostly elderly, who were circumambulating the temple. She told me many of them do this several times a day, no matter what the weather. We passed an old woman who walked so bent over that her head nearly touched the ground. "Or no matter what their health."

Inside the temple, Choedon took me to the room where Mahakali stands, fierce and blue, and explained that she is a wrathful form of Tara. "Wrathful does not mean angry; it means strong and protective." I placed my offering of rupees and a white silk scarf at Mahakali's feet, and asked that she favor me with her strength and protection.

THE TALKING FROG

ONCE AGAIN, CHOEDON and I separated for the day, and I walked back to my hotel alone, past monks in twos and threes headed to the monastery, perhaps for dinner; past the beggar, with his sitar and his dancing marionettes; past the shopkeepers folding their shutters; and I thought: Do I want to marry again? It was a disturbing thought. I had  walked away from the only real marriage I'd had. After that, my relationships were mutual rescue missions: You save me from my chaos, and I'll save you from your politics or your unawakened mind or even your unhappy marriage. And for a little while, it would seem as if we had found refuge in each other. But then, when the illusion faded, we'd both feel betrayed, hoodwinked. Is it possible I still could get it right?

"HAVE YOU HEARD the one about the talking frog?" I asked Father Bob, who was on his way to the patio to watch the sunset. I joined him, and we ordered beers. "A woman is walking in the woods when she hears a voice call out, 'Hello! You there! If you kiss me, I'll turn into your Prince Charming.' The woman looks down and sees a frog. 'Really, I'm not kidding,' it says. Doubtful, the woman walks on. The frog leaps after her. 'Please, you won't be sorry. I promise. It's I you've been waiting for your whole life.'

"Finally she bends down, picks him up, and tucks him into her pocket. 'Hey, wait! You forgot to kiss me!' The woman takes him out of her pocket and looks at him for several moments. 'On second thought,' she says, 'I think I prefer a talking frog.'"

Father Bob threw his head back and laughed, then asked, "Is that your position on prince charmings?"

I told him about Khamtrul Rinpoche and the divination. "If I'm to believe what he said about my health, don't I also have to accept his divination about marriage?"

"I would think so. Why? Don't you ever want to marry again? Aren't you ever lonely?"

"I never give myself time to be," I answered.

He told me about his own marriage, which is strong and steady and lasting. For a moment I felt cheated. My peregrine nature has denied me that.

We watched the sun begin its descent behind the mountain. A hawk wheeled out of the north and swept down into the shadows, its great wings catching the light, and dived invisibly into a ravine.

NOMADIC LIFE

NOT ALL TIBETANS live in towns or monasteries; Tibet's original inhabitants were nomads living in high, open country, grazing their herds of sheep and yak between winter and summer pastures. They lived in large, low-slung tents made of yak hide, and traveled to the lowlands only to trade meat and cheese. They spoke their own dialect and dressed in fleece-lined robes, charm boxes at their necks and long swords at their waists.

Although I would not meet Namtak Yundung and his family until later in Switzerland, he is so much a part of old Tibet that I include his story here.

"I COME FROM a family in western Tibet near Mount Kailash, an area of nomads who lived and traveled in groups. I'm not sure of the exact year I was born, but it would be sometime around 1934. When I was five years old, my mother died. I had two sisters and four brothers. Eight of us lived in one large tent—about twenty meters across—made of yak hide.

"In the middle of the tent was the fireplace, a sort of iron grate big enough to hold two pots. At night, we'd sleep around the edges of the tent, close to the walls. My father slept on a mattress made out of the thick fur of an animal we don't have in Switzerland. Sort of an antelope or a goat. The rest of us slept on cloth sheets with fur coverings. On the floor were Tibetan carpets. We'd dig holes for drainage when it rained so the rugs wouldn't get wet. At night, two people would stay outside to keep watch over the sheep, to make sure they weren't harmed by wild animals or stolen by thieves. The thieves didn't belong to any group. They were more like roaming pirates and would steal an animal whenever they could.

"Our diet consisted mainly of tsampa, yogurt and dry cheese from goat's milk, yak meat, and goat. And lots of butter tea. Then at Losar we drank beer or chang. We didn't grow our food; we lived like nomads always have, on products from the animals.

"Once a year in the spring, as many as seventy families would come together to decide who would go where in the region to graze their animals. The decision was based upon how many animals in the herd and how big the family. Some had to go quite far away to the north. These groups would always help one another when anyone ran into trouble."

Up until this point, most of the people I had met centered their lives around monasteries and temples. I wondered whether the nomadic communities ever got to experience spirituality and monastic life, being constantly on the move.

"Nomads are quite religious. We do practices and pujas daily. We used to invite lamas from the regions to visit us and give teachings. We killed only old animals who were too weak to follow the herds. But nomads did not normally learn to read or write. It was believed that reading caused too much stress on the eyes. If someone wanted to learn to read or write, they had to go to the monasteries. My friend Tenzin Dolma, who would later become my wife, and I learned to read in the backyard. My sister, who had learned in an abbey, taught us. Since we had to work with the sheep all day, we studied at night.

"By the time I reached seventeen, I wanted to do something more with my life, so, without asking my family's permission, I went to a monastery. I was ordained as a monk at a Bonpo [pre-Buddhist animistic tradition] monastery, which was more than two thousand years old.

"In the monastery, my lama had been having visions for ten years that the Chinese would invade. When we got the news that they had invaded Lhasa, the lama already knew it."

Namtak showed me a picture of his Bonpo lama wearing a yellow pointed hat and a yellow-and-red robe. When I asked him to tell me about the mystical Bonpo religion, which predates Buddhism in Tibet, Namtak seemed reluctant.

"My lama knew many shamanic practices, but he was against teaching them because many of the rituals involved killing. My main teaching was Nyingma."

"When did you decide not to be a monk?"

"I was a monk for five years. Then I gave back my vows and married. Her family was much bigger than my own. They had two or three tents, as opposed to my family's one, and more than a thousand sheep, twelve yaks, seventeen horses, and many dangerous dogs that were bigger than sheep. These long-haired dogs would herd the sheep and protect them from thieves and wild animals. Very aggressive in nature, the dogs were more effective than any human when it came to protecting the herds.

"We decided to leave Tibet because when the Chinese came, I could not practice anymore. More and more I saw lamas leave the country as the situation got worse. Even though we didn't have any direct contact with the Chinese, I'd heard many stories of the things they were doing. Also, I had an instinctive feeling that the Chinese were bad for Tibet.

"Five of us started to escape together in 1962. We had a few horses, which we used as pack animals, while we ourselves traveled by foot. We wanted to go over Nede pass, but after the first day, the horses started to slip backward on the icy track, so we had to go back down the mountain and walk around it. It was very hard going. It took us eight days to reach the border of India, near the Upi district. At the border were three check-points. We couldn't go through the first one because none of us had a passport. We had to fill out papers saying who we were and wait for pass-ports to be issued. These we took to the second checkpoint. But the Dalai Lama hadn't arrived yet in Dharamsala to negotiate with the Indian lead-ers about the flood of Tibetan refugees coming into the country. Finally, after two months, we received permission to cross into India.

"We were sent first to a region called Puri Bopaka, where, because the Dalai Lama had organized support from the USSR and other coun-tries, many Tibetan refugees had settled. We lived in the camp about one or two years. Our son was born there in 1963. He made the whole journey in his mother's womb. That's why he looks so strong! My wife had no problems during our escape, and she gave birth in a hospital. She'd never been in a hospital before. She found it wonderful, a great experience.

"A year later we were sent south to Orissa, where we found a house with a little bit of land and began farming. But it was so hot, and as no-mads we knew nothing about farming, so this didn't really work. We left Orissa and went on a pilgrimage to Bodh Gaya, Benares, and other holy places, and finally up to the north. We went by train to Manali, using the last money we had. We were relieved to be in high altitudes again, out of the heat. My wife and I were put to work, along with many other Tibetans,

Namtak Yundung and Wife

building roads. My wife worked with the baby strapped to her back. It was hard, but from the time of our escape, all during the stay in India, we didn't have time to think of anything except how to get through this period in our lives, how to survive. We worked for three rupees a day, and that was barely enough to eat on. We had to repair our trousers nine or ten times because we couldn't afford to buy new ones.

"While we were in Manali, the Red Cross from Switzerland would come and talk to different families to see which ones wanted to emigrate. Most of the families wanted to go, but many of the families were too big to be taken to Switzerland. We were only four—my wife and son and his younger sister, who was sick. But I told them we couldn't travel because of our little girl. In time, she died; two years later, another was born. When the Red Cross asked us again, we agreed. I was hesitant at first because I'd heard that in Switzerland we couldn't practice Buddhism, that we could do only Christian practices. But that turned out to be untrue."

I asked Namtak Yundung how he felt about being so far away from his homeland.

"Our family is very happy living in Switzerland. We have everything we need. Of course, I would like to be buried in Tibetan earth, and like all Tibetans, I would like my country to be free. I can show you a text where Padmasambhava prophesied [in the eighth century] that the Chinese would invade Tibet and the people would have to flee. The text doesn't say anything directly about the people returning to their country, but it does say that if the Nepalese and Chinese begin to have conflicts, then Tibet can become more hopeful about getting their country back. Recently we heard that the monastery where I had studied, which the Chinese destroyed, has been rebuilt.

"We are very happy also that people around the world have been exposed to Buddhism through our refugees. Our one concern, though, is that the younger generation of Tibetans does not seem to be as interested in Buddhism as they would have been had they grown up in Tibet. We're afraid that they won't continue the profound path of our elders. A whole new generation of Tibetans is getting teachings from Western lamas rather than Tibetan lamas. This is depressing.

"On the other hand, my wife, who never had much of a chance to study Buddhism when we lived in Tibet, has had the opportunity to hear many teachings and to do intensive practice here in Switzerland. Her main practice is not to harm other beings, and to avoid negativity in thoughts and action; and my goal is to have a better rebirth for myself and all sentient beings and, eventually, to reach enlightenment. My wish is that all people who are able to read would read about Buddhism and think positively about the future of Tibet."

THAT EVENING, AS I sat writing in my journal, I thought, Is it any wonder these people fell prey to the Chinese Communists? They don't belong in the real world, God help us, they belong to another time, to Shambala.

I made a stab at meditating. Over the years I had tried various techniques learned mainly from books, and my success had been hit-or-miss. Then, on Indian reservations in sweat-lodge ceremonies, I was forced to control my mind to survive the excruciating heat. It was either concentrate or be cooked.

I sat cross-legged on the floor and quieted my mind. But very soon my sick stomach took over. My mind, it seemed, was no match for Delhi-belly.

MEDICINE AND
ASTROLOGY

JAMPA KELSANG TEACHES astrology at the the Institute for Medicine and Astrology. I had been given his name as a translator for my interviews with the two doctors and the astrology professor I had scheduled; as a fellow teacher, Kelsang would be more familiar with the terms.

My first interview was with Dr. Tenzin Choedrak, the Dalai Lama's personal physician. Delhi-belly had worsened; I told Kelsang-la I had better cancel my appointment. But Kelsang-la wouldn't hear of it. "What better place to take your sick stomach than to the greatest doctor in the world!" John Avedon wrote extensively about Dr. Tenzin Choedrak in his book *In Exile from the Land of Snows*. He had survived twenty-one years of beatings and torture and starvation in a Chinese prison, using advanced methods of Tantric meditation and visualization. My experience with critical illness had given me some understanding of the enormous power of the spirit. I had witnessed with my own eyes a woman's malignant tumor "miraculously" cured—later documented—in a peyote ceremony, and I believe my own recovery was profoundly helped by healing techniques taught to me by Native American medicine men and women.

So with considerable curiosity—and a very sick stomach—I was taken to see Dr. Tenzin Choedrak.

DR. TENZIN CHOEDRAK entered the Lhasa Medical Institute at seventeen, one of only fifty students, where he studied for thirteen years. He also devoted eight years to the study of medicinal formulation, a difficult field of science taught only to selected students.

In 1953 Dr. Choedrak was appointed senior personal physician to the Dalai Lama's mother; following the Dalai Lama's flight to India, he was imprisoned in his own country by the Chinese for twenty-one years, until 1980.

Two years later, the doctor was able to go to India, where he became physician to the Dalai Lama and joined the Tibetan Medical Institute in Dharamsala as chief medical officer and head of the research department. Since 1984, Dr. Choedrak has been involved in research programs with Harvard Medical School and has participated in conferences on global health throughout Europe and the United States.

DR. CHOEDRAK'S OFFICE is across the square from the large building that houses the Institute of Tibetan Medicine and Astrology. We entered through a narrow, curtained doorway to an office at the end of the hall.

The doctor sat at his desk, his head lowered over papers. When he looked up, I was suddenly staring into the tragedy of Tibet. It was written on the doctor's face, the twenty-one years of beatings, torture, and starvation in a maximum-security Chinese prison. His left eye was damaged during one of those prolonged beatings, the retina detached, the eyeball knocked into the upper left side of its socket.

But it was also the face of a man who, when he was released from prison and stood on the red line that marks the border on the Nepal-Chinese Friendship bridge, turned and shouted, "Now all you Chinese can go to hell!"

We were about to begin the interview, when Kelsang-la explained to the doctor that I had a "very bad stomach." Immediately the doctor reached for my right arm and placed three fingers on my wrist. "I press the skin with the first finger," he explained, "the flesh with the second, and the third I press just hard enough to feel the bone. Each finger has twelve divisions, each of which reads the pulse that corresponds to a particular organ."

Then he looked at my tongue. He told me I had a microbial infection that could easily be cured by "precious pills," which detoxify the blood. Precious pills are made from gold, silver, and jewels that first have been boiled with certain plants, then ground into powder and dried in a cool place away from sunlight. The powder is then mixed under the full moon of the eighth Tibetan month and made into pills.

I told the doctor about my bout with cancer and asked if Tibetan medicine had a different understanding of the disease than Western medicine's.

"There is not a different understanding, it is the same. We can't find a cure, and it is difficult to find an effective treatment. I am familiar with radiation and chemotherapy as a treatment for cancer, and feel that these methods are good in one way, but are negative in that they have a powerful effect on the blood, so you get weak. I found some patients in France who had cancer. When I gave them Tibetan medicine, it helped to strengthen their blood."

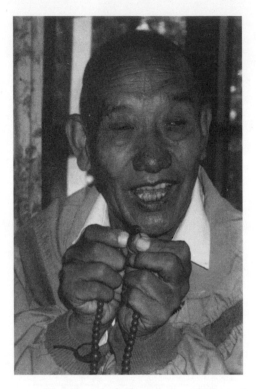

Dr. Tenʒin Choedrak

Dr. Choedrak then proceeded to give me a brief explanation of the history of Tibetan medicine.

"TIBETAN MEDICINE IS 2,500 years old. In the Bonpo tradition, a famous teacher taught medicine near the time of the Buddha. In 253 A.D., an Indian sage came to Tibet and taught his medical system, which was then practiced by a single family who were part of the royal Tibetan court. Around the sixth century, another famous medical scholar came, this time from Iran, and taught his system in Tibet. Then between the seventh and eighth centuries, the Tibetan king Trisong Detson, and the Tibetan father of medicine, Yuthok Yonten Gonpo, organized the first medical conference and invited many doctors from Persia, India, Kashmir, Nepal, and other neighboring countries like Mongolia and China to participate. They held this meeting in a place in Tibet called Samye. The different medical scholars talked about their own specialties. They compiled a very important textbook at that time and established Tibet's first medical college, Melung, or Country of Medicine.

"Then in the tenth century, another burst of medical energy appeared, producing a major medical textbook, which listed 2,243 different medicinal plants and classified diseases into 1,600 categories. At that time, the question arose about what would happen in the future. It was prophesied that in the coming time there would be a great change, the coming of industry, which would result in pollution of the air, water, and environment; and that eighteen different diseases would appear. People would find it impossible to maintain their diets and behaviors properly during that period.

"Our era seems to be the time prophesied. So many chemicals are used now, and people often have negative reactions to them.

"Our medical text has classified almost 1,000 different types of poisons. There are various animal poisons, like those carried by snakes or dogs; and plant poisons, as when one touches certain plants and the hand develops a rash. Another type occurs when one eats food that is not in itself poisonous but, when not digested properly, transforms into poison in the stomach. Then there is a kind of poison that is external, often in the form of vapors or gases, and sometimes transmitted in the atmosphere that comes down from the sun.

"When I visited Russia, I learned about many gas poisons. There are 600,000 people suffering in Russia due to gas or chemical poisons resulting from the Chernobyl disaster. I treated many people there who were working as officials at that time, survivors who suffered poisonous disease.

All of my twenty-four patients were completely cured by Tibetan medicine. Our system worked so well that they hope to create a branch clinic in Russia, though there is a problem in getting the proper medicine there. I am formulating the crucial medicine here, but it is very expensive. The ingredients call for gold and several ground-up jewels, including emeralds, rubies, and diamonds."

I had read of the complexity of the Tibetan system of medicine. To understand how all of the interrelated parts fit together, students at Mentsikhang (Medicine House) have to study the Illustrated Tree of Medicine, which has three roots, nine trunks, forty-two branches, two hundred twenty-four leaves, three fruits, and two flowers. After learning this diagram, they are taught how to associate the appropriate chapters of the tantras with different parts of the tree, and then go on to study each root, branch, and so on. Buddha explained in the first, or Root Tantra, that three humors control the physical condition of all human beings. I read that the three humors of the body are lung (or subtle energy, something like *chi*) bile, and phlegm, and I asked Dr. Choedak to describe the system to me.

"Subtle energy accounts for the movement of the body, bile for warmth, and phlegm for flexibility. There are five types of each of these three humors in the body, and if they get out of balance, then sickness results. The movable part of the body is controlled by lung, sometimes translated as wind; the heat part of the body responds to bile; the fluid or watery factor in the body is phlegm. These three we classify, when we want to analyze or study, into a hundred different types. If still we need to deepen the analysis, we go up to sixteen hundred subtypes. So you have to study many, many years.

"If the heat part of the body is excessive, then you get fever or your body gets hot. If there is too little warmth, then your body starts shivering, gets cold. Phlegm is by nature like the water element. So if you have a disorder of phlegm, usually such a person doesn't have enough heat, and the extremities or the abdomen get cold.

"You can recognize lung energy by movement. When you open your mouth, close your eyes, operate any of the movable parts of the body, this is due to healthful lung energy. Lung functions like an electric current which you connect so something can move. Healthful lung energy pushes the blood and gets it circulating throughout your body. This is, in general, a very easy way to understand lung, although in further study it gets very complicated.

"Lung is also intricately connected with the mind. Disturbance in the mind affects lung activity, and disturbance of lung affects the mind. When you have a problem in the mind, like unhappiness, if you are frightened, then your heart starts to beat very fast. That is lung affecting the body.

"When a person eats too much beef, the blood gets very thick, and fat forms in the body. Then the passage through which the lung energy is moving becomes very narrow, so it can't circulate properly. Alcohol also has the effect of slowing down the blood. These people have reddish complexions.

"When people become obese, their blood grows stagnant and they suffer from shortness of breath. You won't find much blood in their systems, mostly fat. We call these people phlegm-character persons. When this kind of person eats something, it goes into body fat, not toward body energy. As a consequence, he or she isn't very energetic. Often when a person is obese, the color of his complexion is very pale.

"Many of our health problems, in short, stem from our diets. The stomach can be divided into four categories. Ideally, one part should be empty, one should be liquid, two parts should have food. This is the correct pattern of diet to help us digest and get more energy. In the West especially, many people eat raw foods, like vegetables and cheese, which can't be digested properly.

"Now we come to bile energy, the main energy that helps with digestion. If bile is out of balance, then one has a digestive problem. If that energy works properly, then you have good digestion. Usually, the person with healthy energies will have normal body heat. The bile is the factor responsible for body heat.

"The body's fluid or liquid part is phlegm. If the phlegm proportion is normal, the joints are flexible. A correct proportion of pleghm also helps with the stability of mind. If there is too much phlegm, you develop a fever; if there is too little, you begin to shiver. This is a simplified explanation of phlegm, of course."

He told me that surgery, including brain surgery, was once a widely practiced art in Tibet, that they had developed many surgical implements and methods of anesthesia. But when the mother of King Muni Tsenpo died after an operation to lessen the water around her heart, surgery was officially banned. The operation had damaged her heart *chakra* so badly that it impeded her death, because all energy gathers at the heart level before consciousness leaves the body. Dr. Choedrak cited a reference to an ancient textbook that talked about surgery. He added that Tibetan doctors believe in surgery now, but lack much specific knowledge.

In addition to humors and an elaborate pharmacology, Tibetan doctors must learn also how to read pulses, which takes a whole year of study at Mentsikhang. The most effective place to take the pulse is on the wrist, just over the radial artery. If the patient is female, the right pulse is taken first, then the left; the reverse order is used for men. The doctor presses the middle three fingers of each hand on the flesh and bone of the patient. Each finger monitors "inner" and "outer" pulses—hollow organs being read as the "outer" and solid ones as the "inner"—thus twelve pulses are taken altogether. These relay information about the conditions of a patient's organs. For example, with his right index finger, the doctor monitors the heart of a male patient; with his left, the lungs. Again, the order is reversed for women. The doctor also determines the "constitutional pulse" of a patient—whether he or she is dominated by wind, phlegm, or bile—as well as the "seasonal pulse," since the weather also affects the organs.

Through an analysis of the pulses, the doctor then is able to conclude if the illness is "hot" or "cold," after which the state of the humors in the body can be investigated. Each humor—and there are five variations of each of the three humors—has a characteristic pulse. The pulses for various conditions also are taken. The pregnancy pulse, for instance, is soon apparent, and—after six weeks—the sex of the child can be determined. Descriptions of the various types of pulses range from "limping" and "quivering" to "like a vulture attacking a bird" or "like a hen eating grain." Imminent death also may be diagnosed through pulse reading.

Although the Chinese burned several rare but critical Tibetan medical texts during the Cultural Revolution, they have recently shown an interest in the value of preserving Tibetan medicine.

WITHIN THREE HOURS of taking the first incredibly bitter-tasting pill, which must be partly chewed then swallowed with hot water, I was symptom-free. I returned the following day to learn about the role of astrology in Tibetan medicine.

TIBETAN MEDICINE AND ASTROLOGY are as inextricably linked as the mind and body. They are taught in conjunction with each other. Although astrology students are not required to study medicine, medical students must study the astrological sciences. Unlike European astrology, which describes the personality based on the natal situation, Tibetan horoscopes chart the unfolding of a person's life. The life span is calculated and divided into nine periods, each ruled by one of the heavenly bodies. Each period is interpreted in relation to its ruling planet, the natal chart, and the age at which it occurs.

Four major themes appear in the Tibetan horoscope: life span, overall bodily and physical condition, economic and political power, and overall luck in business or career. Astrological calculations are always made for marriages and births. Astrologers also forecast the general welfare of the country.

Physicians consult medical astrology when determining the best day of the week for treatments such as moxabustion or gold needle acupuncture, for a patient. The patient's life-force and life-spirit days are determined from their natal animal sign.

Most Tibetans wish to know the time of their death, so that they can prepare for a good rebirth. However, even though a person's life span can be calculated, one's life can be extended with prayer and good deeds. A person's life also can be shortened by such external events as earthquake or war or a terminal illness if one does not have the karmic potential to survive such events. The Tibetan word for star is karma; one's karma is written in the stars.

As I seemed to be sampling morsels of Tibetan culture on this journey, I willingly agreed to have my astrological chart done by Jampa Kelsang. The two charts I'd had done over the years were interesting but for the most part unimpressive. Here I learned that I have a windy and phlegmatic nature; that I promote frequent changes of feeling and residence(!); that I love to meet new people and exchange ideas. My weakness could be impatience, and my life could "end up with poison, so always be aware"; I use lots of money unnecessarily, and I am advised to control my temper; I overcame many obstacles, separated from partners, and my health was in danger (all dates were correct), but I am coming now into a time of great peace and happiness. Jampa Kelsang also told me, "You have good children who are dear to you, with upbringings free of problems, who are supportive of your work. You have a much better and closer relationship toward your maternal side than paternal side" (this to the original daddy's girl—although I had no way of knowing then what the planets had in store for me).

On the whole the reading was surprisingly accurate. I requested that he not give me the date of my death, lest I wake up on that day and be literally frightened to death. Jampa Kelsang didn't, but the chart does come to a rather abrupt end somewhere around the age of seventy-four. We'll see. . . .

LATER, OVER A LUNCH of spicy noodles and tukpa at the Hotel Tibet, I began my interview with Professor Dakthun Jampa Gyeltsen.

"I WAS BORN in 1939 in Lhasa. My father was district governor and had to travel a great deal, so after I completed my middle school education, my parents invited teachers to our home to tutor me in the studies of astrology, poetry, and grammar. In order to study for the higher science of astrology, I went to a special university.

"Our village was close to the border with Bhutan. After the Chinese invaded in 1959, each time I went out to care for the animals, I began to study the shortcuts and got to know all of the passages for the time when I would make my escape. I had done the astrological calculations to determine when the most auspicious time to leave would be. If a Tibetan cannot begin a journey on an auspicious date, he will often take a small piece of luggage and move it a little down the road so as to begin the journey symbolically on that day.

"I left Tibet in December 1960. I waited till dark, then I strapped my luggage to my back and started walking. I walked all night to the top of the mountain, and all the next day to the Bhutan border.

"In Bhutan I was appointed to the office of His Holiness the Dalai Lama, where I served until 1967, when I came to Dharamsala. When the Tibetan Institute of Medical and Astrological Sciences was formed, I completed my studies, and I am now teaching.

"Tibetan astrology and medicine are based on the same concept of five elements: Wood, fire, earth, metal, and water. We believe that all visible objects are composed of these five elements. Even the wind contains five elements.

"These five elements are related to the external elements of the universe: the water you drink, the fire you use for cooking, the earth on which we live, the metal we use for chopping, the trees you see.

"In our bodies, muscles are the wood element; blood and fluids are the water element; heat is the fire element; the flesh is the earth element; the bones are metal. As for our vital organs, the liver is the wood element; the heart, fire element; the lung, metal; spleen, earth element; kidneys, water element. When a Tibetan doctor makes a diagnosis of a weak liver, he says there is a disorder of the wood element. At the same time, when a Tibetan astrologer makes a calculation and finds an imbalance in the wood element, he says there is a problem in the liver. Thus, a Tibetan astrologer makes diagnoses according to his astrological calculations, and a Tibetan doctor reads pulses but also thinks about the patient's animal sign, when he was born, and so forth.

"Astrologers are also consulted before marriages are arranged, to make sure the combination is good. We consider the situation from four different angles. First, we look at the couple's life span; second, their health; third, their financial status; and fourth, their success. Traditionally, the husband has to go out and find food for the family. So for him, his life span and success are very important. The mother has to give birth, so her health is very important, plus she'll have to take care of the financial situation, so that aspect is significant in her chart as well. So we compare these four different aspects in each of them, and calculate their compatibility.

"If for example we find the man's success is unfavorable, we might suggest to him he wear an amulet, which we make according to his birthday. Or if the woman's health situation is unfavorable, we would make an amulet for her. In some cases, the aspects are so unfavorable that we have to say, stop, a marriage would not be good, there will be too many problems."

I wanted to know if those already married would consult the astrologer if they felt the marriage wasn't working. Would they come to find out if they should part?

"I have found this problem in this modern time more and more. There are couples who are very much in love, who go ahead and get married without first consulting an astrologer. Then, after they have a problem, they come to me for help. So I draw up their charts to find the area where they are having the problem, and according to the problem, we make an amulet for them or ask them to do a certain puja or to read a certain text to free them from their obstacles.

"In the olden times, the amulet would contain a scripture or mantra of the astrological deity and the animal signs of their birthdays. It all would be drawn in ink made from medicinal plants. Nowadays, we don't have as much time, so we make the mantra from block print, then we write the mantra of some deity. Each sign has its special deity. Usually this

is kept secret. This amulet should be worn by the astrologer first, so that he himself is protected from any negative forces."

I asked if it were true that his calculations can predict the date when someone will die.

"We can predict when a person is going to die, but generally it is not good to be that specific. Instead we recommend certain pujas or prayer offerings be made, and to save the life of an animal. That might be the antidote for that year to create good karma. We do this to create good karma for ourselves, too.

"In our system, we calculate the time of birth from when the cord is cut, when a person is separated from the mother. We believe that the child's life begins when it is breathing on its own.

"We also look at a child's potential for education and capacity for spiritual growth, whether the child will do spiritual practice and if it will bring fruitful results. The chart can tell us which career would be best and if the work will be wrathful or peaceful. If peaceful, then which kind of work would be best suited. We also advise which animals would be best to raise. And we look to see if there will be some big loss in the child's life."

I asked if they do horoscopes for whole countries. "Have you done one for Tibet?"

"Since there is a problem in Tibet now, we are always looking to see what changes are coming. In the calculations, it would seem that the problem is disunity. Given this situation, there is no chance. In my calculations it appears that maybe this year we are going to have a good result, but in the end, the result is negative."

On that very sad note we brought the interview to a close. If the astrologer's calculations are correct, Tibet will be no more: these masters I was meeting are the last holders of the secrets of Shangri-la.

HIS HOLINESS
THE DALAI LAMA

THE DESK CLERK told me there was a message for me, and handed me a slip of paper. Tenzin Geyche Tethong, the Dalai Lama's private secretary, had called. My audience with His Holiness would take place the following day at one o'clock. I rushed to find Father Bob to tell him. He was on the patio, pacing nervously; he had just received notice of his appointment, which immediately followed mine.

I WOKE AT DAWN the morning of my audience with the Dalai Lama, and sat over tea, filling two pages of my spiral notebook with questions. I read them over; in despair I ripped out the pages. I had no idea how much time I'd be alloted, but I was certain it wouldn't be enough for all those idiotic concerns.

I went for a walk to try to quiet the noise inside my head. The vendors were not yet in their stalls; shopkeepers had not opened their doors; the sky was as empty and cloudless as buddha-mind. I walked on, trying to match that emptiness, until suddenly I heard loud, insane chatter from somewhere up ahead. At the same time, I spotted an open Jeep parked alongside a hotel, crawling with monkeys. They were everywhere, front seat and back, ransacking the car. They flung candy wrappers, underwear, sunglasses out of the car. One little monkey had managed to open a bottle of soda pop, and drank from it. Another scrambled up the hill with what looked like a hairdryer.

I started to go into the hotel to tell someone at the desk about the monkey invasion, when a man, obviously the hapless owner of the Jeep, came running out, shouting. The monkeys left, but not in any great hurry. The man yelled: "They've taken my goddamn car keys!"

I couldn't help it: I laughed. Somewhere here there was a lesson. My concerns . . . The busy monkeys . . . The laughter . . .

I ARRIVED EARLY, as instructed, for quite a thorough security search, which included handbags and pockets, and a pat down. The woman security officer removed the small Swiss Army knife from my backpack, to be picked up after the interview.

I sat in an anteroom until a monk attendant escorted me along a breezeway to a veranda and through the wide doorway that opened onto the Dalai Lama's receiving room. It was explained that a Swiss couple, recently returned from Tibet, would be sharing the audience, and that His Holiness would talk with me afterward. I was relieved to be an observer first.

But the Dalai Lama walked directly toward me, hands outstretched, beaming his famous smile, and said, "Hello, welcome." I fumbled for a katak, my book almost falling, then realized he simply wanted to shake hands. The moment I relaxed and allowed myself to be enveloped in the warmth of his gaze, I was filled with a feeling of lightness, of time suspended, and of being fully present and alive in that moment.

We took our seats in large, comfortable chairs; the Swiss couple sat on the couch, the Dalai Lama in a chair next to a translator, who was consulted only once. And then His Holiness thought a moment and decided, "No, I think I like my word better."

The room was spacious, filled with fresh flowers, altars, statues, and thangka paintings, yet there was no feeling of clutter. The Dalai Lama listened with rapt attention to the Swiss couple's report of what they had observed while in Tibet. They were describing what happened while they toured the Potala, the Dalai Lama's winter palace in Lhasa. While they had stood studying one of the ancient thangkas, bright lights suddenly flooded them, and they realized they were being videotaped.

The Dalai Lama asked if any Chinese were speaking Tibetan. No, they told him, but many Tibetans were speaking Chinese.

WHEN THE SWISS couple finished their story, I gave the Dalai Lama my Native American book and explained that I was writing one on Tibetan elders. "Yes, yes. I know." He leafed through the book, delighted when he recognized faces of individuals he had met. He agreed that my definition of "elder" had less to do with age than with wisdom and compassion, and expressed great pleasure with this current project of mine.

When I confessed my misgivings and explained that I was new to Tibetan Buddhism, he answered, "But that is wonderful! You are an empty cup."

I told His Holiness about the astrology professor's dire predictions for Tibet.

The Dalai Lama nodded solemnly, but did not fully agree. "I believe our beloved Land of Snows will one day be freed. Our dedication, sacrifice, and hard work will eventually lead our captive nation to freedom. However, it is important that our struggle be based on nonviolence."

"What do you say to young Tibetans who want an armed revolution?" I asked.

"Enemies are our most important teachers. They give us the opportunity to practice tolerance, which is the key to compassion. So it is imperative that we meet cruelty with nonviolence."

I had heard the Dalai Lama described as an emanation of the Buddha of Compassion, a god-king, a living deity of boundless love and compassion—descriptions that have only limited meaning to a person who is not a Buddhist. Sitting across from me was a man of such ordinariness, such unself-consciousness, a man so open and simple that one instantly forgets what has been written. All words seemed to dissolve. I was in the presence of pure light.

AFTERWARD, ON THE WAY OUT, we stopped on the steps, and a monk attendant offered to take a picture. I stood a step below the Dalai Lama, but he jumped down, took my hand, hugged it to his chest, and said, "We are on the same level, you and I." He looked at the Tibetan ring I had just bought at a stall. The small, aged woman who had sold it to me said that it was quite old and that I must wear it when I go to see His Holiness (I don't know how she knew I was having an audience). She sold me this oddly shaped turquoise-and-silver ring for very little, compared to the prices of the others. "Where did you buy this ring?" the Dalai Lama asked.

"From one of the women in the stalls," I answered.

"I know this ring," he said quietly, and blew on it to bless it.

I then received the red sacred blessing cord, which I will wear around my neck until it disintegrates. And this strange ring that now held a mystery. Whatever had gone before and whatever lay ahead, I thought I would never be quite the same. Along with the blessings, I had received an education of the heart.

OUT OF INDIA

I HAD TO RETHINK my plan to apply for a Chinese visa to go to Tibet when news came over the BBC that two Americans had been arrested and detained there in a Chinese prison. They had been seen giving an audio cassette of a teaching of the Dalai Lama's to some Tibetans as a gift.

 After a four-day interrogation, they were finally released and told to leave the country. I needed very little persuading to change my plans; entering Tibet with my recording equipment and camera, even with "housewife" written on the visa, would be testing even the kindest deities.

Still, Mahakali must have been watching over me in Delhi when I tried to get on a flight to the States. The bubonic and pneumonic plagues had broken out in a village south of Delhi only days before. Now people were flocking into Delhi, and tourists were scrambling for flights out of the country. Unable to reach the airline representatives by phone, I walked several blocks from my hotel to the airline office. The sights on the street were terrifying. People wearing hankerchiefs tied around their mouths and noses crowded the sidewalks; the heat was suffocating. Splatterings of spit on the sidewalk looked ominous. I hurried past beggars, who stared at me with haunted eyes, and gasped when a little girl reached out and grabbed my skirt. Too cowardly to look into the face of such suffering, I turned away.

At the airline office I was told that all flights out of Delhi had been canceled. An English businessman standing behind me suggested, in a quiet voice, I try a folded five-hundred-rupee note (less than twenty dollars). Shutting out the faces of the beggars on the street, I slipped the well-groomed official the money. I was then given "the last seat on the last flight out of Delhi." When I looked to thank the Englishman, he was gone. I thanked whatever deity it was who had come dressed as an English businessman, and dashed back to the hotel to collect my bags. On the way, I gave a ten-rupee note to each of the next five beggars I saw, but it did little to ease my conscience; the little girl was not among them.

I felt as if I'd just had a glimpse of the lower realms.

CHINESE INVASION AND OCCUPATION:

THE TAILOR, PART II

IN 1959, THE CHINESE illegally annexed Tibet, and the Dalai Lama, along with 100,000 refugees, fled to India. Others were not so fortunate—like the tailor who had given me a picture of old Tibet. What follows is the horrific story of his arrest and imprisonment.

"WHEN THE CHINESE attacked Chamdo, we were attending the annual Kashag picnic, a week-long grand affair held in huge tents, with fine food served from porcelain dishes. We saw our hosts suddenly ride off toward Lhasa on their horses, and knew that something was wrong. We didn't find out until later that the Communist troops had arrived. In December 1950, I was asked to make Gyalwa Rinpoche [the Dalai Lama] some Tibetan-style pants and a shirt, and a layman-style chuba, but not to tell anyone. When I delivered the clothes to him, he told me to come to the Potala the next day and to wear an ordinary chuba and leather shoes, that we would be leaving at four in the morning.

"As we mounted our horses at the foot of the Potala, I noticed tears in Gyalwa Rinpoche's eyes. He was dressed in the lay person's clothes I had made for him; no one recognized him, and we were able to slip away from Lhasa. I thought that we'd be gone a few days or maybe weeks, but we stayed in Dromo for nearly a year. Since we had brought little with us, I had to make His Holiness some new clothes. We were close to the border with India, so I ordered some American wool from Calcutta. Since it was khaki, a very unsuitable color, I dyed it before making chubas. Many negotiations were going on, but I was so busy with my sewing that I never really understood them.

"The Chinese presence in Tibet was strongly felt. Houses were requisitioned for their use, prices went up, and our work was usurped. The Chinese, who hadn't brought much with them, ordered the local tailors to make them new uniforms, often using as many as thirty tailors at a time. The Chinese paid well—up to twelve silver dayan a day—while our own government paid less than a tenth of that. Furthermore, our paper currency was eaten up by inflation. Tension developed between groups of tailors and myself, which was defused in 1954 when Gyalwa Rinpoche asked me to accompany his entourage to China. We left two days later.

"It was a difficult journey. Rain had washed out many of the roads, and we often had to travel by mule or on foot. General Chiang Chin-wu, who had led the first delegation into Tibet, came with us, and when we put up a red cloth fence around Gyalwa Rinpoche's tent at night, the general demanded one as well. We explained that this would be against Tibetan etiquette, but he insisted, and I made him a white one on the sewing machine that I had brought along. He wasn't completely pleased, for he suspected some sort of discrimination, but he didn't say any more about it.

"About five hundred of us accompanied Gyalwa Rinpoche to China, including lamas and their disciples, government officials and their families, cooks, valets, and various other people. When we entered China, no one was lined up as usual to see Gyalwa Rinpoche and to receive his blessings. They seemed indifferent to his presence. While part of the entourage continued overland with our luggage, three planes carried the rest of us to Shingang. After this noisy and cold journey, we were joined by the Panchen Lama and his bodyguards, although ours had not been allowed. Finally we got to Beijing, where Gyalwa Rinpoche settled into a two-story house in a complex built by the Japanese, which had a lovely garden.

"The Chinese provided everything we needed: cooks, servants. Our own servants and cooks were sent along with us to see many factories, schools, and other sights. At night, they would take Gyalwa Rinpoche out with only his interpreter. We'd stay up late, drinking tea, worrying if they had taken him to an inappropriate place."

"Did you have much contact with Mao?" I asked.

"Mao Zedong never appeared at meals, and we rarely saw him. Once he came to visit Gyalwa Rinpoche quite suddenly, and the Chinese seemed terrified. We peeked out into the hall to catch a glimpse of him.

"In the winter we went on a grand tour of China, and Gyalwa Rinpoche began to make public speeches. At first he seemed tentative and unsure of himself, but by the time he had talked at a number of factories, schools, and stores, he gained confidence. The Chinese speeches were all about how much material progress China had made, how poor the Tibetans were, and how much we would benefit from "help" from China. Some of our party were impressed with the new things they saw in China, but my lama, Phabongka Rinpoche, had told me some years before that I should watch out for all of the modern technology. Even though airplanes and modern machines made things go faster, it also meant that if we didn't have good motivation, we could get to the three lower realms—the hells, the hungry ghost, and the animal realms—a lot quicker. So I was not impressed when the Chinese told us how destitute we were. To me, they looked quite poor and undernourished in their drab cotton clothing. And the factories, with the intense heat and molten metal, seemed like a hell realm. Then, too, there were crowds everywhere.

"It seemed obvious to me that we were terribly fortunate in Tibet. Our temples—with all of their beautiful statues and lavish ceremonies—were open for everyone to view. The air was pure, the pastures spacious, we had enough butter and cheese for everyone. Also, for centuries, anonymous artists had created beautiful objects for the sake of enlightenment or a better rebirth. Where else in the world could you use your talent or your money to attain [spiritual] merit? I remember all of our treasures—the rich brocades, the gold-washed statues, the splendidly detailed thangkas and murals—and felt that we weren't the poor ones.

"After our return to Lhasa, I buried myself in work but could not help but be aware of the mounting tension around me. As the years passed, things got worse and worse, until, in March 1959, I was asked to attend a meeting at the Tsuglakhang. A rebellion was mounting, and rifles and guns were being distributed from the Norbulinka. The tailors had heard this and wanted to arm themselves. But I refused, saying that as tailors we served our government and people with needles, not guns. I advised them to stop sewing for the Chinese and to help prepare the temples for our rituals.

"It must have been my fate to stay behind, because at the time Gyalwa Rinpoche and his party left Tibet, I had gone to visit my mother, who was old and feeble. He had sent a message for me to come to the Norbulinka immediately, but by the time I got there, he had already gone, although not everyone knew this. With a heavy heart, I returned to Lhasa. Anxiously, I watched the Chinese shell the Potala, and was relieved when it did not burn. From my window, I could see many people being killed and others being arrested and tied together into long lines.

"After the generals had put down the resistance around the Norbulinka, they came to my house and set up their quarters in my upstairs rooms. They installed a portable telephone system and began calling different places. I served them tea, thinking that it might be useful later on. When they left, they thanked me for my hospitality and told me they had been very comfortable at my house. Later I found out that they were part of a group trying to catch up with Gyalwa Rinpoche.

"The Lhasa rebellion was soon over. When the Chinese found their way into the Tsuglakhang, they shot the people who were holed up there. Many people were killed in the last pockets of resistance. The Chinese celebrated their victory by releasing thousands of paper flowers from a plane as it circled over the Potala.

"A few days later, just as I was leaving my house to go pay some bills, a Chinese official and Tibetan translator came to my door and told me to report to Taring House, which had been turned into a prison. They knew all about me already, so there was not much to say. At the prison, they took my money and put me in a room with fifty other prisoners. The conditions of our imprisonment were dreadful: we were packed in like animals, given only a little bad food, and all forced to use a single bucket in the middle of the room for sanitation. The stench was overpowering. In Tibet, we were used to quick punishment, like whippings, nothing like this.

"Since I couldn't sleep, I had a great deal of time to think. I remembered all the rolls of beautiful brocades that I had worked with over the years, the satisfaction of turning out perfect garments to satisfied clients, the blessings of being able to serve Gyalwa Rinpoche. At first I did this just to keep up my morale. Then I started to realize that all of these things had put me in prison. It made me shiver to think that the Chinese would punish me for contributing to a way of life they wished to eradicate. I vowed if I ever got out, I would make an offering of brocade robes to the great temples.

"After ten days, I had fallen into despair. Although several people had died, the Chinese kept bringing in more people, so still we were over-crowded. And the food had gotten worse. People's families used to be allowed to send in food, but after a message was found in a thermos bottle, that policy was changed. They began to give us food from the old store-rooms left over from the Thirteenth Dalai Lama's time, most of which was inedible. I felt that if I could manage to accept my situation, I would not waste my energy on fear and resentment, but could devote it toward survival. I began to concentrate on getting out.

"When I was called for interrogation, the head of the prison, a fierce-looking man, told me that I had spent most of my life exploiting the masses as the Dalai Lama's tailor. He scowled and banged his fist on the table as he talked to me. Finally, when I got a chance to talk, I told him that he could bang his fist all he wanted to, but I was only a tailor. When the Chinese had asked for uniforms, I had complied. I had cooperated in every way and had not gotten involved in politics. He got very angry at this and was about to dismiss me, when I said, 'I am considered the best of seven hundred tailors. I'm no good to you in jail. You could use me. I would be happy to work.'

"Where I got the courage to say all that, I don't know. Then I added that I had been in the Dalai Lama's service for thirty-eight years, since I was eight years old, and I could sew anything. When he asked if I could sew Chinese clothes, I said of course I could, they would be nothing at all after the cutting and fitting of the brocade friezes for the temples. A few days later, he brought me a shirt that had bullet holes in it to mend, then a pair of Chinese trousers, and some other work. I was given a place to work, and they let me send home for my sewing machine. In time, he boasted that he had the Dalai Lama's tailor working for him. Orders and requests came pouring in so fast that he decided to set up a sewing unit. I recruited other tailors from the prison, and some who weren't tailors but were having a bad time. We often had to work seventeen and eighteen hours at a stretch, but we received more food and no longer had to live packed in a cell.

"In mid 1959, I was told that I had to undergo a public trial. These harsh affairs of the work units involved being insulted by your friends and neighbors, then beaten. The prison authorities had told me that they wanted to exempt me from this, but since they could not, they would recommend that things didn't get too carried away. During the trial, I had to stand on a platform while the Tibetans hurled insults at me. In order to get a good work record with the work units, people were encouraged to denounce their fellow Tibetans. They called me the Dalai Lama's dog, and a few of the women said that when they had been apprenticed to me, I had mistreated them. This was ridiculous, for I had never had a woman apprentice. They tore my clothes, beat me with their fists, and pulled my ear until I was sure that it would come off. I think they would have killed me except that my nose began to bleed profusely. Then they remembered that the officials had recommended that things not go too far with me, so they let me go back to prison.

"After about a year, I dreamed one night that I was back in the workrooms and everything was the way it used to be. Gyalwa Rinpoche appeared and gave me three oranges, which I put in my chuba. The very next day, we were sent to Meru and given our prison sentences. Most people received ten- or fifteen-year sentences, but mine was only three. Still, the idea of spending two more years in the jail made me feel desperate. The food continued to be bad, and many people died. Although their deaths were supposed to be kept secret, one of the men who had worked for me as a tailor was assigned body bearer, so he told me about it. His job was to hide the dead in the outhouse, then take them at night to the cemetery. We counted sixty-one bodies.

"I was released from prison in 1962. My house had been sealed, and my things confiscated, so my mother and I found rooms in another house. While I was in prison, the Chinese had given me red wool taken from the monks' storerooms to make into chubas for the prisoners, and I arrived home in my red chuba. My mother's friends told me not to wear this in public, that anyone dressed in what seemed like a monk's robe would be punished.

"After a few months, I was summoned again to Meru. This time I, along with a few other people who were also labeled 'reactionary,' was told that I had to 'wear the hat.' This was almost like being in jail, because three people assigned to those who wore the hat were to report whatever we said or did. We had to ask permission to do everything, and my watchers were always nosing into my life to get information from my friends: if I recited prayers or not; how much money I made as a tailor. And if they found that I made a mistake, it would give them credit for 'revolutionary behavior' with the work unit authorities. This was a dreadful method of instilling hatred and mistrust among people. In addition to this isolation, I was required to do all sorts of odd jobs, such as watering someone's vegetable garden or cleaning their toilet. This work took up so much time that I couldn't make much money sewing. Furthermore, people would demand that I sew for them, and then not pay me.

"The Cultural Revolution was a time of intense destruction. Red Guards roamed the city, visiting different families and carting away whatever they could find. They all were Tibetan, for the Chinese didn't take part in this devastation, they just organized it. The beautiful brocades that I had made for the temple statues already had been taken down and distributed as loot. Now the statues were being destroyed, as were the paintings and murals. The metal statues were separated from the clay ones and carted off to the Chinese. We heard that they were made into bullets. The clay statues were thrown into the rubbish heaps and used to fill in the swamps. The statues wouldn't sink immediately, but would float in the swamp for several months, their heads visible, eyes looking out, creating an eerie effect. So many books were burned that some of the fires smoked for two days. The chapel of the Tsuglakhang, once so beautiful, was turned into a pigsty. Anything reminiscent of former times was now defiled.

"I couldn't help but think that all of the political intrigue and bad things that had happened before the Chinese invaded created the bad karma that we reaped during the Cultural Revolution. But the Chinese, whether they knew it or not, were also accumulating collective negative karma that would ripen at some future date. Even knowing this, I found it very painful to see everything that I had believed in and worked for go up in flames. I tried to accept it in order to retain my sanity.

"By 1967, it had become extremely difficult for me to earn a living. In addition to all of the odd jobs I had to do as a hat wearer, I was required to go to many denunciation or ideological meetings and self-criticism sessions. Lhasa itself was in turmoil, with two factions of the Red Guard warring with each other.

"In 1969, I was asked to join the sewing cooperative. Although many of the workers there had been my apprentices, I worked as a cutter and was given various menial jobs to do, such as fixing the tea. Despite my experience, my salary was eight times lower than others in the cooperative. Still, it was an improvement over the past few years, and there were no more of the dreadful renunciation meetings. It wasn't until 1978 that those of us who wore the hat were once again rounded up and brought to the Meru courtyard. This time we were told that our hats had been removed and once again we had the right to talk to whomever we wished and to go wherever we wished. In 1980, we were allowed to apply for passports, and mine was granted almost immediately."

I WAS HEARING more and more firsthand accounts of the terrible ordeals undergone by the Tibetan people following the Chinese invasion. The International Commission of Jurists, a Geneva-based human-rights monitoring group, reported the atrocities Tibet suffered at the hands of the Chinese: hundreds of public executions aimed to intimidate the population, including dragging the accused to their deaths behind galloping horses and throwing them from airplanes. It was reported that children were forced to shoot their parents and religious teachers. Monasteries were destroyed and looted, their sacred images desecrated; monks and nuns were forced to copulate in public. The People's Liberation Army annihilated entire villages with air strikes.

When the Chinese first entered Tibet in 1950, Dorji Wandu Phala was chief commander of the Tibetan Government Regiment, as well as in charge of security for His Holiness the Dalai Lama. His is one of the voices from the occupation:

"ON NEW YEAR'S DAY 1950, Radio Beijing announced that the People's Liberation Army would liberate Taiwan, Hunan, and Tibet. Our army, only a few thousand troops, had only a small amount of artillery and

Dorji Wandu Phala

a few hundred machine guns and mortars. Appeals to Great Britain, the United States, India, and Nepal drew negative responses.

"When the Chinese invaded Chamdo, headquarters of Tibet's eastern front ten months later, the entire country erupted in panic. The war between China and Tibet lasted only eleven days. Our cabinet cabled the United Nations to plead for intercession, but to no avail. The UN's position was that Tibet's international legal status remained unclear.

"In December 1950, fearing capture of the Dalai Lama by the Chinese army, some of us accompanied His Holiness to the border town of Yatung, near India, where, if necessary, we could get him into India quickly. It was our responsibility to protect the Dalai Lama. Our government sent a delegation to try to negotiate with the Chinese. Prime Minister Zhou Enlai offered a ten-point plan for Tibet's "peaceful liberation," which our delegation refused to sign. They instead offered us a Seventeen-Point Agreement threatening all-out war against Tibet, so our delegates, cut off from all communication with the Dalai Lama and our government, were forced to sign. The document was certified with seals of the Tibetan government that were forged in Beijing. With the signing of that so-called agreement, Tibet lost its identity as a nation-state.

"We returned to Lhasa in August 1951. The Dalai Lama had just turned sixteen in July. The following month, three thousand Red Army troops marched into Lhasa. By December there were twenty thousand troops.

"Soon after the Dalai Lama returned to Lhasa, more than ten thousand refugees from outlying areas set up tents around the Holy City, while guerrilla forces maintained strongholds in the mountains.

"Several of us shared the responsibilities. We oversaw about 440,000 people. The army had about 8,500 military personnel. There were two services, divided into twelve different sections. One service operated solely for the protection of the Dalai Lama and followed wherever he went, from summer palace to winter palace, or to various ceremonies at the monasteries. The other service, national defense, consisted of 500 people, who accompanied the Dalai Lama on trips outside the country.

"In July 1954, I was one of 500 dignitaries to accompany the Dalai Lama on a seven-month trip to China. The Chinese government organized a tour for us Tibetans while we were there. We saw how poor the common Chinese people were, and how severely they were controlled by Mao and Zhou Enlai (they used to call him Chew 'n' Lie). That whole year, I felt very unsure. I wanted only to get back to Tibet. Although everything was very well organized, I was afraid the whole time. I wasn't afraid that the Dalai Lama would be kidnapped, but I felt extremely uncomfortable. The Chinese did not mean us well, and the future was something to be feared. I felt this very strongly.

"On March 7, 1959, a Chinese general issued an invitation to the Dalai Lama to attend a theatrical performance inside the Chinese camp. On the morning before, the chief bodyguard was informed that His Holiness was to come unaccompanied except for two or three unarmed bodyguards. The general also insisted the Dalai Lama's attendance be kept secret.

"We could not agree to this. News spread quickly, and a rumor swept through Lhasa that the Chinese planned to kidnap the Dalai Lama. Things grew very tense. Weeks earlier, four high lamas had been invited to theatrical performances without their attendants, and were immediately arrested and imprisoned. Three were executed.

"At that time, the Dalai Lama was in the Norbulinka, the summer palace. The people decided that if their ruler was expected to go to the performance alone, they shouldn't let him do so. We took eight days to answer the Chinese, and during this time the people of Lhasa surrounded the palace. They wouldn't let the Dalai Lama leave the palace because they were so afraid. It became clear to us then that the Dalai Lama must flee Tibet. During those eight days, evenings were spent planning the escape. It was very secret. We didn't even have time to go to our families. By then, I was already married and had ten children. But I didn't tell anyone, for fear of starting rumors. An announcement was made to the crowds gathered at the Norbulinka's front gate that the Dalai Lama would decline this and any future invitations to PLA headquarters.

"The city was in a state of turmoil; demonstrations decrying the Seventeen-Point Agreement were taking place, enraging the Chinese. The PLA mounted heavy artillery around the entire Lhasan valley. The Dalai

Lama later wrote in his autobiography: 'I felt as if I were standing between two volcanoes, each likely to erupt at any moment . . . My most urgent duty was to prevent a totally disastrous clash between my unarmed people and the Chinese army.'

"On March 15, a platoon of Chinese soldiers stationed themselves at the southern wall of the Norbulinka, and hundreds of Tibetan soldiers positioned themselves to take aim. Two days later, the first shots were fired. Mortar shells fell within yards of the Dalai Lama's residence.

"This was the moment. With no belongings, only one cup in our pockets, we left the palace that night at ten o'clock. The Dalai Lama disguised himself in a layman's robe and hat, a gun slung over his shoulder, and removed his glasses. One of the soldiers carried a bag of tsampa, butter, and some meat, all the provisions we could bring. The Dalai Lama's two tutors and members of the Cabinet rode hidden under a tarp in the back of a truck.

"Exactly how we left is still secret, but we did. Near the border, the Khampas, underground fighters, were waiting with their horses. The Khampas followed us and protected us until we got to the Indian border. The trip took more than two weeks by horse. At one point, Chinese planes flew overhead, and we knew we had been spotted. We expected they'd be on us in no time. But a sandstorm suddenly blew up just behind us, concealing our column, and we were safe."

Dorji Phala paused, remembering. His eyes were fixed on a mental image of that moment when he, a secular man, witnessed an act of divine protection. I asked him how that incident affected him. He closed his eyes and nodded silently.

"Some officials were sent ahead to the Indian border to request asylum. Nehru agreed that the Dalai Lama and his followers could come into

India. We settled first in Musoori. There we organized schools and settlements until the government-in-exile moved to Dharamsala in 1960. We were grateful to the government of India.

"At that time, officials were spread around in different places. I went to Kalimpong, near Darjeeling. My main job was to set up a school and to help the refugees. Other colleagues shared these duties.

"In Tibet, I'd always served our government. Transferring to Europe was a big change, but looking back, it wasn't so bad. First I went to Sussex, England, where I acted as adjunct to the house father at the Pestalozzi Children's Village for three years.

"My brother, Thupten W. Phala, who had settled in Geneva, Switzerland, became the first representative of the Dalai Lama in Europe and my son had also moved to Switzerland. So eventually I came here as well.

"When I first arrived here, I helped my brother, who had become ill. Afterward, I went to work in a textile factory, and continued there until I retired. Now I live an ordinary life. I get up at seven. It takes me more than an hour to say my prayers. Then I have my breakfast and do some shopping, take my walk, and write letters. After that, I read scriptures. I have a lot of Tibetan neighbors, and we visit each other. It's a large Tibetan community. The next village has a monastery as well. The time passes quickly."

I was always curious to know what each person I interviewed thought about the future of Tibet. Namtak Yundung's concerns were about the next generation of Tibetans, who are growing up in the West and receiving their teachings from Western-educated lamas; while Mr. Phala's were about the next generation of Chinese, who seem to be more Western-thinking and thus perhaps more willing to consider Tibet's freedom.

"I have a feeling that the internal political system in China will change. The younger generation of Chinese seems more open, and perhaps doesn't see things in strictly black and white. They also seem more interested in material gains.

"I would love to spend my last years in a free Tibet, but if you ask if Tibet is going to be free, we must say we don't know. We can have hope. My attitude toward the Chinese and the situation in my homeland is based on Buddhist philosophy, which is how I can face the situation. With that, I can face any hardship. The Tibetan community has the Dalai Lama, so there is a deep comfort. This is our privilege. Other nations don't have this. I tell my children they must care for each other and not lose their cultural heritage.

"The Dalai Lama sets an example for the whole Tibetan nation. We listen to him and we feel much better. No other leader of a nation makes his people feel like this."

I WAS BEGINNING to understand how this small enclave of exiles had managed to bring enough of Tibet with them to sustain themselves.

WAR HEROES

NGAWANGTHONGUP, KNOWN AS KUNO, was the hero of the March 20 uprising in Lhasa in 1959. Called the "incredible revolt," it took place three days after the Dalai Lama's escape to India. Twenty-eight years old at the time, Kuno was the youngest member of the four-man Council of Lhasa, a post to which he had been appointed after joining the government service at age eighteen. He had fought nobly for the holy city of Lhasa, but his greatest victory, he said, was to overcome his longtime hatred of the Chinese.

Educated as a monk official in the Dalai Lama's government, Kuno held key positions for twenty-five years, both in Lhasa and in Dharamsala. In 1952, he invented the Tibetan typewriter, which was produced in India by Remington Rand in 1976. He has taught and lectured in universities throughout the world, and has published numerous books and articles in Tibetan, English, and Chinese. In 1983, Kuno became the official biographer of His Holiness the Dalai Lama. Tall, reed thin, with an aquiline face, his long gray hair worn in a ponytail, Kuno now lives and works in Thekchen Choling, the headquarters of the Dalai Lama in Dharamsala.

"MY PERSONAL NAME is Ngawangthongup. My nickname, Kuno, is a Tibetan word, a title of respect, but when I taught foreign studies at the Tokyo University in Japan, I learned that the Japanese also have a word with the same pronunciation. Later, I found out that it also appears in German, but with a different meaning. According to my horoscope, I needed to change the name Ngawang to get rid of obstacles in my life.

"I was born in 1931. My father and mother divorced early; I was their only son. Later I realized that it was good for both of them to divorce: my mother was very religious, while my father was business oriented and went out a lot.

"As a child, I lived with my mother and grandmother in the family home in the country. It was a three-story stone house, similar in construction to most Tibetan houses, but higher, wider, and larger than most. Across the front there were two big steps, then a courtyard.

"I received a good education from that side of my family. When I was three or four years old, my grandmother began teaching me Tibetan reading and writing. She also taught me that when you eat, you must look at the food, observe its color and shape, and ask where it came from, who produced it. In Tibet, all rice is imported from China or India or Nepal. My grandmother would say, 'A single grain of rice represents at least one drop of the farmer's blood. And how many insects died for this one grain of rice? Think of the people who died working in the fields. If you waste a single grain of rice, you are really not valuing it or the labor that went into producing it.' Then she'd say, 'Taste things individually, don't mix them together. And give thanks for the food and those who brought it to your table; pray for them and generate a determination to return something, at least a prayer.' It was she who first taught me how interdependent the world really is, and to value everything in it.

"Then my mother married a Nyingma lama. That family had a tradition of learning Tibetan medicine, so my grandmother and mother brought a Tibetan medicine practitioner to teach me.

"Later, my father took me from my mother's home because he wanted to put me in school in Lhasa. My grandmother and mother were training me as a medical doctor, you see, but I wanted to be a monk. Everybody wanted to go to the capital, the center of Buddhism. I had heard of people going on pilgrimage to this holy place, so I wanted to go, too. I became a monk when I was six years old.

"You know, in Tibet, we have polygamy and polyandry. If I married somebody, after that, if I could manage it, I could have another wife, or two or three. Also, one woman can have two or three husbands. Therefore, I have four mothers. My father traveled a great deal to different parts of the country, so after he and my mother divorced, he had three wives. Sometimes all three wives would gather together, even live together. Each woman took care of all of the children as if they were her own, and we called them all 'mother.' "

I asked him if it was hard for him to leave home at such a young age.

"At first, I cried every day. I wanted to see my [biological] mother. Particularly at sunset, that's when I became most homesick for her. I also loved my grandmother very, very much. But in Drepung monastery, the college had fatherless brothers, so they took turns taking care of me.

"Drepung monastery is like a whole university, with four colleges. Each monastery would chose nine candidates, and from these, three would be selected, with the approval of the Dalai Lama or his regent. I was one of those young monks who were brought to the Potala palace school, where I lived from age ten to seventeen. Although I would see the Dalai Lama, I could not talk to him. Nor could he make contact with us. But we'd see him at certain times when we were giving him blessings, like the New Year, when we all went to offer him scarves.

"At the school, we received a newspaper published in Tibetan. Until then, very few of us in Tibet understood much about the far reaches of the world. We knew only China, India, Russia, Mongolia, Japan, and England. We knew nothing of the Americas. We didn't know about other indigenous people. In our view, the world looked like this: Russia, Mongolia, China, India, and Tibet made up one whole face; then on this side was Japan, like an ear; and England, as the other ear. It was only during the Second World War that we found out how much we didn't know. I wanted to see something of this world.

"After completing this college, one would automatically become a monk official and, depending on his qualifications, could get a job in different offices. I was placed as a clerk in the secretary's office in charge of the monasteries and all religious sites. That was in 1948."

I remembered what the Gadong oracle had said about Tibet's political system as a combination of church and state. I asked Kuno to explain this to me.

"Only in Tibet do they have this system where monk officials and lay officials join together in their work, like a coalition in the government. Every single office has both monk officials and lay officials—except the judicial office that involves punishment. Since the Fifth Dalai Lama, 1642, and to the present, the Dalai Lama is the head of the Tibetan government. But before that, the government was made up of all the families of the aristocracy, with the ruling class exacting a great deal from the peasants in a sort of feudal system. The Fifth Dalai Lama invited all of the

Kuno

children of the aristocracy to reform the government. At that time the lay-men who made up the government weren't working efficiently. The Dalai Lama thought the government should work for the peasants and the no-mads—the majority of the people—for their benefit instead of for the benefit of the aristocracy. So he invited monks and lamas from different monasteries, who had good educations or were outstanding in some way, to join in the government to serve the general population and to strive for justice.

"At first, those monks were elderly, and the system worked very well. Then the Dalai Lama and his assistants, who were like prime ministers, thought it would be a good idea to train monks to collaborate with lay of-ficials of the aristocratic families. So at the Potala palace, they established a kind of institute or school that trained monk officials. They selected monks from traditional monasteries who didn't have any physical handicap and who were very intelligent. These monks came from varied backgrounds—peasants, nomads, and common people, even bankers' sons.

"During the early fifties, the government was very conservative politically, and the aristocratic families very much afraid of reform. The Thirteenth Dalai Lama had tried various reforms, but they didn't succeed. In Lhasa, we already had some kind of underground movement organized among the students within the school. And later, when I had become an official, I felt we needed to move in a different direction. The whole world was going toward democracy, and we needed to change as well. The present Dalai Lama also wanted these reforms.

"At that time, the Tibetan government sent delegations to the United States, Britain, Nepal, India, and China. Being the clerk of the staff member selected to go to the United States, I was to accompany His Holiness there as monk official. We had already departed from Lhasa when they telegraphed us, ordering us not to go farther. They told us to stay and wait. We waited almost seven months while the negotiations went on. We arrived in the winter and celebrated Losar there. In summer, when the negotiations failed, we returned to Lhasa.

"After the Seventeen-Point Agreement with China, the Tibetan government agreed to send young Tibetans to China to study the language. The goal was to foster good communication and a better relationship between our two countries. The Dalai Lama even gave us money for the trip, like pocket money. We went to Beijing to the so-called National Minority Institute. At first, we Tibetans had special privileges. The Seventeen-Point Agreement specified that the Chinese must respect all Tibetan traditions and culture. In Tibet, we don't have beds, just cushions, like a futon. Also the custom is never to step over someone, even over another's clothes. Other students, even Mongolians, had bunk beds, but Tibetans had single beds. The Tibetans were given a separate kitchen because we don't eat seafood, only yak meat or mutton.

"But in 1956, things started to change rapidly. At first we were allowed to teach Tibetan religion, language, and culture to the Tibetan students. Even the Chinese were learning the Tibetan language, but not our culture or religion. They taught us Maoism, Marxism, Leninism, the Long March, and the goodness of China. In the beginning they were afraid to say that Tibet belonged to China. Later, when they began to claim that Tibet was part of their country, everything changed.

"The Chinese had a saying: 'A hundred flowers can bloom together all at once, and a hundred scholars can express their thoughts freely.' At that time, people were allowed to criticize Chinese policy, and we were the first ones in the school to make a poster that questioned the Chinese policy on Tibet. In the autumn of 1956, we organized meetings. Then the trouble began. About 800 Tibetans were living in Peking, and gradually we began to realize that we were in danger. I had already scheduled a four-month vacation to go back to Tibet to see my mother. If that had not already been planned, I could not have gone back, for I was on a blacklist. We had established an underground movement among the teachers and students, and the officials found us out. One of my teachers, a Chinese who had lived in London and Paris, advised me to leave. He had to guarantee the Chinese government that I would come back, but he knew that I didn't plan to return. So I went to Tibet, pretending that I'd return, but I didn't go back to China. That was 1957."

"At what point did you finally meet the Dalai Lama?"

"The first time I met the Dalai Lama was in China. The so-called Communist Chinese constitution had to be translated into Tibetan, Mongolian, and a few other languages, and I was on the committee that worked on the translations. When the Dalai Lama went to Beijing at the end of 1954, he learned that the constitution was going to be published as a book, and wanted to know about the project. He also wanted to hear about our experiences in China.

"For almost four hours he conferred with me alone. He had democratic ideas and told me that he wanted to bring more changes to Tibet. Actually, the Thirteenth Dalai Lama had outlined the democratic constitution and even invited village people to Lhasa to be specially trained, but they did not stay long. They didn't want to offend the aristocratic families. The monks were also manipulated by the aristocratic families who supported them and acted as their benefactors.

"At the time of the invasion, in 1959, I was on the translation committee in Lhasa City, living at the Jokhang temple. We never thought that the Chinese would shell us, so we were not prepared. And the Dalai Lama had not advised us to fight.

"We were able to erect only two barricades. One, made of timber and sand bags, provided a machine-gun post at the rear of the cathedral. For the other, we tore up the old cobblestones from the square, and reinforced them with old chairs and tables and bales of cloth from the nearby Nepalese shops and anything else we could lay our hands on. On top of that we put hundreds of flower pots and tin cans already filled with earth—some early flowers blooming in them.

"Just after two in the morning, we heard the machine guns—in the distance at first, then nearer and nearer; early in the morning, they shelled the Jokhang; about dawn, we heard them on the Norbulinka side, the western side of the building; just before sunrise, we saw that they were shelling the Mentsikhang, the medical institute; within hours they had totally destroyed it, the main school, and the apartments where many people lived—totally destroyed . . . That was the worst; that evening they started shelling the Potala. They destroyed all of the electrical poles. The soldiers came, and we wanted to fight, but there was no way. Then the people started flooding the temple, including many women. We all worked together. We had only a few guns. Mainly we threw stones. The women were so brave. They brought us tea and kept encouraging us. The temple was on fire, and the women went to help put it out.

"Then, at about nine o'clock the next evening, the Chinese came in closer, found an open area, and charged about twenty women who had taken cover from the shelling. In the meantime, I was with two men on the upper part. I was very encouraged, because we were fighting for Tibet's freedom. We all hoped that the Dalai Lama had already escaped from Tibet, but we had no way of knowing. We thought that maybe if we could keep the Chinese out of the temple within the Potala, he could make his escape. We didn't realize that he was already gone.

"There was one among us who knew how to fight, and we followed him. He was in charge. We called him Gurgur, 'The Hunchback.' Others and I didn't hold out much hope after the failure of the uprising. But we never thought that the Chinese would be so hard on the Tibetans or that they would destroy so much.

"There was no way we could win. Even if we surrendered to the Chinese, they would either kill us there at the temple or we would be put into prison and tortured and killed. There was no way we could have been successful, but I still believe we did the right thing in trying.

"Until 1986, I was very angry at the Chinese and really wanted to fight them again, but that was wrong. I thought that we had to fight, but now I follow the Dalai Lama's teachings and no longer think this way.

"They talk about the Chinese brainwashing. I think the Dalai Lama washed my brain. There was the Kalachakra initiation I fully received in Bodh Gaya. I learned how to go within and deal with my mind, to counter anger and hurt with compassion. I had studied this before, but it hadn't moved my mind. Now I understand if we hold anger for a country or on a personal level, it cannot bring good. If we practice patience and tolerance, then there'll be peace within. When we have that kind of peace in every single person's mind, then the world as a whole will have true peace. Since I have dropped my anger, I've had this inner peace. If we can't love our enemies, we should at least pray for them.

"Before 1986, I even used to pray negatively. I'd hope that there would be earthquakes in China or mud slides or some other disaster. Now I pray for the Chinese in a positive way.

"They say, 'Think globally; act locally.' Locally is wherever you are. Local is your mind. You can clean up the environment in every way, but you also need to clean up your mind. In order to take global responsibility, you must take local responsibility, for your own self."

IT COULD NOT have been so simple, I thought, given what these people witnessed, to erase all negativity and anger toward the Chinese from their minds. Where in the West would one find such mental discipline? I thought back to Denma Locho Rinpoche's description of his flight from Tibet, which he had told to me on my second visit to him in Dharamsala:

"SINCE I HAD spent so much of my time studying, I wasn't really aware of the Chinese presence in Tibet, although I began to hear things that disturbed me. About the time I finished with Gyume Tantric College, the situation in Lhasa had gotten very bad, and I began to think of returning to India, where I had gone on pilgrimage in 1956. One day Gen Nyima called me into his room. He burst out, 'Are you going around saying you are leaving for India? Maybe you just want to enjoy a ride in a train or an airplane?' I told him I thought the situation was getting worse, but he just shrugged and told me that Gyalwa Rinpoche [the Dalai Lama], his tutors, the Ganden Throneholders, and many other great beings in Tibet were not talking about going to India, and said, 'So what's up with you?' I didn't know what to say, so I just sat there, silently.

"Chinese spies were everywhere, even in the monastery. Once a monk from Drepung Tantric College, whom I knew to be a spy, criticized Communism and asked my opinion. I told him that I thought Communism was really all right except it didn't accept religion. I added that the PLA [People's Liberation Army] in Kham had behaved well and paid the local people the price they had asked for food and so forth. He didn't reply at all. I always made it a point never to criticize the Chinese in public.

"In the second month of the Year of the Earth Pig [1959], the abbots went to consult the Gadong oracle. I went with Gen Nyima on horseback, carrying only a bowl and an offering scarf. When I asked the Gadong oracle what would be the best for me, he said I should stay right there. That night the shelling started. A family gave us tsampa, tea, and horses, and we started out for the Indian border. At one point, we were going over a pass that would not have been impossible to cross if it snowed. When the villagers came to ask if I could do anything to help, I used an amulet from Sakya Dagchen, which contained a small charm for stopping snow. The charm was very powerful, and the sky cleared. Otherwise, we would have been stuck there. Beyond the pass, the snow was very deep, but fortunately we met a yak coming toward us and were able to follow the channel of its path through the snow. We did a divination and decided to press on through a few more passes. We finally reached the Indian border and were among the first group of refugees to cross over."

I had once seen a Native American shaman divert a storm, so I knew such things were possible. I believed then that it was a gift, but now I was beginning to see that it is also the intensity of the practice.

Denma Locho continued: "Then in 1967 His Holiness's two tutors asked me to go to Manali to serve as the abbot of a small monastery, and in 1978 I spent a year at the University of Virginia in Charlottesville, where Jeffery Hopkins translated. The university students were interested in the *prajna paramitas*, the Six Perfections. I can't generalize about people, but I felt that Tibetans tend to be contented people, while Westerners are so involved with possessions that they find it difficult to leave the materialistic way and attend to dharma.

"I went with His Holiness to California when he gave the Kalachakra initiation, and to New Mexico when the choir monks performed. American Indians danced for us, and when the monks performed religious dances, there was a rainbow in the sky. These Indians liked it so much! They are very fond of rainbows."

I smiled, remembering that I had attended that ceremony; it was the first time I had seen the Dalai Lama. Many Native Americans interpreted the appearance of such a spectacular rainbow as a blessing from the Great Spirit for both the Tibetan and Native American peoples.

I mentioned to Denma Locho Rinpoche that so many of the teachings I had heard tell us that the practices begin with transcending selfishness and anger and jealousy, but that nobody had explained what the first steps are in getting rid of anger.

"Anger makes you and other persons unhappy, and creates enemies and animosity. When you get angry it is very difficult to think in terms of compassion, for compassion is the opposite of anger. Don't say anything, just concentrate on calming your breathing. After about ten breaths, you will feel a little bit more calm; then you will think and think and see that maybe there is a misunderstanding. Besides, if you show anger to the other person, he is only going to become more angry. Instead, you should try to understand him better. You have to think and to use your compassion."

He reached for his dog, Champa, who jumped onto his lap.

"If you hit a dog with a stick, the dog will bite the stick because he doesn't know that the stick has no control over itself. So if you think that the other person is showing anger to you, it is not that person doing that, it is the anger inside of him.

"If you just feel regret, it is of no use, but if you feel regret in your heart, that will contribute to your not doing it again in the future. So if that sort of regret comes, then it is very fortunate.

"If you have commited some sin, your regret will prevent you from doing it again. This particular idea about sin and regret, I think, is the same with the Christians. When I went to a church in London I saw this seat, a place where you could make confessions. In Tibet, if you confess and commit not to do it again, this leads to purification."

I asked what future he saw for the Tibetan people and for the world in general.

"Both my teacher and I feared what would happen to the monastic structure in exile, for it seemed to be like a turtle without its shell. I've seen the lives of many monks blown about like feathers in the wind. Many young tulkus have been totally disoriented and have had to turn away from their studies in order to cope with an entirely new way of life. Many have gone to live abroad. I kept thinking that I'd be able to go back to Tibet. That hope sustained me even though others who spoke English told me that the possibility didn't look very good.

"But I think the world in general is heading for better times. My fears have been a little bit lessened now that the Cold War is over and there is less danger from nuclear war.

"My main interest is to help this world. Since there are so many conflicts and controversies and new diseases, I pray that my meditations—morning, noon, and evening—will be to end all this suffering. Since I am in this world and have connections with this world, I pray that this sort of suffering will go away, and that everyone, including myself, will be safe. Always I pray that way."

And I, in turn, would pray that these people of Shambala get back their country and continue their noble lives for the benefit of all beings.

SURVIVING
THE INVASION

THE CHINESE ARMY targeted monks and nuns as the most threatening group in Tibetan society, but it was the women of Lhasa who took to the streets and dared the Chinese to fire on them. And in the spring of 1959, when a Chinese general demanded the Dalai Lama's at-

tendance at a theatrical show inside the Chinese camp—without bodyguards or soldiers—it was the women who lay down on the road to prevent His Holiness's vehicle from taking him to certain captivity. These same women finally spearheaded the revolt that led to the Dalai Lama's escape to India.

"RIGHT AFTER THE UPRISING," Newang Choezin, the former head nun in Dharamsala, had told me, "a movement was started. Two ladies—one was a nun—moved many Tibetan ladies to Dharamsala. Someone turned in their names for starting this movement. The nun was shot later on by the Chinese. They stood her up and shot her, and she fell in the pit. A nun from her abbey was imprisoned and grew very sick. She died in the hospital. Another nun was shot by the Chinese.

"I feel that truth and justice should prevail, and I am praying for that. I am also praying that the Chinese people's anger and their lust for Tibet should be lessened. And I am teaching the younger nuns to do the same. If there is truth and justice, we Tibetans should not be suffering so much. Also, the world should understand that the Chinese are wrong. So I pray for that too. If the whole community can accumulate good merit, things will go in a positive direction. I teach the young girls to avoid hatred. I think to myself that maybe I've created bad karma, or maybe we as a people have done bad collectively, so we have to suffer at this time. Please, may the feeling of compassion and the feeling of goodness grow in the hearts of the Chinese so this suffering doesn't have to last for a long time.

"When it came time to escape, it was always in my mind that if the Chinese caught me they would do very bad things to me, since I was involved with the women who started the movement. The border in the area of Sikkim was not closed, and there were traders, Muslims, and other non-Tibetans going in and out. I joined a small group of them, and they were helpful, but I had to be careful to stay hidden.

"Usually the journey took seven days, but it took us fifteen days to reach India. Since nuns were not allowed to go through, I had to dress up like a beggar. Everyone was in such a sorrowful mood that begging wasn't so hard; people would always give you a little something to eat. At the border, guards couldn't always tell who was going into Tibet or who was coming out, and we managed to slip by. We were on foot almost the whole time. It took three months to reach Dharamsala.

"In Kalimpong there were other Tibetans, and they treated us well. Also at that time, Christian missionaries were giving out milk powder and oil and other things that were very useful. I'm still grateful for those alms.

"In Dharamsala, His Holiness held two public audiences each day. Everyone had problems and wanted to talk to him. In one of the public audiences, His Holiness asked who had just come from Tibet. I said that I had been a nun in Lhasa. He told us to stay for a bit afterward. When His Holiness learned that I knew how to read and write Tibetan, he gave my name to his sister. She had already started a nursery school in Dharamsala; I was offered a place to live in exchange for teaching the children and looking after their health. I stayed two or three years. Then an offer came from Sweden to bring young girls there as students, to learn nursing, so I went to Sweden for four years and studied.

"I was surprised at how big the people were, and how blonde! And the bathing suits and the things they wore, everything was so different. My sponsors taught me how to make a Western cake, and I taught them how to make momos and tulpa and other Tibetan dishes.

"Thirty-six of us went to Sweden. Of those, some went on to England, some got married, and others came back into the Tibetan settlement in India to serve as nurses or teachers. I was put in charge of the nursery. After some time, I came here, to Dharamsala.

"At first we were very poor here at the abbey, but the Tibetan people are extremely religious and made many offerings, and we were able to build and make repairs. We also got gifts from the West. I received enough donations of food so that I could do a meditation retreat. I was one of the lucky ones."

I asked her what she meant. It was then that I heard about the one we will call "Dolma."

DOLMA IS STILL YOUNG—twenty-four—though in her eyes, which are dark and enormous in the small face, one can see centuries of humanity's unspeakable capacity for cruelty. Yet, strangely, the compassion in those eyes transcends pain. In that compassion, one glimpses true spiritual heroism.

"IN THE SPRING of 1988, five of us nuns started poster campaigns to protest the continued persecution of our people by the Chinese. On May 15, nine of us, along with two monks from a nearby monastery, held a secret meeting. We decided to stage a protest march calling for Tibetan independence and the release of Tibetan political prisoners. We vowed we would keep our activities peaceful in accordance with the wishes of His Holiness the Dalai Lama. We also vowed that if any of us were arrested and interrogated, no one would divulge the identity of the others, no matter what they did to us, and that we would sacrifice our lives if necessary for the sake of our country and our religion. Then, one by one, we secretly left our abbey.

"At ten o'clock on the morning of May 17, we met in front of the Jokhang temple. We circled the temple three times, shouting our slogans. On the third round, Chinese armed police arrived and dragged us onto their trucks to take us to prison. They made us stand with our hands raised in the air, but still we kept shouting our slogans. That made them angry, and they began to kick us and beat us with rifle butts and truncheons. One monk began to bleed profusely.

"We were taken to Gutsa prison in Lhasa. Guards photographed us and took our names and the names of our nunneries and monasteries. Then they began to interrogate us one by one.

"They asked me for the names of the ringleaders. I said we all were ringleaders. When I wouldn't answer their questions, they brought in a dog to attack me. The dog would bite my arms and legs whenever I moved.

"Then they took me to another room, where I was handcuffed and stripped. Two women beat me with truncheons and prodded me in the vagina and mouth with electric cattle prods. They did this in full view of some male prisoners who were watching from windows. I felt such humiliation and shame, and the pain was so great I lost consciousness. When I came to, I was in another cell, still naked.

"Sometime in the night they came for me again. They said I was too young to have planned the demonstration, and they wanted the names of the people who did. I refused to give them any names. They made me lie down and stomped on my body. Then they brought in a chair and made me squat, balanced on my toes, with my chin resting on the chair. Each time I fell, they beat me. Five more guards came in and beat me and kicked me. They twisted my arms behind me until I fainted.

"The next morning I was alone in a cell; there was blood on my face and all over my body. The pain was excruciating. During the next ten days there was blood in my urine. I asked to see a doctor. When two women doctors came to see me, I told them about the blood. They slapped me in the face and walked away. I had no food for two days after.

"On the third day I was taken for interrogation again, and beaten and tortured once more.

"Three months later we were released and ordered to our abbey. When I arrived I discovered the Chinese had begun daily "re-education" sessions to indoctrinate our nuns about the virtue of the Communist system and to convince us that Tibet is an irrefutable part of China. The head nun and administrators were threatened that they would be held responsible for any future demonstrations by the nuns. During the six months the Chinese were there, we were forbidden to follow our religious activities.

"On February 11, 1990, the Chinese expelled forty-three nuns from the abbey, including myself. We were ordered not to undertake any religious activities, to stay home, and work in the fields, and all other nunneries were forbidden to admit us.

"When I reached my home on the outskirts of Lhasa, I found my mother desperately ill. She had been made to stand naked on the ice for three days for shouting slogans against the Chinese for their policy of banning religion in Tibet. My sister had served a nine-month term in Gutsa prison for taking part in another demonstration.

"I decided I must escape and tell the world what the Chinese are doing to our people. I left home without telling my parents where I was going, for fear of bringing more punishment down on them. I went to Lhasa, collected some money, and headed for Mt. Kailash in western Tibet. From there, I escaped to Nepal with five nuns and eight monks. We all wore lay clothes. I reached Dharamsala in the summer of 1990."

In October 1993, fourteen nuns, serving up to seven-year sentences in Drapachi prison, were given additional sentences of up to nine years each for having recorded songs on a tape recorder smuggled into the prison. The songs were laments addressed to their parents and relatives. Copies of the tapes were circulated among the underground movement in Lhasa.

The Root Lama of Tibet is the Panchen Lama.
When he lived, prisoners could be liberated immediately from
    Tibetan prisons:
The barbaric Chinese eliminated him.

Our food is like pig food;
We are beaten and treated brutally,
And prison sentences imposed are limitless.
But this will never change the Tibetan people's perseverance:
It will remain unfaltering.

There are bars on the windows,
And iron on the doors.
Inside the prisons of Tibet,
The Chinese beat us.

Where is the freedom we once enjoyed?
Now under the Chinese we no longer are free.

Sacred Conqueror,
The snowland of Tibet is your birthplace,
All of the Tibetans are like your children.

There are beatings without end;
Under the Chinese there is no freedom.

From my embittered mind
I sing a sad song.

The Chinese have transformed our land of Dharma
Into a giant prison;
The unending torture which the Chinese have inflicted on us
Could not destroy us:
We did not die.

The woman with the shortest sentence is not due for release until 1998; the last one will complete her term in 2006.

ARISTOCRACY

Tibet's aristocrats trace their origins directly to the Yarlung kings, who held their ancestral estates by grant from the government. Men and women dressed in lavish silk robes; the women braided turquoise and coral in their hair and wore elaborate jewelry; and they employed a large ret-  inue of servants. They also hired monks to perform pujas at household shrines and to teach their children. Government positions kept the nobility in Lhasa most of the year, but all had country estates, where four-day picnics and archery contests were held amid magnificent gardens. Guests were served on silver plates and jade bowls and serenaded by chang girls.

"When we heard that His Holiness the Dalai Lama fled in 1959, we discussed the situation and decided to flee as well. The Chinese had caught our cousin's brother, and we thought that we had to go at once.

My mother was too old to travel; my daughter decided to stay behind with her grandmother and look after the house.

"We traveled by horse, but we weren't able to bring anything with us, just a little food.

"We went first to India for about a year, then to Sikkim—the queen of Sikkim is a relative—where my husband taught Tibetan. But then all government officials were called to Dharamsala. Tibetan people needed jobs, and the Indian government put them to work building roads. My husband supervised the more than 600 people who were assigned to road construction in the Chamba Valley in India.

"We lived in tents in a settlement village. Everything we had came from donations from America and other countries. Life was difficult. During storms, stones would fall down from the mountains, killing many of the workers. In the meantime, my husband had an administrative position in Dharamsala. We saw the Dalai Lama often, but usually in a group. We were always working.

"In 1962, we left Dharamsala and went to France, near the Pyrennes, to teach and look after a group of Tibetan children: ten boys and ten girls. We stayed there three years; then we moved to a larger city for another five years. We all were sent by the education department of the Tibetan government-in-exile to a government school, where my husband taught Tibetan language, culture, and religion. We lived with the students in a dormitory or boarding school, but in a separate apartment. The expenses were paid by the French government.

"The idea for the school came from a Frenchman who had come to a Tibetan school in Musoori and seen the hardships the children were suffering. He went to see the Dalai Lama and asked him if he would consider sending the children and teachers to France. His Holiness consented; the

Frenchman and his friend, a naval officer, presented the plan to the French government. President De Gaulle agreed, and supported this idea.

"In France, the children would attend classes in the morning, then they would work in the fields, do the washing, cooking, everything. The French students as well. Teachers worked too, cutting firewood and washing and cooking. When all the twenty Tibetan students were grown and had completed their studies, we came to Switzerland.

"Finally my daughter got out of Tibet. She lives here in Switzerland now. But for twenty years we had no contact. When the Chinese loosened up a little bit, we received news from a Nepalese trader that my daughter was in prison. I kept asking anyone who went to trade in Tibet, 'Have you seen my daughter?' until I found someone who knew her. He told me that she was still alive.

"The Chinese had put all members of aristocratic families to work in the fields. They were sent to the river to fetch water, and had to wade in even in the wintertime. They were treated very badly; they were even forbidden to look up at the Chinese. My daughter, who was only thirteen years old, was sent to prison, where she was kept in forced labor for fifteen years. She never did develop properly, and even today she has medical problems. She is married now.

"I feel anger and hatred for the Chinese Communist government, who harmed my country. I'm sorry, but I do."

Mr. Norgay brought out a collection of embroidery done by Tibetan students in the school in France. They depicted scenes the children had witnessed in their villages in Tibet when they were little, scenes that remained vivid in their memories.

He explained the stick figures: "This man's hands are chained to a plank; his legs as well, spread-eagle. The red spot over the heart is for tar-

The Norgays

get practice, and the people watching are his neighbors. The woman standing behind him is the mother, who would be made to dig the grave.

"In this one, these children are being forced to shoot their parents. In this, a young man is committing suicide." There were perhaps a dozen, each carefully wrapped in tissue.

Mrs. Norgay added, "In Tibet, my husband was a government officer; in France, he was a teacher; here, he has to work in a factory. But compared to the people still left in Tibet, we live extremely well."

THE MORE I HEARD about life in exile, the more my heart broke. I wondered if, in their place, I could feel the kindness toward the Chinese, for their accumulation of collective negative karma, that so many Tibetans have learned to develop.

MOVING ON

I DON'T KNOW at what exact moment I made the decision to
move on to California to continue my research. Several Tibetan Buddhist
centers in Los Angeles draw visiting teachers and lamas from around the
world, and for all the traveling that lay ahead, a major airport was an important consideration. Los Angeles also held one of my
sons. I was in the middle of putting books and files into
boxes when I remembered the Wanla oracle and something
about my moving to a place near a great ocean. Had the
seed been planted in my mind then, or had a seventh-cen-
tury spirit dwelling in the Himalayas sensed I would hear about a perfect
apartment that would become available immediately on my return to the
States? Are we really just characters in some other writer's story? If so, who
is the author? Karma? Destiny? It seemed I was even willing to go to the
land of earthquakes, fires, and mud slides to look for answers.

SOON AFTER ARRIVING in Los Angeles, I flew north to see my stepdaughter Wendy. San Francisco's Green Gulch Zen Center is the oldest established Zen center in the United States, and Wendy has lived there for twenty years, many of them as head gardener. Married, mother of two, she has prematurely gray hair, which was now snow-white and framed a face deeply tanned from her years outdoors.

We spent the weekend strolling through her gardens, visiting the *zendo* (meditation hall). Wendy told me that the standing life-size figure of Jizo Bodhisattva, with the uplifted big toe, represents active wisdom, the one who guides unborn children and travelers from one world to another. The seated Manjushri Bodhisattva, in the center of the room, listens with settled compassion and awakens wisdom in those whose gaze rests upon him, she explained.

I told Wendy about my travels to Ladakh and of the terrible three days and nights of my demons. "One of them," I said, "came dressed as you."

She listened caringly, her deep brown eyes reminiscent of her father's and my son Billy's, and said, "It stands to reason, since I'm the Buddhist in the family and there you were in a Buddhist country writing a book on Buddhism. The demons, though, are yours." With a gentleness born of the bond we had created when Wendy was a young girl, we explored our feelings about my divorce from her father. It was a necessary step, she felt, for my own path. "And don't forget, each of us has our own karma," she reminded me.

She had grown wise and compassionate in this garden of hers.

I WAS EAGER to see Lobsang Lhalungpa again. Tenzin Wandrak had given me a package to deliver to him, and I called soon after I returned to Santa Fe to ask Lobsang when I could come by.

He greeted me as an old friend, delighting in my travels and listening with great care to my reactions to the people I had met. It was summer when last I had visited Lobsang's Santa Fe home. The Sangre de Cristos, dwelling place of the Native Americans' ancestors, had been as thickly forested as the foothills of the Dhauladhars, where the deities of the East dwell; now, the Aspens had turned gold. "Quaking Aspens," they are called, for the flattened leafstalks that catch the least breeze, causing the leaves to flutter. The mountainside glittered in the afternoon sun, as if robed in ceremonial dress studded with tiny mirrors.

As before, an array of birds gathered on the railing of his deck, reminding me now of the flocks of the small, young monks that swarmed the hillsides of Dharamsala.

I told Lobsang I had been extending my meditations by only minutes at a sitting, tentatively, and with a certain degree of distrust. Most of the time I felt like one of those slugs stuck on Ani Gomchen's steps. Would my progress always be this slow, I asked, or was I perhaps trying too hard?

"A person recognizes his spiritual potential when he looks at the problems of his existence—growth, old age, sickness, death—and sees that these are things he cannot change. But what he can change is his own attitude, his own way of looking at life.

"And that's only the minimum level of spirituality. But when true spiritual life is begun, one becomes concerned with much more than his own growth. As growth takes place in the spiritual realm, in the realm of consciousness, a person widens his concerns—not just to his limited family, but to society and the entire sentient world. Even if he is not in a position to do anything, at least he has a moment when he has this sense that, oh, God, there are so many suffering beings, and I have the potential to develop my spiritual strength and vision and power so that one day I may become one of those great masters who can help others. This vision has to do with the dharma. Dharma is my source of spiritual growth. Eventually it opens out into universal concern and compassion. That is the heart of spirituality.

"It is not enough to say, 'I'm a religious person,' or 'I'm meditating,' or 'I'm worshiping in a temple,' if it is only self-concern. To pray for happiness for oneself, to want God's blessing for oneself to be someone important: this, from a Buddhist point of view, is materialism. Pure and simple.

"On the other hand, a layman, a poor man, sitting in a corner without much material support, may have an extraordinarily sensitive mind, and thinks, 'I don't care how poor I am; I'm surviving; but there is so much suffering in the rest of the world.' This is a way one may want to grow spiritually so as to be of help to these suffering beings. That is spirituality. So you see the distinction? That is what Buddhism teaches."

I thought of the suffering of Dolma and Dr. Choedak and all those still in Tibet, and wondered how my tears could ease their pain. Or how the meditations of ten yogis sitting twenty years sealed off in caves change the world.

"Many people in the West do not understand that attaining enlightenment is not itself an end; it is only a beginning. The true task of helping others lies ahead. The bodhisattva vow is, 'I do everything possible to achieve enlightenment so I can work to alleviate suffering of all sentient beings, and help them to achieve their own enlightenment.' That was the vow that Buddha took, the vow that many other buddhas before him took, and the vow that many others now are taking and will take in the future. Notice that we say buddhas, not just a Buddha. Out of the great mass of sentient beings many, many have achieved buddhahood. Therefore, it is for the practitioner to recognize this as their source of inspiration. You can achieve the same thing and become like them, join the army of the great masters who work for humanity.

"Buddhism provides a basic education about life: Life and the living environment are precious, fragile, requiring care and nurturing. Humans have the truest potential for spiritual development, which includes a deep understanding of life and the environment, universal concern, and compassion. Unbridled quests for material wealth and sensual gratification only feed an insatiable craving for more and cause serious destabilization and distress.

"Buddhism makes people responsible for their own lives and for what they do to others; turning away from the mentality that says, 'I can do what I like and I don't have to concern myself with its impact on society or the ecology.' Buddhism has this totally integrated view of life. A view that is a protection from the impact of disease when it comes. When we understand why we get sick—of course, there are so many factors—if a person says, 'I'm so sick; I'm so miserable,' then the illness becomes worse. The more confusion, depression, and fear, the more suffering.

"But if this same person says, 'Of course, sickness naturally comes. I may have done something wrong—wrong habits, wrong diet, or maybe there is some other cause. In any case, now that sickness is here, I have the pain, how do I remain calm?' that is where the training in meditation comes in. It frees the mind. When the mind is free and calm, it has an impact on the body apart from conscious efforts to face the problem. People who practice take these things very seriously and are benefited in many different ways, in terms of overcoming physical illness, mental distress, emotional prostration.

"Appreciating the fragility of life protects one from false hope and disillusionment. There is no guarantee anyway that you're going to live long enough to enjoy your wealth. You might pop off suddenly because of

Lobsang Lhalungpa

a heart attack. I think we should seek only the materials we need to sustain this body, and fill up that other half with spiritual devotion. Then you will have the combination of a well balanced material and spiritual life. Materialism should be only a support for your spiritual growth. You can attain this balance as long as you have that clear in your mind, as long as you know that you can use this extraordinary vehicle for spiritual purposes. The Buddha's Middle Way avoids both pure materialism and self-indulgence on the one hand, and drastic self-denial on the other."

Realizing I had never really interviewed Lobsang, I asked him now about his early years.

"I WAS BORN in 1924 into a good family—not that rich—but a good family. My father was very learned and had a great influence on me and my personal life. After a brief secular education, I became a monk at the age of five. For a while I continued secular education with my school-teachers for different subjects, but at the age of nine or ten I began to study more closely with my monastic teachers.

"At the age of sixteen I became a monk official—the youngest. Soon after, I was appointed to the staff of the grand secretariat at the Potala palace, an office directly responsible to the Dalai Lama and to the regent. The regent ran the country on behalf of the Dalai Lama, who was still a minor.

"Fortunately for me, as a member of the staff I had easy access to His Holiness's two tutors, and for many years received advanced teachings from them. I also studied with other lamas, including a great woman, Jet-sun Lochen of Shukseb Hermitage and Nunnery.

"My background in secular and monastic education seemed the basis for the regent later to appoint me to the new assignment as director for the Tibetan and Buddhist studies in the Indian Himalayan towns of Darjeeling and Kalimpong. The year was 1947. The government decided to add a number of students to the group of private students already in the modern schools in India—the first cautious step toward Tibet's modernization. I left for India, traveling on horseback for three weeks. This was a turning point in my life. I was not to return to Tibet.

"From 1947 to 1951, I ran the education program with utmost devotion. The pay was little, benefits none, and the life lonely. My students numbered more than a hundred. Not only Tibetan, but Bhutanese, Sikkimese, and Bhotias [local Tibetans] as well. Then, under pressure from the Chinese, my students were called back. For myself, I refused to comply with the cabinet's order to return and report to new duty, a most painful decision, for consequences would be serious, both for myself and for my family in Lhasa. In 1950 and 1951, I lost my country to the massive Red Army of China.

"During the early years in exile, I faced lack of employment and means of support for myself and my new family. At that point a new chapter in my life began. I started to teach numerous foreigners: historians, scholars, linguists, and anthropologists who, because the Chinese would not permit them to visit Tibet, came to Kalimpong, where I lived.

"Since the regent had rejected my 1948 proposal to set up a Buddhist monastic university in Kalimpong, His Eminence Dardo Rinpoche, abbot of Bodh Gaya and Ghoom monasteries, and I decided to set up the Buddhist Cultural Center there. We also organized a school for local Tibetan children who were already receiving free education (and indoctrination) at the Chinese Communist school, funded and managed by Beijing. Before long, the children joined our charitable school. That made the Chinese headmaster furious. This was our cultural challenge to the Chinese!

"By 1956, the Indian government realized that Tibet represented a great loss to them: with the Chinese border so close, India felt very vulnerable. Although they still maintained friendly relationships with China, they were nervous. India could do nothing for Tibetans politically or militarily, but wanted to help the Tibetan people in commercial and cultural pursuits. The Indian government set up a new cultural office close to the Tibetan border to help Tibetans in whatever way they could, to give them some relief—food to eat and clothes to wear. Thousands had taken this terrible journey and were seriously run down and weakened from it. Some were suffering from TB and all kinds of health problems; and they published material in our language to send back to Tibet. I was asked to start a Tibetan radio program from New Delhi to inform Tibetans in and outside of Tibet about conditions in India and in the rest of the world; how India and other world aid agencies were helping the Tibetans. The program also included topics concerning education, religion, and our difficulties in the political arena.

"I started the Tibetan Broadcast in 1956, and it continued as almost a single-handed operation for three years. I worked without an assistant, without taking weekends off. It soon became very popular throughout Tibet, so popular that everybody began buying radios and batteries so they could listen to the program. The Chinese tried to jam it. I ran the program for fifteen years, devoting all my spare time to helping Tibetan refugees.

"In meetings with His Holiness the Dalai Lama and the ministers during 1959 and 1960, we discussed many things. I emphasized what I felt most strongly: 'We are now facing an unprecedented catastrophe in Tibet, and a trauma in exile. Our political situation is hopeless, with no nation supporting our cause. Nothing should discourage or distract us. We need to rebuild our lives, re-create our religious and cultural heritage. Let us first and foremost establish monasteries, nunneries, and schools. Without these vital foundations, nothing else can save us. These institutions should serve as the nucleus of our resurrection as a nation.'

"In 1970, I decided to move with my family to Canada. I taught at the University of British Columbia for a year. Then I began to translate Buddhist texts. I've translated many important books, but I haven't published all of them. Tibetan Buddhism was being introduced to the West, but with so much misinformation, so much distortion, that I wanted to wait until people had a proper introduction to the fundamental teachings before publishing serious doctrinal books.

"While the loss of Tibet is great to us Tibetans and also to the world, the good that came out of this tragedy is that many of the great teachers escaped with their followers, the monks—which is how Buddhism reestablished itself in India and partly in Nepal.

"But I believe that when you lose the people—their language, culture, religion, and natural honesty and sensitivity—then Tibet is gone. Tibet is a spiritual essence, the living dharma!

"We're gradually losing that essence, both in and out of Tibet. And that's very sad. What will survive? Certainly there will be Tibetan people, but how much of that essence of Tibet will survive is anybody's guess.

"That is how things are: impermanent. Still, without saying that it is hopeless, we have to go forward and do whatever is best for us and for our children."

I told Lobsang that while I was in India, people—and spirits—kept telling me I must find a teacher. And I felt I probably should. But I didn't know how to go about it.

"It is very hard to find a good teacher. I think we will see more and more Eastern gurus coming to the West, and, unfortunately, some self-appointed masters will emerge locally. People from India or Tibet who were not recognized as good teachers and who had no following in their own community or areas see that the West is opening, and they come with their titles or their connection to somebody and declare themselves a guru or a lama. They are publicized and develop a following. That is the problem now. I'm not saying that there are not good lamas, but a teacher is more than a learned person. A teacher is very different. A teacher has to embody the essence of all the teachings he has learned. A learned man can give a message, but he is only a messenger; he brings the message that he has read in books or learned from other lamas. That's one service. I'm not excluding that. But Buddhism is much more than a message. Buddhism is an intimacy between teacher and pupils. Teachers work with students, sharing their ups and downs, telling them in terms of dharma: 'This is the way you work, and these are the pitfalls you avoid.'

"But there are a lot of people who want to make their lives more meaningful. People honestly seeking a simple truth, applying it, and going on about their lives. I don't expect anybody to change their name or shave their head. This is not necessary. Change has to take place inside. Buddhism doesn't care how many people convert to Buddhism. It cares only how each individual is benefited."

WHEN I FLEW east I stopped in Boston to see Mark, my eldest son. Of the three boys, he has always been the most spiritually curious. He goes to church regularly, and he meditates. He also has trouble with relationships, for which I am quick to take blame. For the first time, I stopped now to consider that maybe my children's karma is not necessarily subsumed by mine.

I gave him a copy of *The Tibetan Book of Living and Dying* and told him about Sogyal Rinpoche. He listened, fascinated, then asked if that meant I would improve my relationship with my mother, whom he had always defended. We had had conversations like that before, and I always felt betrayed, as though his loyalty belonged with me. Couldn't he see how unfair, how cold, how impossible my mother was to me?

The issue was often money. Ever since my father's death, my mother controlled the purse strings. She did not feel the need to support my writing, as my father had, or my habit of marrying and divorcing. Mark pointed out that his grandmother is a very independent woman, and that I am her worst nightmare: an unmarried woman determined to pursue a career that does not support her. (Me to my mother: "I would have to write *Gone with the Wind* to get out of debt!" My mother: "Then write *Gone with the Wind*. Or get a job.")

EDUCATING

A YOUNG MONK

GESHE THARCHIN IS the abbot of the Rashi Gempil Ling Kalmuk Buddhist Temple in New Jersey. He was born in Lhasa in 1929, the Year of the Water Dog. His full name is Khen Rinpoche Geshe Lobsang Tharchin.

 "NOW I AM SEVENTY-FIVE years older. I entered the Sera monastery at eight. At its peak, Sera had more than eight thousand teachers and disciples studying the ancient books of Buddhist wisdom. In one house, there might be six hundred to a thousand monks.

"We young monks were mischievous. Our house tutor would send us up to the rock cliffs behind the monastery with buckets to fetch water from the spring, and we would dawdle for hours, throwing rocks. We liked to tuck our feet into our maroon-colored robes and slide down the long boulders until the cloth was ripped to shreds. On our way back, a favorite trick was to put tacks on the path leading to the front gate. Some of the monks liked to walk barefoot, and we would hide behind the wall and wait for a victim. Then we would race away, robes flapping and flying in the wind, before he would catch us.

"We also had a game called pakda, which means an arrow of dough, a kind of a dough ball. I was very good at firing dough balls at our teachers, especially in the middle of chanting, when their mouths were open. Then they'd begin choking and spitting, and we would roar with laughter—until the housemaster came at us with his stick.

"My house proved to be a very good scholar's house, but I was a terrible goof-off and had a rather bad reputation. They were about to give up on me and let me bow out before the toughest course of study, when a glorious master, Phabongka Rinpoche, came into my life.

"Phabongka Rinpoche was a reincarnation of a Khenpo of the small monastery atop the famous rock formation, which was about three miles from our monastery. It was there a minister, Tonmi Sambhota, created an alphabet and grammatical system that lasts to this day.

"Rinpoche's voice was incredibly powerful, and he had an uncanny ability to relate to his audience. But his most famous tool was his humor. Public discourses could sometimes go on for ten hours or more without a break, and many people would begin to nod off. Then he would tell one of his jokes and startle the daydreamers.

"He spent long periods of meditation in a small cell built around the mouth of a cave in the rock formation. The central chamber had a high vaulted ceiling, in the center of which was an odd natural triangle that looked exactly like the shape of one of the mystic worlds described in our secret teachings.

"In the corner of the cave, an underground spring flowed, and above it was another natural drawing, this one just like the third eye that we see painted on the forehead of one of our female buddhas. We believe this third eye stands for the spiritual understanding in one's heart, and that the cave was the home of a *dakini*—a sort of Buddhist angel.

"It was here that I first met Phabongka Rinpoche. As a wild teenager, I had the distasteful job of quartermaster. Rinpoche had just returned from a teaching tour, and I was sent with firewood and supplies. When he saw me he put his hand on my head and said, 'Now this one looks like a bright boy!' From that day on I felt I had received his blessing, and with it some special power to pursue my studies. I suddenly realized the preciousness of human life, and how fortunate I was to be a student at one of the greatest Buddhist monasteries in the world. Why was I wasting my time? What if I suddenly died?

"In my heart I made a decision to master the teachings for the benefit of myself and others. I remember going to my house teacher, Geshe Namdrol, and declaring my change of heart to him. He laughed. 'Now the bad boy is going to study and become a master geshe! The day you become a *geshe* is the day I become the Ganden Tripa!' The Ganden Tripa is one of the highest religious personages in Tibet. He holds the throne of Lord Tsongkapa, attained only by reaching the highest rank of geshe, the *lharampa,* and then serving as head of one of the two colleges devoted to the study of the secret teachings.

"I got angry and swore to him that I would not only become a geshe, but a lharampa geshe as well (a rank which he never could reach). In my later years, after I had passed the lharampa examinations with highest honors, Geshe Namdrol used to ask me a little sheepishly if I would help him pick a good topic for the day's debates.

"Before my final exams, Phabongka Rinpoche passed from this earth. It is our custom to cremate the body of a holy person and preserve the ashes in a small shrine, and I still remember the day when they brought Rinpoche's remains back to his mountain hermitage. A shrine was constructed, and a great many of us monks came to pay our respects and make our final offerings.

"We Buddhists believe that although the body dies, the mind—since it is not destructible, like physical matter—continues on and eventually comes into a new body, within your mother's womb if you are to be born as a human. We believe that great saints can select their birth, and that out of compassion they will choose to return and teach their disciples again if this will benefit them. Thus it is a custom for the disciples to seek the help of some great wise men and go out to find the child who is the reincarnation of their teacher.

"A reincarnation of Phabongka Rinpoche was discovered in Darjeeling, India, and is now a promising young monk at the new Sera monastery in south India.

"We believe that there are many buddhas in the universe, and that they each can appear on one or more planets at the same time, if this will help the beings who live there. We believe that a buddhahood is the ultimate evolution of all life; that a buddha can know all things, but does not have all power. The Buddha did not create the universe, for example (this we have done by the force of our own past deeds, good and bad), nor can he take all our sufferings away from us by himself—these too we believe come from our own past actions, and must be stopped by ourselves.

"By studying and practicing the teachings of the Buddha, we ourselves can become buddhas, as can every living being. Therefore when we speak of enlightened beings appearing to a saint directly, we mean that any being who has removed all his suffering and gained all knowledge can appear to any one of us, in any form that may help us to reach this ultimate state ourselves.

"At fifteen, I started the actual training, which continued until I was thirty years old. I finished my Lharam Geshe degree in 1953.

"When it came time for the final Geshe examination, I had to read so many books that I developed an eye problem. I couldn't even see light for two weeks—very painful, some sort of infection from the paper. I got unbelievably sick. My mind became crazy with fever. I imagined people coming out of their houses, dancing, playing, reciting poetry. And I saw all these different creatures. I couldn't study, so my teacher told me to go home, a two-day trip by horse. This happened several times.

"I wasn't frightened. We had been taught to study karma. The results of our actions can't be avoided; these were obstacles, blockages that were disturbing me. Overcoming them helped me to become stronger.

"The final examination was held in Lhasa, in the main temple. All of the scholars from the largest monasteries were gathered there. They would ask us questions and we would have to give answers from the morning until ten o'clock at night. His Holiness, who is a great scholar, was there. By extraordinary luck, I was given highest honors. After that I automatically went to the Tantric College at Gyume monastery. When I finished there, I worked as an administrator.

"For several years I'd been afraid that the Chinese would begin killing the scholars and monks. They had been talking to the monks and geshes, trying to get them to publicly criticize the Dalai Lama. If they were to question me, I would have to say what I believed, and they would kill me. If I said what they wanted me to, then I'd be going against everything I'd worked for and believed in my whole life long. So in 1959, I chose to go to India.

"Five students and I traveled on foot, without shoes, over the moun-

Geshe Lobsang Tharchin

tain to India. The snow was hard high up, but when we began our descent
and the snow would get softer, we'd sink into the snow and be unable to
walk. With the melting snow, the water would be icy cold, and people's
feet would get frostbitten. Some lost their toes later. It took us almost a
month to go over the mountains from Lhasa to India. We'd set up a tent
to sleep at night, or sometimes there would be little farmhouses we could
stay in. At other times we would have to find empty places in a little cave.
The only thing I carried was food and fire-making equipment. Do you call
them bellows? That was very important. In Tibet, we make them out of
goatskin. We'd use a stone to strike the spark.

"We saw Chinese soldiers in the distance. We had decided that it
would be better to get killed on the road than to stay in Lhasa. Seven or
eight times they spotted us from airplanes. Twice it was very close. They

shot at us. Rat-tat-tat, like that. Some of the yaks were killed, but none of the people were hurt. We covered ourselves with blankets so they couldn't see us so well. We would find the casings from the shells and use them for candle holders.

"I went first to Assam, in India. Then to Delahousie, and eventually on to Calcutta to the university there, to teach and translate. Nehru agreed that the young Tibetans needed an education, so he arranged several schools for them. His Holiness asked me to teach in one of these schools. After several years, I told His Holiness that I wanted to learn English, so I came to the United States, here to New Jersey, in 1972. A friend had come earlier to start a monastery and requested a teacher from His Holiness.

"Buddhist philosophy teaches that when you change your body [die], your body's consciousness continues. When the consciousness goes to a bad place, this is a result of karma. Only karma. My previous life must have been a good one, because I'm very happy this time around, many good things have come to me.

"Dharma has many levels. Every day I have to take it from the top. I want to teach the people who want to learn as much as I can teach. There are not too many members of this temple—fifteen or twenty families, a hundred in all—but they are devoted."

He asked me if I had a teacher; I told him I did not. If I was to have one, I had not yet found him or her.

"How to find a qualified teacher is a long process, but I can make it shorter. Find a teacher who has strong compassion for his followers. Second, he must be highly trained in Buddhist teachings, otherwise it is only entertainment, hollow. Third, he should have patience." He laughed. "And if he doesn't have patience, then he should have courage."

Geshe Tharchin continued: "We are refugees from Tibet, driven out of our Shangri-la by the Chinese armies. The halls of Gyalrong house, where Phabongka Rinpoche gained his knowledge and I played my tricks on Yeshe Lobsang, have been bombed out and burned. The Rinpoche's mountain hermitage stands like some strange skeleton—only the front wall of stone remains erect, for all the rest were ripped down by the Chinese for firewood. The monk's cell at the mouth of his wonderful meditation cave was smashed to rubble, which so fills the opening that no one can even find it now.

"As Buddhists, we Tibetans do not feel anger at the Chinese, only a deep sadness at the loss of our country and traditions and at the deaths of more than a million of our friends and relatives. In a way we have become more aware of how precious and short life is, and how we should practice religion while we are still alive to do so. Our loss too is perhaps the greater world's gain, as teachings will now reach the outer world for the first time. I pray these teachings will help us all to defeat our real enemies—the emotions of like and dislike and ignorance within our own minds."

A LESSON
IN JUDGMENT

I HAD ASKED each elder I'd met for suggestions of others I might talk to, and I was developing quite an impressive list. I also kept checking back with Lobsang Lhalungpa, to ask his opinion. Often he thought of someone too, and had another name and address for me.

 Back in Los Angeles I contacted a teacher everyone seemed to hold in high esteem. He is called Geshe-la. He was shy when I reached him by phone; he was not sure that he was important enough to be in a book. I told him that it was okay, I wasn't important enough to be writing one. He laughed and agreed to see me.

A TEACHING CAME in an unexpected way the day I met with Geshe-la. Before our interview, we'd had lunch at an outdoor café near the studio where he meets with students. At the adjoining table sat four men bantering back and forth about business in voices loud enough to all but drown out Geshe-la's soft, accented voice. The men spoke cynically in the hard-edged way people do when they are trying to top each other's stories. I strained to hear Geshe and tried to block out these other voices, my mind all the while madly judging the men.

The waitress had forgotten to bring milk for Geshe-la's tea, and I went inside to get some. When I came back, one of the men was looking at Geshe-la, commenting on his monk's robes. "Must be hot in that getup," he said. "What are you?"

Geshe-la smiled happily and explained he was a Tibetan monk, and that no, it wasn't terribly hot today. "Quite pleasant." He chuckled as I fumed.

After a while the men got up to leave. One stopped at our table and said, "I must tell you, sir, I couldn't take my eyes off of you. You have such a spiritual aura, I've never seen anything quite so extraordinary. . . ."

Geshe-la beamed, extended his hand, and introduced himself. The man mentioned that he had a friend who did business with the Chinese and made frequent trips. "They're changing, you know. The new guard wants to put an end to Communism. I bet in five, ten years you'll get your country back."

Still smiling, Geshe-la's eyes had misted over. He took the man's hand again and thanked him profusely. The man's face was full of wonder. His whole demeanor had changed. Slightly embarrassed, he suddenly bowed like a schoolboy and then rushed off.

I had witnessed a transformation of a sort that I would have sworn could not have been possible.

"I WAS BORN in 1943 in eastern Tibet, on a farm about twelve miles from the town of Chamdo. Not a big farm, but we had a number of cows,

yaks, deer, dzomos, donkeys, goats, horses. My father was a good and religious man. He would go to the local monastery, Ganden Jambaling, which
means 'land of love,' for teachings for months at a time, no matter how
busy things were at the farm. We were a very close family. My mother, such
a very kind lady, was quite young—only sixteen when I was born—yet she
understood how much my father needed a spiritual path and never criticized him. I'm very lucky to have had such good and gentle parents.

"I was the oldest of seven, eight including the one we lost. When I
was six, my father and mother brought a teacher for me from the
monastery, an older learned monk. He lived with us for a year and a half.
During those eighteen months I learned many of the sutras by memory.

"When I was eight, my father asked me if I wanted to go to the
monastery. Most first sons go to the monastery unless they are needed in
the home—then the next eldest would go. Since I wasn't needed, I chose
to go. My uncle, my father's brother, was already a monk, so I could share
a room with him. The first few weeks were hard. I'd think about my
mother and my home. Many of us boys were homesick."

I marveled at the stories I heard time and again of the incredible
knowledge imparted to the people when they were only children; the
time, attention, and devotion of the families and teachers to the spiritual
education of the young. Gelek Rinpoche would later explain that the reason for the focus on children is because it is easier to change karmic im-
prints in the young before habitual patterns are formed.

"The founder of Ganden monastery," Geshe-la continued, "was
Lama Tsongkapa, a great fourteenth-century master and founder of the
Gelugpa sect: the emanation of Manjushri. I studied there for twenty-
three years, every day, winter and summer, without a break. Sometimes we
would be invited to a benefactor's house and we'd be given food and a
place to stay.

"My studies would have been finished in 1960 but for the Chinese invasion. I left from college on March 14, after I had gone to the evening session. One monk close to me in the dormitory asked where I was going. I said I was going to session. He said, 'If you are going away, you should go now, because the Chinese soldiers will soon come into the monastery.' He gave me some light clothes and a coat. It was very difficult to leave my robes.

"My practice *pecha*, study book and daily practice book, plus something to eat, was all we took. And barley flour for tsampa. Three days we were in the Himalayas. The strongest person went first, to make a narrow footpath through the snow, and one by one we followed. It was very dangerous because you can sink in the snow.

"At night we dug a hole in the snow to keep warm. There was always the fear that the Chinese would chase us with machine guns from their airplanes. From a distance I could see them shooting and crowds running in fear. Finally we crossed the Himalayas to the Indian border, where the grass was new and it was warm. People in the countryside welcomed us and gave us food.

"I went to Delahousie until 1962, and finished my degree. His Holiness had asked the monks to continue studying just as they had done in the monastery.

"I heard nothing of my family until 1981, when the government-in-exile sent a fact-finding delegation to Tibet. They found my sister, and I learned then that my father and uncle had passed away under the hardship of Chinese rule. Since my family were farmers, they were not tortured, but it was hard for them to get food; they were of the more than one million Tibetans who lost their lives under the Chinese occupation.

"In some areas of Tibet now you find more Chinese than Tibetans— some places twice as many. As part of the plan to obliterate Tibet, the

Chinese are changing the names of the cities, the streets—even the mountains.

"In 1963 His Holiness asked me to go to Sussex, England, to be the teacher for Tibetan refugee students sent there. When we arrived at the airport we were overwhelmed by television cameras and excited newspaper reporters who had never seen Tibetan children before.

"What surprised me the most was all the many lights at night. In India we were in the mountains and didn't go into town very often. I had never seen so many lights.

"Some years later, when I traveled to the United States, it was the cars that amazed me. And I had never seen the ocean before I came to California. I had only read about it. There were so many people at the beaches; everyone seemed happy, taking things easy. I thought how very good it is that the people have so much freedom here.

"At first, as a teacher, I had a very difficult time communicating with my Western students. I had many ideas and so many things to say, but I lacked language skills. In those days, people really wanted to hear the dharma and would appreciate even one word of dharma I could tell them. Sometimes, one word is like having a whole session of dharma teaching. When I think about those days, reflect on those early retreats, I am quite amazed. Somehow the students were able to understand. We'd get together and chant, or do prostrations, paying respect to the Buddha, Dharma, Sangha. And I would give instruction in meditations.

"As to the difficulty of practicing dharma in the West, with its busy lifestyles, it's not just in the West that people are busy. Everywhere in the world there are families to be taken care of and jobs to go to. That is not such a big obstacle. The problem I see here in the West is that people have no patience. They want results right now! They think the dharma can be accomplished in just a few years. Even with great concentration it takes many years of practice to gain positive results. This impatience is the biggest obstacle for Westerners. So many start to practice, but they soon drop it. They lose energy because they didn't practice long enough to see results. People all want to get something, they want some power, but they want it to come like a miracle. A miracle is not such a big deal. Even if someone can fly around the room or read minds, this is not a big deal.

"What in fact is a big deal, and what we need most, is to get rid of our negative mind. If a person wants to see how much progress he or she has made in practice, then they should just check to see how their mind has changed from beginning the dharma practice up to the present. If there is no change, then they are not practicing correctly. The dharma is pure, but if it isn't practiced correctly there will be no positive result. If there is a positive change, if there is less desire, less anger and hatred and more calmness, that is the mark of good practice. That is a useful result. It may not look like a miracle to show off to others, but if one becomes a better person, more positive, then that is the right result. It works. But for many Westerners, if the result doesn't come immediately, they go try something else. And do the same thing all over again.

"There are some people who live very happy and successful lives without practicing the dharma. Many people ask me how this can be. The reason is that though they do not practice in this life, they did in a past lifetime, and that created the good karma for their present life. But if they don't continue to create positive actions in this life but instead do negative deeds, they will experience the result of the bad karma in their next lifetime."

"Geshe-la, here in the West, the 1960s saw a spiritual revolution among the young people, who rejected their parents' traditions and religions. Many turned to Buddhism for answers, and some parents took this to be just another form of rebellion."

"One's birthplace can often be like a prison, and one's parents the jailers of that prison. Our parents can show us great kindness, which we must remember and be greateful for, but from another point of view, parents sometimes create obstacles and mislead and misguide us. From that point of view they can be said to be like jailers.

"When you read the life story of Sakyamuni Buddha, you find that when he wanted to leave the palace and begin his spiritual practice, his father did everything he possibly could to stop his son from doing this. So, even our teacher had to run away from his birthplace.

"When parents do this sort of thing, it is out of love and affection. They think what they are doing is for the best. But from a spiritual point of view, it is like telling one's children to stay with them in samsara.

"In the Lamrim texts—the Stages of the Path to Enlightenment—it is stated that faith precedes the attainment of realizations. Faith is to realizations as the mother is to the child. If you practice the dharma from the bottom of your heart, then the basic necessities of life, what you need to sustain you, will somehow come your way."

"That is not so easy, here in what must be the *capital* of samsara. Did you know there is even a perfume called 'Samsara'?"

Geshe-la laughed. "You should abandon friends who stimulate your delusions. Instead, cultivate friends whose company inspires you to create positive actions. These are your dharma friends.

"All the activities that you engage in are endless. You will never complete them. So you should try to relax a bit, try to be less busy so that you are more relaxed to do something for your future lives. Do something that is meaningful for your spiritual betterment."

THE TEACHER

GURU DEVOTION IS a concept I have a hard time understanding. When I was in France and I met with Sogyal Rinpoche at his retreat center, I asked him to explain it to me. I remember it was the scene itself that raised the question.

Lerab ling is Tibetan for "sanctuary, place of enlightened action." Sogyal Rinpoche, teacher, author of *The Tibetan Book of Living and Dying*, and spiritual director of Rigpa, an international network of Buddhist centers, gave this name to the retreat center he founded in southwest France. Situated in the Languedoc plateau, between the Cevennes and the Mediterranean, Lerab Ling sprawls across 359 acres of meadow and woodland.

I arrived at this spiritual paradise in the middle of a summer retreat with more than 400 students, many of whom stayed in tents and referred to the summer sessions as spiritual boot camp. Rinpoche's secretary, a young woman from California who is a longtime student, explained they would have to fit me in between teachings. She had reserved one of the dozen or so recently built two-bedroom "chalets," which I would share with a retreatant. Built of cedar and simply furnished—bed, chair, and table—the chalets line the path to the swimming pool, a natural mountain spring. I shared mine with a tall, shy German fellow who smiled and bowed imperceptively when we passed each other in the hall.

Families with small children occupied the chalets on both sides. Dharma kids grew wild there; they were everywhere—chasing one another through the trees, splashing in the pool, in the cafeteria sneaking salt into water pitchers—and seemed to be of little distraction to the meditators.

I was invited to attend some of the teachings. The first evening, at twilight, I walked up the hill to the enormous shrine tent where Sogyal Rinpoche was giving a teaching. He is a young elder—in his forties. I recognized the round, bespeckled face from the movie *The Little Buddha*, in which he played one of the lamas searching for a tulku, a reincarnation of an important master.

Here, Sogyal Rinpoche sat on a stage, under a brilliant yellow canopy, on a large raised platform furnished with altars, six thangkas, and a pair of red-lacquered chests, on which rested blue vases filled with fresh-cut flowers, brass butter lamps, and framed photographs of his teachers and of the Dalai Lama.

The rinpoche's chair and table were of lacquered orange; beside them stood an imposing throne used for ceremonies. Underneath lay a beautiful Tibetan rug of yellow, blue, and gold. He wore a gold-colored robe over a yellow shirt; his slightly graying hair fell in soft waves around his ears.

A small microphone was fastened to his robe; a video camera on a tripod rolled tape. Two more microphones were placed around the room for simultaneous translations in French and German. I sat on the floor near the entrance. In front of me was a woman with a child at her breast, an infant so tiny that I wondered if the woman had given birth during the retreat.

Laughter rippled through the group; Sogyal Rinpoche was telling a story about his days in a Jesuit school in Delhi, where he kept hearing what he thought was some sort of an incantation: "Please, father, water," but which turned out to be a simple request: "Please pass the water."

His students clearly adored him. They listened, amused and delighted and with rapt attention, to teachings sprinkled with personal stories and shared confidences. When he fumbled for a word or forgot a date, Rinpoche called on his oldest students, who occupied the first few rows, for help.

The talk was followed by a meditation session. Someone had been kind enough to pass me a cushion, and I decided to stay. I sat cross-legged, spine straight, and tried to concentrate on my breath. But my mind buzzed and flitted like a fly, lighting on one thought, then another and another. Like many Westerners, I could not help but be bothered by this open display of guru devotion among the followers. Yet his teachings are precious; no other word will do. His book has reached countless people whose lives have been profoundly affected by the wisdom and compassion in his writing. He has probably done more to bring the dharma to the modern world than any other teacher.

I DID NOT GET my appointment with Rinpoche until the fourth day. But the staff was attentive, and I used the time well, writing in my notebook on the wooden deck of the chalet. I watched, amused, as the rotund rinpoche walked past in his bathing trunks and sandals on his way to the swimming pool for his daily late-afternoon swim. He was always accompanied by part of his entourage, one of whom hurried along behind him, carrying his towel.

THE FIRST MORNING I was jolted awake by a loud crash that shook the foundations of the chalet. My mind raced; my heart pounded. *I'm in Los Angeles, and it's an earthquake.* Another crash, the chalet shuddered, and I forced myself to open my eyes. *No, I'm not; I'm in an earthquake in the south of France.* What does one do? Run outside? *Crash, shudder.* I reached for my shoes.

Suddenly I realized these crashes had a definite rhythm; it couldn't be an earthquake. It was the student in the next room doing some Wagnerian calisthenics! It continued for perhaps another twenty minutes. *Crash, shudder.* Really, couldn't he do this outdoors?

At breakfast I stopped him as he passed the table where I was sitting. He was carrying a tray. With elaborate politeness, I asked if he would please do his exercises outdoors. He smiled and, peering shyly from behind thick glasses, he said, "Yes. I suppose I can do my prostrations in the shrine tent."

I looked over at the others at the table, who were smiling patiently, and dropped my head in my hands. "I have no business doing this book," I mumbled miserably.

ON THE AFTERNOON of the fourth day, Zanna, Rinpoche's secretary, appeared at my door to escort me to the garden of Rinpoche's private residence. Rinpoche and I sat across from each other at a table in the shade of a large ash, flanked by his secretary and his assistant, Patrick Gaffney, whom he'd known since his days as a visiting scholar at Cambridge. A copy of my book rested on the table next to a copy of his own.

After a brief exchange of pleasantries, I told him that the whole issue of guru devotion puzzled me, and asked if this very Tibetan tradition were really possible in Western culture.

"YES, IT IS. Correctly understood, devotion is actually a way of finishing with your past, and of healing it. Our task in life is really to learn to let go, to change and grow, and not to remain stuck in the past. Devotion is about us giving ourselves the permission not just to study, but to follow. People who have really followed a master have something in them that makes them go through things. Sometimes I am surprised and moved by the devotion Western people can have, healthy devotion, that is, not blind faith. You may have the karma to meet a master, but you have to develop the qualities to follow him."

"What is it that makes devotion possible, then?"

"Devotion is possible when you really engage in a training, when you really work with a living master. Sometimes people follow a master from a distance and without actually participating in the training. They'll say, 'The Dalai Lama is my teacher.' Of course he can be your teacher, but it will be difficult for you to follow him. He is the master of all the masters. Some people also claim they've studied with this master or that, when all they did was go to a few talks or a few seminars. Whatever they claim, they could not have fully studied, because their basic being is not trained. Then they often have a lot of difficulties on the path."

"What happens to what you describe as pure guru devotion when it comes to the West? Doesn't it become distorted, corrupted?"

"It can be corrupted in the East, too. Not everything is automatically corrupted once it gets to the West! The only thing about the West is that there is not the right environment; it's not part of the culture, so it lacks stability.

"When you show devotion, you show everything of yourself, including all of your history and all of your projections. Sometimes students project onto the teacher all kinds of things. For example, people relate to the master like the father or mother they did not have, and it gets mixed up with a lot of emotions, which can only lead to frustration. They assume that the teachers are there to solve all their problems, and so students hold them responsible for their whole lives. They expect the teacher to be grateful because they have followed him or her. They get frustrated when they can't talk to the teacher whenever they want. But the relationship with a teacher is not an ordinary one; it is spiritual and is based on, and lives in, the teachings.

"Even when you address this openly and tease people about it, I am still amazed at how many projections and expectations there are. This is what distorts and contaminates the master-disciple relationship."

"And the guru ends up becoming a rock star. . . ."

"Frankly speaking, I don't think this is so much the case with Tibetan Buddhism. If they had wanted to, if they had gone all out, there are masters who could have become like rock stars. They have the wisdom and the charisma . . . but the teaching itself seems to discourage that. In order to have the clear discernment to follow the teacher, we need a good understanding of the teachings—because the real teacher is in the teachings. What does the teacher teach but the teachings? It is not following the teacher's personality, but the message that he gives.

"Also, in the West, there is often a lot of fear: When you follow a master, is he trustworthy? Is he going to lead us down the wrong path? But when we meet a master, such questions don't even exist. Sometimes it becomes very clear how much these fears we have are our own fears and need to be purified.

"You see, on the spiritual path, all kinds of difficulties can come.

Why? Because, inevitably, the teacher and the teachings mirror us. A master can bring up all our weaknesses. If it's a special master, he or she can push many buttons. That's normal. Even a master who's very calm and gentle and fits the bill will push all the buttons nevertheless. Sometimes peaceful masters are more wrathful than the wrathful masters. They show us things about ourselves that we may not quite like to acknowledge. It is like looking into a mirror and seeing a terrible, ugly face. We deny it, get angry, and hit the mirror; it breaks into a hundred pieces, with a hundred ugly faces.

"When we get really angry with ourselves, we refuse to accept and we lash out against the master. This is a very Western phenomenon. Again, in this case we really need to know the dharma and understand it.

"It says in the great *Ornament of the Mahayana Sutras* taught by Maitreya Buddha: 'Rely on the message of the teacher, not on his personality. Rely on the meaning, not just on the words. Rely on the real meaning, not on the provisional one. Rely on your wisdom mind, not on your ordinary, judgmental mind.' "

"What exactly is the nature of the master-student relationship?"

"Very simply, it depends on the master and on the student. As for the qualities of a student, the great Dzogchen saint Longchenpa said that a good student has trust and is highly discerning, diligent, conscientious, and mindful; follows the teacher's instructions; is disciplined, compassionate, and deeply concerned about others' well-being; and is open-minded, patient, generous, visionary, stable, and deeply devoted.

"The student is someone who is able to see a gem, to be able to recognize when a master is special. Usually we have a particular concept or idea about how a master should be. If you look at the history of India, the great Vajrayana masters often did not appear in a conventional way. Tilopa, the forefather of the whole Kagyu lineage of Tibetan Buddhism, appeared as an outcast and a beggar. Sometimes these masters had only one disciple.

"We need to be able to see beyond the form, straight to the essence. If we have this capacity, it means that we have something special. When you go to McDonald's, you know exactly what you are getting. You cannot expect the master to be like a McDonald's, purveying something that fits your concept exactly.

"If a master is an authentic master, he will manifest as such in every situation. The traditional teachings speak of many qualities for a perfect teacher-realization: learning, discipline, compassion, renunciation, skillfulness, having the blessing of the lineage, and so on. The remarkable nineteenth-century master Patrul Rinpoche said there is one quality that stands above all the rest: that the master has a heart that is filled with *bodhicitta*—the real desire to become enlightened for the sake of all sentient beings. Compassion is the most important thing.

"Of course it is difficult to meet authentic masters. When there is a lineage it is easier to find them, but even then, to find a master with very special qualities is rare. You can find masters, but among the masters too there are masters. I can speak from my experience. You could say that my life has been filled with masters. I've been so fortunate: I've met master after master, all owing to the kindness of Jamyang Khyentse, my first and principal master. Even though he died when I was quite young, somehow he took care of me, and I kept on meeting masters who have continued to reveal to me what he had sown in me.

"Without the masters it is not possible for people to understand the teachings. It is only through their direct instructions that we can come to understand the meanings; they bring the teachings alive. Authentic masters also embody the blessing of the lineage. So devotion to the masters begins with gratitude. If you have authentic devotion, you see with a new clarity, certainty, and faith; you feel such an extraordinary joy and sense of celebration. I remember times when I received certain teachings, I felt as if I was no longer on this earth.

"What you also realize is the tremendous compassion, love, and care they have. And how selfless they are: they just go on and on, giving, giving, giving. They give you the greatest gift, the gift of wisdom. What does that do for you? It frees you from yourself, from your own ignorance. You begin to discover your real nature. Till then, you did not know who you were, but now as you come to discover yourself, all your frustrations begin to dissolve. That's why there have been so many great *dohas*—hymns, songs of experience, and prayers of devotion—composed spontaneously in the moment of realization. That great gift of wisdom is actually the gift of yourself.

"The more you realize the truth of the teachings, the more you'll find that the very beings of the masters resonate with the truth. Whenever I think of Guru Padmasambhava or the masters I have been close to—Jamyang Khyentse, Dudjom Rinpoche, Dilgo Khyentse Rinpoche, Karmapa or Kalu Rinpoche—or any of the masters, I see them all as the same. Because they all are showing the same truth; the same as all the buddhas, the same as Guru Padmasambhava.

"This means that the master is no longer a personality; he is the embodiment and the human face of truth. This is really what an incarnation is—a compassionate vehicle for touching the minds and hearts of beings. When you have been touched by a master in that way, things happen for you, quicken, and progress. You may even find that you don't need anything else; if your devotion is pure and focused, you're okay.

"And what's interesting, you may find that the more devotion there is in your life, the richer and more fulfilling your life becomes. Because devotion is the means to purify all the negative emotions and to work through particular psychological patterns. Really to work with devotion like this is a means of development.

"If you have this devotion, you can become enlightened more quickly. It is said that there are three means through which we can realize the nature of our mind: meditation, the accumulation of merit, and devotion. For me, devotion is the path, and it is only because I have this devotion that I can communicate the teachings—because I know that when there is devotion, there is also the blessing. If the teacher does not have devotion, it is questionable whether the lineage will last.

"So it's the greatest human relationship, the teacher-student relationship. It is something that makes you transcend from the ordinary to the spiritual. It's such an amazing dynamic. It purifies; it empowers; and, in a sense, it is the only way of learning. It is an extraordinary path, rapid and direct.

"When we talk about the teacher, it is something universal; it's a principle. The outer teacher, the master we meet, is the key, the master who shows us, but actually life itself is also a great teacher. But we don't know how to listen to its teachings. This is called the 'universality of the teacher.' Once the master teaches us and we know the teaching, then we'll have learned how to listen to life and how to read the messages life is always giving. Because ultimately what is our teacher? The truth is our teacher, and the truth is what we have to become."

I understood what Sogyal Rinpoche meant, and I was moved by his sincerity, but still I had doubts. We are such a young society, too hungry for idols; inevitably we turn our masters into rock stars.

HEALING

On a Wednesday morning in late May, just before Memorial Day weekend, I went to a doctor, new to me, for my yearly checkup. The physical exam proved fine; in another year I would reach the five-year mark, the doctor cheerfully reminded me. She then ran the usual blood tests, among them the standard tumor marker, used to measure a tumor if there is one. The office would fax me the results in two days, she said.

I was out much of the day that Friday; when I came home there was a message on my voice mail from the doctor. She had called at 4:45 to say she wanted to talk to me about one of the tests, the tumor marker, which was elevated. I could reach her in her office until five.

I froze. My body went numb. Time hung suspended in that strange other place remembered from four years before, where one is instantly removed from all that is life to the holding place; not yet death, not quite decided.

I looked at my watch: 4:55, just time to catch her. But the receptionist told me the doctor had already gone. I explained the reason for my call and asked if there was anyone else I could talk to. The indifferent receptionist was afraid not. Outrage all but obliterated fear. "Is there no way to reach the doctor for even a brief conversation?" I asked. She would leave a message on her exchange, but as far as she knew, the doctor would be out of town until Tuesday.

Cancer creates its own particular paranoia—catch a cold and it must be nose cancer—so a mysterious phone call about a blood test on a Friday of a holiday weekend promised long days ahead in which to contemplate impermanence. I reminded myself of Khamtrul Rinpoche's divination: "The illness you were stricken with a few years ago will not return. You are fine." Did that mean never? He said I was fine then, but what about now?

Lobsang Lhalungpa had told me about his bout with cancer a few years earlier. His words came to mind: "If you look at life as what it is, then you have no illusions. Life is not always a beautiful garden. Even in the garden itself, there are harmful things, poisonous plants, and thorny bushes. So looking at things as they are means that life itself is unreliable. But a mind that is calm and free of fear has an immediate impact on the body."

I found I was taking notice of each thought, each word, each deed in a new way, for each would be my legacy, in each would lay the foundation for the future. I discovered I was thinking in Buddhist terms about karma and rebirth.

Chagdud Tulku Rinpoche, in his book *Gates to Buddhist Practice*, tells the story the Buddha used to illustrate the rarity of human birth: "Compare the 3,000-fold universe to a huge ocean with a wooden yoke floating somewhere on top of it. At the bottom of the ocean lives a blind turtle. Once every hundred years it comes to the surface for a gulp of air, then goes back down to the bottom. The laws of chance are such that, sooner or later, the moment the turtle surfaces the wind will blow the yoke over its head and the turtle will poke through. That this will happen is just barely conceivable. According to the Buddha, the chances of someone finding a precious human birth are even less likely."

I took notice of my moments of impatience, of selfishness. Why had I never noticed them before? I resisted the urge to give in to the drama; I just watched and thought and, yes, prayed.

I do not fear death, only the way it may come: helplessly and with the indignities of a long illness. And before I have had a chance to fully understand the nature of life.

When Tuesday finally came and the doctor called me, she suggested I have the test redone, as labs can sometimes vary in their testing procedures. I had good reason to be angry. She might have mentioned that major caveat in her message and spared me a weekend of wondering. But by the end of the week I had new results that were perfectly normal.

I also had a new mind.

I turned once again to Lhalungpa for the Buddhist view of illness and health.

"HEALING IS AN ESSENTIAL part of Buddhist meditation. We don't always talk of healing, but when you work with the mind, when you make it peaceful and sensitive and compassionate, the body is impacted and you feel at peace. At the same time, you impact others; it influences how you look at other people. You don't have to pretend when your inner world is secure and you understand what you are doing. When you look at other people with concern, you need no pretense. Your face reveals what you are inside. There is no division. But when your inner world is not clean, not pure, not sensitive enough, then you pretend to be kind, sure, but you present a different kind of face, a different kind of smile. Very soon sensitive people discover that that smile is not sincere. Dharma is not pretense. Dharma is really being what it is. Pure inside and outside, everywhere.

"From a Buddhist perspective, the deeper cause of disease is in the settled, unresolved mind or unresolved karma. There is something there that then works with the conscious mind. Somewhere along the way, this mind did not focus inwardly on these problems. Therefore, the problem is gradually built up with images—through the environment, through contact with an unhealthy environment—which all together result in disease.

"Therefore there is a need for something specific in terms of medicine, so Buddhism doesn't say that only meditation will work. A balanced approach is needed. The power of the mind is such that when you take medicine with the understanding and trust that this medicine has some property that is going to work, this gives confidence and peace of mind. The combination of mind and medicine speeds recovery.

"This is true even in serious cases, like my own cancer. Fortunately, because of my lifelong devotion, when my doctor told me, 'Mr. Lhalungpa, you have cancer, a very serious one,' I said all right. I had prepared myself for decades to understand how natural things work, how disease can overcome us. I had prepared myself all along for this kind of situation. For health is unpredictable. Even thirty years ago when I enjoyed extraordinary health, I didn't take it for granted.

"But some people, when they heard I had cancer, asked, 'What did you do?' as if I had committed some crime and was being punished for it. This is a misconception, that there is somebody out there with the rules: somebody is a good boy and he gets wonderful things—more money, more wealth, more friends. When somebody gets cancer, it's a punishment. This is so foreign to our tradition. It is a total misunderstanding of how nature works.

"I didn't feel any shock when the doctor told me, I just said, 'Okay, let's go ahead with the surgery and the treatments.' I had a long course of radiation. I was losing weight every day—I became almost like a skeleton—but still, my mind was peaceful, I slept well. Even when I lost my country—it was a great loss, a tragic shock. But I had learned how to understand things. I learned to take things as they come and ask, 'Is there something that I can do or not?' If you see that there is something that you can do, do it.

"When I had radiation, there was an immediate impact of how powerful and destabilizing it was. The first day, I was fine, but the second day, I felt so nauseous and weak that my wife called the doctor and he sent me some pills. I took four or five pills that day only. Then I said to myself, I can't take these pills every day. So every morning, before going to the hospital for radiation treatment, I did my meditation practice. Then I would go to my doctor's office for chemotherapy. I thought, Something else needs to be done because this is so powerful. It needs a stronger counterforce. So I did my meditation at home, then I went to the doctor's office and sat outside in the corridor. I told the nurse I would sit there quietly for five or ten minutes before the treatment.

"I meditated until the time they called me in to the radiation room. This meditation is unlike anything. It's very calming and peaceful. On the table, they took measurements and drew a chart on my stomach while I lay there doing my meditation to counteract the ill effects of radiation. I paid no attention to what the doctor and nurses were doing. I was doing a healing meditation. When they said I could get up, I got dressed and went and sat in the corridor again for another period of meditation. I did that every day, and soon that destabilized feeling that I'd had the second day was gone. I had protected myself from the ill effects of the radiation. At the end, I was a little weak but I never was mentally worried. It is a waste of time, worrying. What's going to happen? Is it going to work? Is it not going to work? I never questioned any of these things. If it works, okay. If it doesn't work, okay.

"I've long accepted the tradition that says that when your body is unwell you need to do something physically—physical therapy, medicine, plus spiritual and mental work. You need to combine them. And that is, I think, a very healthy thing for modern people to look at. People have a tendency to look for magic sometimes and exclude conventional methods of treatment. If the unconventional methods don't work, they are lost. But when you combine medicine with spiritual and mental work, it is more effective than either method by itself.

"My practice never stops, which doesn't mean I sit in the corner doing my meditation. My practice means whatever I am doing, daytime, nighttime, even in my sleep. In this way, dharma is an incessant flow of generosity, understanding, and compassion that ensures stability in the inner world. When the mind is still and clear, when you see things without confusion, there is always joy."

I WAS NO STRANGER to the power of prayer. When I was in the hospital and I knew Pete Catches was praying and doing ceremonies for me, I felt safe. The night before my operation, I had a dream in which a faceless voice said the words, "You will get well, you must get well. You have to build a sweat lodge for George Bush." I woke laughing. The nurse, hearing me, poked her head in and asked if they'd already started my medication. "No," I said, still chuckling, "but would you hand me the phone?" On the off chance that Pete would be at his son's house, where there was a telephone, I called. I shouldn't have been surprised when it was Pete who answered. I told him the dream and, knowing his dislike for the Republican administration and for George Bush in particular, waited for him to burst into laughter. But he was silent. "Isn't that funny, Grandfather?" Finally he answered, "But that is exactly what you must do, Granddaughter. You must build sweat lodges for all the George Bushes of the world, and you must do that with your books." He then told me he would be doing a pipe ceremony during my operation.

DHARMA DYNASTY:

FROM TIBET TO THE WEST

I HAD BEEN READING about the Sakyas in "Cho-Yang," a series of books on Tibetan history and culture, which Tsering Choedon introduced me to when I was in India. According to history, the Sakya family descended from gods of the Realm of Clear Light, who entered the human realm more than one thousand years ago and has remained unbroken  since then. Rulers of much of Central Asia for many years, the Sakyas descended from the Sakya Pandita, thirteenth-century religious leader of Tibet and spiritual advisor to Kublai Khan. Because the lineage is inherited, the men are permitted to marry.

In June I flew to Seattle and Vancouver to see three members of the Sakya family, all great teachers.

HIS HOLINESS JIGDAL Dagchen Sakya is the founder of the Sakya monastery in Seattle and author of *The Sakya Principality*. Born in

1928 into the Phun-tshog branch of the Khon lineage, he is the imminent successor to the throne of Sakya. He is one of seven children—two boys and five girls.

Sakyas receive a special education, and since Dagchen Rinpoche was to be future head of the Sakya School of Tibetan Buddhism, his was carefully planned by his father, H. H. Trichen Ngawang Thutop Wangchuk, the last throneholder in Tibet. Dagchen Rinpoche was not to enter a monastery until his tenth year.

Rinpoche and his family were the first to settle in the United States, in 1961. They came at the invitation of the University of Washington, sponsored by a Rockefeller Foundation grant. His Holiness offered teachings in their home and in rented facilities until a building was found on the outskirts of Seattle. In 1974 Sakya Tegchen Choling, a dharma center and monastery, was founded. The large white building flying the Tibetan and American flags serves as temple, library, and offices, as well as residence for some of the members.

I wondered if Jigdal Dagchen Rinpoche might have some advice for developing the calmness of mind which enabled Lobsang Lhalungpa to face his illness with such utter serenity.

"WHEN I AM ASKED how to approach the dharma, my teaching is to practice with the body, speech, and mind; to think of the body and speech as servants to the mind, the mind as the master. When you die, the mind leaves the body, so think of the body as a temporary dwelling, a hotel. And speech is like an echo off a mountain; it just resounds.

"Mind is foremost. Its actions decide whether one will become a buddha or descend to the hell realms. Mind determines all actions, good or bad. Therefore it is king. The three negative mental factors of the mind are attachment, desire, and grasping. Practice of the dharma is the antidote.

"When listening to a teaching of the Buddha's, we should avoid what are called the 'three faults of a receptacle.' If we don't listen to the teachings, we are like an overturned bowl; nothing can be retained. If we don't put the teachings into practice, we are like a bowl with a hole in it; everything leaks out. If we are lazy-minded and sleepy, this is similar to using an unclean bowl; the holder corrupts what it holds. We should also avoid the six defilements: pride, nonbelief, resentment at feeling obliged to attend the teachings, feeling they are useless, being distracted by the environment of the teaching, and seeing faults in that environment.

"On the other hand, we should practice the four desirable attitudes: viewing the teacher as a physician, seeing oneself as a patient, understanding the dharma to be medicine, and resolving to practice the dharma as our cure.

"In Tibet, a student usually starts with the foundation practices. These include prostrations, purification ritual with mantra recitation, *mandala* offerings, and guru yoga.

"In meditation here at the monastery, I tell practitioners to sit with a straight back. This is the right position for the psychic veins to channel correctly, to put the mind in the proper state for meditation. The legs should be crossed, right over left. The hands should be in the lap in the 'equipoise' position, with the right hand within the left, left on the bottom, the thumbs interlocked.

"The mental attitude for meditation can be viewed in progressive stages. Understanding the dharma engages one on the Path of Accumulation, where beginners learn the difference between virtue and non-virtue and start to try to comprehend the nature of mind. Experiencing the dharma engages one on the Path of Application, which is like seeing the reflection of the moon in water. The realization of dharma engages one on the Path of Insight, like seeing the moon in the sky just after the new moon. Over time, it becomes a full moon, which is buddhahood.

"The mind should be kept in its natural state without thinking of past, present, or future, and without excitement, depression, or distraction. The mind should maintain a union of clarity and emptiness in a calm, unperturbable condition.

"The base or ground of the mind is our buddha-nature. All beings have buddha-nature, but we can't be enlightened until we are free of incidental stains. These stains can't be removed like spots from a teacup. To remove them, one must view the Root Lama as inseparable from the Buddha himself. Then, having faith, devotion, and sincerity when meditating, one can reach complete buddhahood and become free of all incidental obscurations and stains."

It still amazes me that Tibetans see people as originally pure, as having the nature of enlightened beings.

"At the end of every practice, we always dedicate the merit. We do this to express our joy and gratitude at being fortunate enough to be able to study the dharma. Also, the dedication is not done just for one's own sake, but for all sentient beings as well, for their happiness, the fulfillment of their wishes, their freedom from suffering, and attainment of buddha-hood."

At that moment, the door burst open and a small boy—barely more than a toddler, with dark, close-cropped hair—rushed into the room and clambered onto Dagchen Rinpoche's lap. A moment later, his mother appeared, looking apologetic. But Dagchen Rinpoche was laughing, delighted.

"Meet our littlest lama," he said. "Tulku-la. He is the reincarnation of my wife's uncle Deshung Rinpoche, who founded this monastery with me. Tulku-la, this lady is writing a book about us. Her name is Sandy."

The boy, dressed in sweatpants, Mickey Mouse shirt, and bright, multicolored sneakers, hopped down from Rinpoche's lap and came toward me, hand outstretched. His large dark eyes were serious.

Thinking what nice manners these Tibetan children are taught, I extended mine. But it wasn't my hand the boy was reaching for, I realized. It was my head.

"Tulku-la wants to bless you," Rinpoche explained.

Dutifully, I bowed my head low enough to make the crown accessible to his reach. I smiled—a bit patronizingly, I admit—as I felt the small hand gently touch my head. But then I looked into his face, and to my astonishment I saw not a child's expression, but that of someone wise and mature—and yes, compassionate.

I looked over at the mother, whose name, I learned, was Caroline Lama. She nodded matter-of-factly. An American who married a Tibetan student of Dagchen Rinpoche's, Caroline was told by her teachers that the child she was pregnant with was "special." The prophecy was confirmed in her dreams. Only months before, when Tulku-la had turned two, senior lamas in Nepal (Deshung Rinpoche's monastery-in-exile) pronounced the boy the reincarnation.

Shortly after, his father was killed in an auto accident. "Not unusual," Caroline said. "Many tulkus lose both parents when they are young." Caroline would soon lose her child too, in a sense. In a few months, she would have to take Tulku-la to the monastery in Nepal to begin his studies. She would visit him only twice a year during the ten years when he would learn to take his place among the great Tibetan masters.

It was time now for Tulku-la to go home to bed. With a promise they could stop at McDonald's for a shake, he flew out of the room and came back carrying his miniature ball jacket, the words "Lil Monster" written on the back, and handed it to me.

"He wants you to help him on with it," Rinpoche said, smiling.

"I am honored," I said, strangely meaning it.

As I left, I was handed this poem Rinpoche wrote in the Year of the Water Pig (1983) at the conclusion of a lecture he gave in Olympia, Washington:

The pure, cool water of Tibet's previous history
Has the auspicious marks of an orderly flow of elegant sayings.
From within the precious vase of my mind,
Can not your thirst be quenched by study and reflection?

Therefore, I delight in drawing you a picture,
To make universally known without obstruction in the three
        worlds,
The beautiful form of the circumstances and events.

Consider a place enclosed, an extensive lotus garden
With the thousand movements of dancing bees,
Who search and delight in the taste of the lotus-knowledge;
I also see the hive where I and others live.

Accordingly, having defeated the army of dark ignorance
With the honey of great intelligence which studies
The great and profound stories of former times,
I imagine this lecture should have some benefit.

—HIS EMINENCE JIGDAL DAGCHEN SAKYA

FROM MY EARLIEST memories I have been plagued—or blessed, depending—by strong, vivid dreams. So vivid that in my early childhood my parents took me to doctors, one of whom suggested the dreams were an indication of *petit mal*, a mild form of epilepsy. The idea must have so horrified my mother that she refused to hear any more of my dreams, and I, with my child's innate sense of survival, stopped talking about them. They continue still, and I have learned as best I can to understand and to heed their teachings.

One morning I woke in tears from what I perceived to have been a terrible dream. In the dream I had met an all-seeing, all-knowing spirit and asked him about my karma. He answered that I would never be happy, not in this or any other life. I was stunned. "But," I asked, "is there nothing I can do to change that?" "No," he said. "You can't change your karma." "But wait—" I called after him in vain. He had evaporated.

The dream left me enshrouded in a cloak of doom. I felt as if I had been dealt a terrible sentence. But then, as the day wore on, the feeling of gloom began to lift and was replaced by a strange feeling of relief: If I'm never going to be happy anyway, then I can stop trying. No need anymore to look for happiness; I am free to get on with my life.

That afternoon, as I boarded a plane to Vancouver, where I would meet with Jetsun Kusho, I wondered if the dream had something to do with my readiness to give up samsara. I was beginning to feel the desire to meet a teacher.

HER FULL NAME is Her Eminence Sakya Jetsun Chimey Luding. The sister of His Holiness Sakya Trizin, Jetsun Kusho was born in Sakya in 1938 into the noble family of the Khon lineage. She was trained alongside her brother, who became head of the Sakya lineage. Jetsun Kusho is one of the three women in the history of Tibet to have transmitted the Lamdre (Path and Its Fruit) teachings, the system of contemplative and meditative practice special to the Sakya lineage. She is also known for her teaching on Vajrayogini, a female meditational deity.

I found her in her modest home in the suburbs of Vancouver, where she lives with her husband. Jetsun Kusho is the resident lama at the teaching center Sakya Tsechen Thubten Ling.

"THEY SAY THAT many, many eons ago, we came from the heavens, from another planet. The god realms, they say.

"In the Sakya tradition, the women don't marry. We all become nuns. The line continues through the men's side. I was eight when I took my first-level ordination. The teacher came to our house for studies. If I had wanted to, I could have studied in the monastery with the monks. Not ordinary nuns, but Sakya lineage-holder nuns. You can do retreats in the house or in mountain caves.

"The palace I grew up in was quite big, with twenty or twenty-five servants inside. There were thirteen farms, each with a manager that came once a year with offerings. The two Sakya lineage-holder families aren't royal in the usual sense, but in a religious sense. A noble family, not royal. Generally the girls who marry into the Sakya lineage are from other noble families, government service people.

"I am married now, but in Tibet, I wore nun's robes and shaved my head. I stayed there until 1959. When we heard that the Dalai Lama had fled, we followed. My brother and aunt and I left with a small party. Maybe twelve people in all. We went first to Sikkim because another aunt lived there. At the time we left, there were no Chinese people in our region, but many spies—Tibetan people who were spying on us for the Chinese. We were quite young, so we really didn't know what was happening. I still don't understand politics.

"It was difficult being a nun in India. In that country, women shave their heads only when someone dies. They didn't understand my shaved head, and they became suspicious, always asking questions. So I decided to let my hair grow. Also, in India, people understood English and Western ways, so I began to study English at a missionary school.

"My husband's family is also from a Sakya lineage-holder family. He was my brother's student, and the marriage had been arranged through my aunt. My husband and I knew each other in school, and we'd gone to the movies together, just as friends. We had a one-week wedding party. A very, very rich woman would have a one-month wedding party.

"Astrologers tell a woman what color to wear when she marries. My dress was a bit awful, a blue dress with a green blouse. It's been a good marriage. We have four boys, and a little girl who died at three months of age. They told me to get pregnant again right away, so I did. I think little children understand past lives better than we do. Then, slowly, slowly, they forget. Sometimes when babies are just a few weeks old, they will start

Jetsun Kusho

laughing or crying in their sleep. They say this is because of memories of past lives.

"Our oldest son is thirty and owns a carpet company; he was married a few months ago, to a Japanese Buddhist. The second, who will be a lama and the lineage-holder, lives in India. The third and forth ones live here; they're twenty-six and twenty-four. The older son is the production assistant for a design company, and the younger works in a photo shop. I'm a weaver.

"It hasn't really been difficult to raise my children in the West. I'm very lucky they never got into trouble. One of them tried drugs, but it made him sick. We are very open in the family and hold few secrets. We don't shout at each other. The children don't like it, my husband and I don't like it, so we don't shout. With drinking, I tell them that maybe they'll have a few hours of pleasure, but then there's the hangover. I tell them to think about consequences.

"People ask me how to instill compassion in their children, but I think that compassion is something that you're born with. You just have to remind children by showing compassion toward others, by displaying patience. Tibetan people tend to have lots of patience, not like Westerners. It's part of the culture. Children learn from their parents and especially from their grandparents. My older son is always quoting something his grandmother told him as a child.

"The role of women in Buddhism, and women's issues as they pertain to the spiritual path, have become prominent right now in this particular culture. I think it is very much a function of the time and place in which we live. When the Buddha taught twenty-five hundred years ago in India, the cultural situation was quite different. We can see historically that a great number, perhaps the majority, of those who followed the Buddha's teachings were men. But that was simply a reflection of the cultural situation at that time and not something we need to regard as inherent in the teachings.

"The Buddha taught for the benefit of all sentient beings, for the benefit of all living creatures; not just human beings, not just men. And as we can see, if we examine the historical record of Buddhism in India and other countries, women and their nunneries play a very strong part in the monastic religion. Within the tradition of Buddhism in Tibet, the vast majority of lamas and teachers have been men. But this does not mean that only men can be the teachers. There have been, in fact, many women teachers. In the Sakya School of Tibetan Buddhism, there is a very strong tradition, particularly within my family clan, of women teachers and practitioners.

"Certainly among the Sakyas the custom was that if people, regardless of their sex, wished to undertake practice and develop themselves spiritually, they would encounter no barriers. In my family, the blood lineage played a very important part. All sons and daughters are regarded as potential teachers by virtue of having been born into this family. Both the legal and social situation in Sakya was such that the women were accorded equal status with the men—in terms of legal powers, in terms of their ability to practice and develop themselves personally, and also in terms of their ability to act as teachers.

"In the Nyingma school, the most ancient school of Tibetan Buddhism, we also find a number of key historical figures who were women. One of the most famous who comes to mind is a woman named Jomo Menmo. Not only was she regarded as a fine teacher, but also as a person who discovered very many 'treasure teachings,' concealed teachings which she revealed to her students.

"Machig Labdron lived in the eleventh century. Her teachings are practiced today by all four traditions of Tibetan Buddhism. Although there haven't been many women teachers in the Gelugpa tradition, still the teachings of women have been revered over the years. Presently, there are a few women teachers in the Nyingma and Kagyu traditions, though not many.

"In the combined histories of all of the schools, women also have played a very important role in the transmission of lineage. As well, the dedication of women practitioners in Tibet, women who were known for the sincerity and the intensity of their practice, was a very strong force in the advancement of the religion.

"In the household, women are often the boss; the husband always obeys the wife. This business of a woman being a slave to the husband and children I don't believe happens too much. Sometimes a woman doesn't have any qualities or isn't very smart, and the husband is in charge, but usually it is the woman who controls the house.

"My husband and I are equals. He works as a school janitor. Every day he travels nineteen miles each way, two hours by bus or forty-five minutes by car. My husband never worked in Tibet. In India, as a refugee, he didn't work either. When we came to Canada, we both worked. For the first few years when the children were small, I stayed at home. But when my older son was twelve years old, he looked after the younger ones and I worked.

"However, women are not considered as important politically as the men, except for the head of a nunnery. We didn't have any women political leaders until the 1950s, when the Dalai Lama's sisters took public roles. In Sakya, as I said, there are women teachers, but Tibetan women tend to be very shy and afraid. My father's sister, my aunt, is a very good practitioner and teacher, but after my father died, when she began giving my brother long-life empowerments once a week, she refused to allow any servants in the room except the shrinekeeper. She'd give the empowerment to my brother and me, but would get upset if I looked at her face. She was too shy."

"Do you think women Buddhists' roles will change, now that they are in the West?"

"It is only natural that people in a different culture, one new to Buddhism, begin to wonder about female role models and stereotypes and so forth. You must remember Western people do not have a great deal of previous experience with Vajrayana teachings, so I'm suggesting to you that in the true spirit of the teachings of the Buddha, there is no fundamental distinction made between male or female. The same processes they observed in India, in Tibet, will also be true in the West: that a student will go to a qualified teacher and receive empowerments, teachings, and direction. And through their own practice they may come to be worthy, at a certain point, of taking the responsibility of carrying on that particular lineage.

"Also, it is conceivable that women in the West will be recognized as tulkus, incarnate lamas. Tulkus, who were advanced practitioners in former lives, require much less training in this one. But it's important that we recognize and respect the authenticity, the validity of the process of a student going to a teacher, receiving guidance and empowerments in the traditional manner.

"Buddhism is so new to this culture. We have to learn patience. We cannot expect things to establish themselves overnight. That's impractical. On the one hand, we might say we want things to get going immediately. On the other hand, we cannot rule out the possibility that there are Western lineages in the process of forming. There are Western lamas who trained in Tibet, and men and women now being trained in retreat centers in the West. Perhaps in the future there will be Western men and women of Sakya, Gelugpa, Nyingmapa, and Kagyupa speaking from the Tibetan Buddhist point of view. But in order for these lineages to establish themselves, the lineage-holder must go through rigorous training. It is also impractical to expect that there will be self-arisen lineage-holders, that, all of a sudden, one pops up and establishes a brand new lineage. It's far more likely to be a process of the old tradition handing its knowledge over to the new, and making that transition from one culture to another.

"Maybe Western teachers will change it, but Tibetan teachers want to keep things the same. Westerners have so many ideas when they come to dharma, and sometimes they tend to make up their own teachings. It is difficult for us to do that; we have to have permission from our own teachers, who check to make sure that changes will be beneficial. But Westerners think that it is like going to the university: when you finish studying, you get a degree. It's not that easy. Sometimes people meditate but they don't get the meaning, so the mind does not benefit.

"Buddhism teaches that everything is in the mind. The mind is very tricky. It does all kinds of things. One moment it goes up to the planets, all over the place. That's why we have the wisdom teaching of how to make the mind stable. If you have a stable mind, then you can learn.

"Your mind can be trained to accept any situation. If it doesn't accept what is happening, then every single minute is difficult. I tell my students that my mind is very dull, not very sensitive, and I'm very fortunate that way. Sensitive minds tend to upset themselves, especially if they pick up on only the bad things. It's fine if they pick up on the good things.

"When something bad happens, I immediately try to understand the obstacle, to view it in terms of karma. What have I done that is coming back now? Some people blame others, but karma comes from many, many lifetimes. You can create good karma by helping, by saving lives. This also tends to create your own longevity.

"For example, I get migraine headaches. The wet weather in Vancouver must not be good for my head, since I've never had headaches anywhere else. The doctor couldn't find any source for the headaches, even though he took X rays. Rice and sour fruits help. Sugar and wheat make it worse. But who knows what karma is involved? Maybe in another life I hit somebody's head or something. It helps me to think like this.

"When I came to Canada, I became ill with tuberculosis. Actually, I think that I contracted it in India but it didn't show up until I got here. I stayed in the hospital six months. The doctor said that I'd have to stay for two years. I had three holes in my left lung; my right one was all cloudy. The doctor told me that if I let them cut out my lung I'd get well quicker, but I didn't want to do that. I did practice in the hospital, like a retreat. After a while, the holes began to shrink. Within five months, they were half their size. My brother and other lamas offered prayers for me, and that helped, plus the Buddha's blessings. If people believe that prayer works, then it does. If they don't believe, it doesn't.

"My husband was sad that I had to spend so much time in the hospital. That part was difficult, but otherwise, the people in the hospital were wonderful. Also, the people in the Canadian government were very kind. Every Sunday they brought my husband 150 miles to see me. Every day someone would come to teach me English. At first, all I did was eat and sleep. Then, after a month, they told me to do things like embroidery, knitting. A teacher came every Thursday to teach me how to do handicrafts. The ladies in the room taught me to play a card game called crazy eights, and we'd watch movies together. My brother told me to do meditation and sent me scriptures. My husband brought me a tiny flashlight so I could read without disturbing the other women in the room.

"In the Tibetan tradition, we are taught to think about death and about the state you enter right after death, called the bardo. Some people, if they are very good practitioners, go right to the pure realms. Others, if they're very bad, go to the hell realms. But most people go to the bardo after the time of their death and before they are reborn into the next life. In this lifetime you practice to keep your mind stable during the coming transition. The bardo is a kind of judgment place, not unlike the Christian purgatory. When you are in the bardo, you encounter the contents of your mind, your dreams and fantasies, as well as places you've visited in your life. Then you are reborn into one of the realms.

"If you are very stingy and very nasty, you'll be reborn into the hungry ghost realm. If you're very lazy, you might be reborn in the animal realm. Your karma decides where you will go. When Christians do terrible things, they say that God will send them to hell. I don't think anyone sends you anyplace. It's your karma that decides. Even if you are not a practitioner, if you are kind to others, not self-serving, then you'll find a good human rebirth.

"You never know about your karmic relationships with other people.

If you don't have a good connection with someone in this lifetime, maybe you mistreated them in a previous one. Buddhism teaches that you should always be mindful of other people. We teach the ten virtues and the ten non-virtues, similar to the Judeo-Christian ten commandments. We have three in the body, three in the mind, four in speech. The three in the body are killing, stealing, and sexual misconduct. The four in speech are lying, troublemaking, gossip, and harsh words. The three in the mind are having a covetous attitude, harboring ill will, and not trusting the teachings. The speech virtues are very difficult to keep, especially avoiding gossip and harsh speech. Killing, stealing, and lying aren't too hard. Slowly, slowly you learn these things. In Buddha's time, he learned and became enlightened. So did his students. If we learn, then, of course, we become enlightened as well.

"If you are guilty of any or all of the non-virtues, you confess to your teacher, whether actually present or visualized, and you vow not to do it again. The teacher gives you teachings that will purify. Buddha said that any non-virtue—no matter how severe—can be purified. When you catch yourself doing something again, don't become excited and worried. If you get excited, then you can't think. Just tell yourself, I made a mistake, I'll try not to do it again. No matter how you grew up, you can slowly learn to have good values and reap the benefits of that.

"Tara, the mother of all buddhas, provides a very powerful practice— her activities are very beneficial in this generation. Female energy is getting stronger now. Also, the female represents the wisdom aspect, and male the method. Now that things are going faster and faster, this female wisdom is very important."

We were interrupted by a knock at the door. A young man wearing an earring, a long ponytail, and torn jeans had come to inquire about teachings. Jetsun-ma and I exchanged smiles.

"When people come to me, I tell them to go to lots of teachings: Hindu, Muslim, Chinese Buddhism, Japanese Buddhism, whatever. All religions are spiritual. Somehow we have karmic connections; somehow we have a good feeling about a particular teacher, no matter if Hindu or Muslim. If you go to see them and you feel very comfortable with them, then you stick with them.

"Once you are into it, you can see the teacher as often as you like. In Tibet, it takes a long time to travel, so you may see the teacher only one or two times in a lifetime. But around here, you can see the teacher at least once a year. If you can see them more often, that's good."

"How do you feel about the onslaught of people who 'try' Buddhism, as if it were the newest fad?"

"Some people who go to dharma centers don't want dharma; they want a husband. Some do want dharma, but they look for other things, too. People think that they are lonely, but they are lonely only in their minds. A lot of people ask me if I was homesick when I came to Canada. I say no. They ask if I was lonely, and I tell them that I wasn't lonely either. In Tibet we say that in whatever country you are comfortable, that is your birthplace. Whoever loves you, those are your parents. We have that, so it doesn't really matter where you are. People ask me if I want to go back to Tibet, but my birthplace was destroyed, flattened. There is nothing to go back to there. But places are the same; people are the same."

As I met more lamas and studied the books they recommended, I began to glimpse the overwhelming complexity of Vajranaya. First, I noticed that things frequently happen in threes: one takes refuge in the Three Jewels: Buddha, Dharma (the spiritual teachings), and Sangha (the community of practioners); practice is done in terms of body, speech, and mind; and teachings consist of inner, outer, and secret levels. Then, just as I thought I was beginning to get a handle on things, I began to hear about the nine *yana*s; ten virtues; ten non-virtues; and seventeen points of mind training. Vajrayana is so full of enumerations that it is no wonder the Geshe degree can take thirty years.

In terms of the teachings, wherever I scratched the surface, I seemed to uncover more and more details, greater elaboration, increasing complexity. But, the Dalai Lama said, it all comes down to good heart, to developing love and compassion.

MEDITATIONAL DEITIES, OR *yidam*s, form an important part of the Vajrayana path. As I understand it, yidam practice is done on the outer, inner, and secret levels. On the outer level, the deity represents an image of purity and perfection. This image can be used as a focus for prayers and meditation. Each part of a yidam's representation—often painted on silk in the form of thangkas—has multileveled meanings. Manjushri's upraised sword cuts through ignorance; Tara's outstretched leg symbolizes her readiness to jump into action; Chenrezig's thousand arms represent multiple ways to assist other beings; and so forth. The colors used, position of the deity, number of heads and arms, whether they are peaceful or wrathful, presence or absence of a retinue, all help to convey the qualities of the deity as part of the meditation.

On the inner level, each deity represents some aspect of the psyche, which is first objectified, then, through the process of visualization and meditation, assimilated. The qualities of the deity one aspires to are thus gradually incorporated back into the psyche and recognized as our own. If a teacher thinks an individual should aspire to cultivate wisdom, for instance, they might have the student take a Manjushri initiation, which gives the practitioner permission to take Manjushri as a tutelary deity, recite his mantra, visualize his form in all of its symbolic power, and generally work with the wisdom-energy represented by him.

On the secret level, deity practice is not separate from our own buddha-nature, which is innate and inherent but often obscured. Yidam practice is used as a technique to rid ourselves of defilements and uncover our mind's pristine awareness, our buddha-nature.

BORN IN SOUTHERN Tibet in 1945, His Holiness Sakya Trizin, Jetsun Kusho's brother and cousin to Jigdal Dagchen Rinpoche, is the forty-first in an unbroken lineage of lamas that reaches back to 1073 A.D. The title "Sakya Trizin" means "Holder of the Throne of Sakya." He inherited the title at the age of eleven, when his father died.

Sakya Trizin has founded numerous monasteries throughout India and East Asia, and established his seat in exile at Rajpur, India. He also founded Sakya College, a school of higher philosophical studies where training is given in logic, philosophy, and Buddhist psychology. Since 1974 he has made several world tours. I met with His Holiness in San Francisco at the Ewam Choden Center, where he would be giving a teaching. I asked him what the subject of his teachings would be.

"I'M GIVING A HEVAJRA empowerment here in San Francisco, a major empowerment in the Vajrayana tradition. Hevajra is the principal deity of the Sakya order. This highest Tantric deity basically represents the union of ultimate method and ultimate wisdom together."

I asked His Holiness Sakya Trizin if he would tell me a little bit about his life.

"The Sakyapas are the Manjushri tradition-holders. When a child is born into the lineage, the letter string DHIH, Manjushri's symbol representing speech and wisdom, is written on the baby's tongue with a special nectar made of saffron, butter, and other substances. An early prophesy says that the Sakya lineage all are emanations of Manjushri, Chenrezig, and Vajrapani.

"I was born in 1945 in Tsedong, about 150 miles from Sakya. I used to have many friends as a child, and we performed many pujas. People think this shows a very good propensity and probably means that I was a practitioner in my previous life. But I personally think it's because such activity is the main thing one saw in Tibet. We didn't have television or any other kinds of worldly distractions. (Though in our summer house in the park, we'd enjoy listening to records on an old windup gramophone. They were mainly British military marches although we also had a few Tibetan folk songs.) Mainly, all one would see were the monasteries and the monks performing. I would mimic the monks as a child, doing pujas with them. I had a full box of religious ritual objects—cymbals and drums and offering bowls that I played with as a boy. In other countries, children would have toys, but in Tibet the children don't have as many toys as they do in the West. I think that how you act early on depends on the surrounding or atmosphere in which you were brought up.

"In the early fifties when I was a teenager, I learned English from an American named Jarod Rhotan. He didn't know any Tibetan, and I knew only a little English, so we taught each other. Then, in 1959, I fled to India, right after His Holiness the Dalai Lama. I didn't have so much difficulty leaving for the border of Sikkim; the border to India is less than a hundred miles farther on, and I was on horseback. But without a road it wasn't so close, after all.

"My wife's family is from Kham, and we had contacts there. They came to visit us in Sakya and also in India. Her father is a cabinet minister,

also a good Tibetan doctor and a spiritual practitioner. My auntie approved of the match. We have two boys and they both will become teachers. My oldest son already teaches and is very serious—almost too serious. We worry about his health.

"I'm living now in Dehra Dun. I teach and administer our college and two monasteries and many other branch monasteries, so I do a little teaching, a little administering, some counseling. I'm meeting lots of people, giving dharma advice. Also when people come and want to know their future, I do divinations for them with dice. I was trained as a lama, and it is one of our duties to give divinations to people who seek help.

"Students here come to me about problems in their relationships. Even the Tibetans who live here come with these kinds of problems. They have learned from the Americans! It's a different kind of society. The more advanced the society in terms of communication and such, the more distractions you will have. So people become attracted to another man or another woman."

I asked Sakya Trizin how he regards dreams and nightmares, if they are another kind of consciousness or have deeper meanings.

"I think dreams are of two kinds. One is a separate sort of consciousness, while the other is like a prophesy. You know the difference through experience. Up until midnight or, say, up till the middle of the night, dreams are more a processing of the day's events. But early morning dreams are more like prophesy; they have a different feel to them.

"I began doing divinations when I was eleven years old. After my mother died, when I was very, very young, my auntie, the elder sister of my mother, took care of me and my sister. She was an extremely spiritual practitioner, and she was the one who handed me the dice. (She's dead now. My father was married to her before he married my mother, but they never had any children. She came to India, and died in 1975.)

"At first I just played with the dice, but then, slowly, I learned how to use them for divinations. It takes a long time because you have the text, you have the dice, but it is not always like the text says, for there are many exceptions. I think that every person who does divination will have a slightly different interpretation for the numbers of each die, depending on individual experience.

"When you ask if I believe that everything is destiny, I would have to say no. I believe that karma has two parts, like a crop that you plant. When things are already at the ripening stage, then you can't change them. If the crop is just beginning, however, then how well it will grow depends on how much care you give it. Thus karma that has yet to ripen can be diverted toward better ends.

"Our present body, for instance, is already in the ripening stage. Whether we are beautiful or ugly or healthy, that we can't change. But karma that has yet to ripen, the life ahead of us, this we can change. For example, being healthy in the future depends on how we act now. If you smoke and drink and do all the wrong things now, then you'll be very un-healthy and shorten your life. At any stage you can change your con-sciousness and thus change your karma. Even if a horoscope says that you're to die in a certain year, that still can be changed. It is yet to come. You can prolong your life.

"When people die, it is because of three factors: your life-force is ex-hausted; your merit is exhausted; your karma is exhausted. If all three are exhausted, then you have no choice, you have to die; if only one, it is eas-ier to prolong life; if two, it is more difficult, but you can still prolong. In an oil lamp, if the light is low, you can put in more oil. If the wick is used up, you can replace it. But if both the wick and the oil are gone and you have no more replacements, then it's over, the light goes out."

"What do you see for Tibet's future, and the rest of the world's?"

"There are many prophesies, and it is hard to interpret them, but I hope for the best. The Cold War is over, so worldly conditions don't seem too bad at the moment. China is changing now, they are making progress. But unless one makes inner spiritual progress, the goals we are seeking won't be achieved. We should try our best to change our inner being be-fore operating on the outer world. This need is easy to see, but it's not so easy to practice according to the teachings. Everything is polluted: the earth, the people, the sky, the ocean. These create terrible diseases, a part of the prophesy. The nagas, the owners of the under earth, and the *devas* and other deities are also very much affected by contamination, and their being affected increases the diseases. I think we should do more purifica-tion rituals, for practice begins with meditation and purification."

I was having difficulty keeping up. Breathlessly, I tried to match his words with what I had read, and thought back to my days in Dharamsala when I decided these people were naive. They are not naive; they are light years ahead of us. Evolved beyond us spiritually, emotionally, mentally—I was reminded of the New Age chestnut "Create your own reality," and it occurred to me that that is Stone Age thinking compared to what these people are capable of.

"All the major world religions emphasize lovingkindness and compassion. In Buddhism, these qualities represent the very root of the practice. The person who practices and possesses lovingkindness and compassion within his mind can establish peace and harmony within himself and help create peace and harmony within his family, his neighborhood, his town, his city. In this way, more and more people's practices can increase peace and harmony throughout the world. So therefore, whatever religion or philosophy you have, I think it is important for the people to practice lovingkindness and compassion toward all sentient beings.

"You can become conscious of the effectiveness of this just from your own feeling. If somebody hurts you physically or mentally, it is a very painful thing. So through this experience, you learn how others feel and wish to avoid hurting them. Other beings, living beings—especially those who share our human nature—are also brought up in lovingkindness. When we were born our mothers looked upon us with lovingkindness and compassion. When we are brought up in the midst of such feeling, I think it is human nature to love the person who loves you, who cares for you. As you love this person, so also you should reciprocate with other beings. It is logical, quite obvious. If you benefit just yourself and hurt other people, then I think that is so clearly wrong.

"Once we create more awareness among the general public, with ordinary people more aware, then there will be fewer people who hurt others and do evil things. But we can't count on everybody learning at the same time.

"Even those who have committed major crimes can be corrected by the teachings. It is Buddha's teaching that people who have extremely negative karma—even someone who has killed his mother; or Buddha's own nephew, who tried to harm him—may be cured through the teachings. With that understanding, all Tibetans always hope that we will get our own country back. We believe that the truth will prevail, always, no matter how long it takes."

I asked how he reacted to the many homeless people here in this rich country of America.

"When the Dalai Lama came to Bodh Gaya—and there are many beggars there—he decided to give five or ten rupees to each beggar. Do you know what happened? Even the owners of three huge buildings came to get these five rupees. So how do you decide who is poor and who not? Of course, you have to try when you see a particular individual in need.

"Sometimes I quite admire the beggars. They're happy, singing songs, they don't worry. Sometimes people who live very luxurious lives have so much anxiety about their businesses. They fly here and there but they have no time even to talk to their families. The beggars tend to have more time. I know people from the lowest to the highest. I've been to restaurants with all the roadworkers and seen them eat, the kind of food they were given, chairs and tables covered with grease and dirt. I've also had lunch in a luxurious hotel with the Dalai Lama. And I have traveled all over India. On the trains, people sit on top or hang off the sides. Also I've traveled in first-class trains in India, with air-conditioning and wonderful foods. And I've flown by air: first-class, and also in army airplanes in Ladakh, where there is no circulating oxygen—you are given a mask. No seat belts. No seats! Just a bench. I've traveled by horse cart and by limousine. If your mind is happy, even in your ricksha, then you are happy. If your mind is not happy, then you aren't comfortable even in your fine limousine."

Jamyang Dagmo-la Sakya

JAMYANG DAGMO-LA SAKYA married into a key noble family of the Sakyas. Dagmo-la and her husband, His Holiness Dagchen Rinpoche, and three sons, as Dagchen Rinpoche had told me, were the first Tibetan family to settle in the United States after the exodus caused by the Chinese takeover. They made their escape from Tibet over a treacherous 24,740-foot-high mountain, Monla Kachung, with Chinese soldiers at their heels. Leaving Lhasa in disguise, the family—the youngest still in diapers—and their servants were strafed by Chinese aircraft. Their horses, many too weak to go on, froze to death in snow 4 feet deep. Weeks later, on the brink of starvation, the family reached the bridge marking the Bhutanese border. But they were refused entry by the Bhutanese, who feared recriminations from the Chinese. As they waited, their food supplies dwindled. The Dalai Lama, reaching freedom in India, heard of the plight of some 1,700 Tibetan refugees and asked Nehru to make a formal request to the king of Bhutan. At last, the Tibetans were permitted entry.

Mother of five sons, Dagmo-la is a much-loved teacher, and author of the book *Princess in the Land of Snows*. I met her in Los Angeles, where she had come to give Tara teachings.

"WE WERE BROUGHT to America in 1961 by the Rockefeller Foundation on a three-year grant. I never thought we would stay here forever. We were sure Tibet would get its freedom and we could go home, but after three years my husband and my uncle began teaching at the university, and we made plans to stay.

"I was twenty-six, a young mother with three children and a fourth on the way. The children attended school, so they picked up the language faster than we did. A year later I had another son—five boys.

"Learning the language was the hardest part, but the University of Washington assigned a graduate student to help us with things like shopping. In America it's so easy—you go to one store and buy everything. The problem was, in India and Tibet we had many servants—here we had to learn how to keep house and to cook for the family. It was difficult to find the kinds of food we were used to, and since we didn't know the measurements, we were confused about how much we needed to buy. We were always cooking too much or not enough. I tried to learn from our cook in India before we left, but it is entirely different here.

"I found Americans to be most friendly, most helpful when you need to ask something. But somehow we had the idea that we mustn't ask too much or people would think Tibetans are dumb. So we got into difficulties—we'd take the wrong bus and spend all day riding back and forth, trying to find our way home.

"American society moves so fast. There's no time for family, for elders.

When the University of Washington found us a house, we had a next-door neighbor, an older lady, who was very nice to us. She knew we were a refugee family with young children, and even though we couldn't communicate, she would leave toys for the children and give us vegetables from her garden. We couldn't even thank her properly. Then we didn't see her for a while and wondered what had happened. We noticed newspapers had piled up in front of her door. Finally, they went inside and found her dead. Her family, who all lived far away, came back to claim the house. They didn't seem sad. They just argued over the things she had left behind—the house, the furniture, and such. That really shocked me. I know all Americans are not that way, but I thought: I don't think I want to live in this country when I get old.

"Tibetans respect their elders—our society looks down on people who don't take care of their parents. I always loved older people—my great-uncles, my grandmother, grandfather.

"I really don't understand Western society's fear of age. In Tibetan society, when you meet somebody for the first time, you ask their name, then you ask their age. In fact it is impolite not to ask someone's age, but in America . . . I made many mistakes. I'd meet somebody like yourself and I'd ask your name then ask how old you are. They would be shocked.

"Of course, all women care about how they look, but the difference is, if you tell a Tibetan woman that she is looking older, that's fine. But I don't think a Western woman would like to hear that. In Tibet if somebody says you're beautiful or your clothes are beautiful, you have to answer, 'Oh, no, no,' because otherwise you would be showing pride. And even if someone says your son is very good or your daughter very beautiful, you say, 'No, no.' In the Western way, you say, 'Thank you.' I had to learn these customs because I was always saying the wrong things.

"If you know the dharma, you know that it is special to be a human being. You know that no human being will live forever; everyone has to die. You die young or you die old. Why try to make yourself seem younger?

"I was raised in a dharma family. My uncle was a lama; my great-uncle was the head of the monastery. Then I married a lama, and now my son is a lama. That was the whole purpose of leaving Tibet—not just to save our lives—we wanted to save the dharma."

I asked Dagmo-la about marriage and divorce in Tibet.

"In Tibet, a son brings a wife home to live with his parents. If there are no sons, then the oldest daughter would bring her husband into the home. He would take the wife's family name.

"I don't know any other country where this exists, but in Tibet a woman can have two or three husbands, maybe brothers. Sometimes a family doesn't want their sons to go to a wife's family, so they might bring in two wives, but it may not work out to have two wives live in one house. They may not get along. Sometimes they bring two sisters to live with two brothers in the same house, but many women have two husbands, and that works well.

"In Tibetan weddings, unlike Western, there is no recitation of what you call commitments. We don't repeat any promises or anything. A couple is wed by the Buddha and blessed by the Buddha, with family and friends as witnesses.

"The modern system of divorce is pretty much Westernized. In the older system, even if the couple stop loving each other, even if they don't sleep together, they still carry the name and continue to live together. Society looks down on adultery, but if the marriage really isn't working, then it is different. I have never heard of Tibetans going to a lawyer. They don't like to make things so public. Instead the two families get together and settle things. If there are children, the father takes the son, the mother takes the daughter. The man will leave and take whatever he has with him. The wife will leave and take everything she brought with her—the dowry, everything.

"In America, the couple decide for themselves to split up. They have counseling here. In Tibet if the parents can't work it out, then they go to somebody close to family. But they would never pay a stranger.

"Marriage in the West begins with desire—they don't look further, into the background. They love each other in the beginning, but when desire fades away the marriage falls apart. In Tibet, once they have made a commitment, not just to sleep together but to care for each other, to have children together, and to know that these children are half of each of you, they stick to it. In America, marriage is to live together for a while and then maybe separate. Divorce is very rare in Tibet. In America people go on to have a second or third marriage. This doesn't exist in Tibet."

"Is there prostitution in Tibet?"

"There is prostitution in the big cities in Tibet. The community looks down on it, but we could never get rid of it. The women don't necessarily live in a particular area, but people know where to find them."

"Since you were the first Tibetans to emigrate, where did you practice the dharma? I assume no temple existed then."

"When we first came to America, there were no dharma centers. When we tried to talk about buddhadharma, people were not interested. Just one of those strange religions, they'd think. They wouldn't take it seriously at all, and I was a little worried. After about seven years, I made a trip back to India. I knew that we weren't going back to Tibet and we weren't going to live in India, so I went and got our things out. At that time, I visited His Holiness the Dalai Lama. He was very kind and loving. I cried, and he asked what was the problem. I said there is no trouble in America, everything is very happy and very easy financially, except that there is no dharma. We have our own chapel and shrine and we do our own praying, but there are no Buddhist monasteries and nowhere to go for teachings. His Holiness said, 'They are coming; there will be some later.' A few years later, my husband and uncle started a dharma center in our own home for people who gathered for teachings. Later, when my husband and I went back to India for a visit, His Holiness said, 'I told you. I told you.'"

I asked her how she feels about the West, and what it was like to raise her family here. After all, her children's generation would be the first Sakyas in centuries not to grow up in Tibet.

"Everything you can wish for is here in this country. In Tibetan Buddhism, we would call it the desire realm. But here it is all taken for granted and people don't think of the future, so things are out of balance. Buddhism says, the more imbalance, the more negativity.

"I think children in the West have too much freedom—and too much money. So they start with drinking and drugs. If they are lucky, they have some religion. I've noticed that many parents don't even have time to take a meal with their children. In the mornings everybody goes their own way, to school or to work. Everyone is too busy. They should at least get together in the evening and sit at the table and talk. And television should be limited.

"I was a very strict mother. Even for birthdays, or any party, I would never have alcohol in the house. I would buy sparkling water, which they would call 'Mother's champagne.' Of course, I didn't know all that they did. They were very careful to hide things from me. I know all teenagers have problems, but my boys were really good.

"They all are grown now. They are educated, they have their own homes, and I don't have to worry about them. I wish only that they would have more dharma. When they were young, I had a very difficult time teaching them. They knew how important dharma is in our background and they liked their Tibetan name, but in society and in school they were embarrassed. It was not easy, because in Buddhism, there are special times, celebration days when we need to pray, and I had a hard time gathering the children together as a family, especially if they had a football game or something. Now they are coming back to the dharma and they are more interested in practicing. So I'm happy.

"I am much happier now than I was when we first moved here. Many students now seem interested in learning from women teachers. They like to talk woman to woman. With a lama, they have difficulty asking certain questions. But women have more feelings and a different kind of wisdom. We are the ones who go through the pain of giving birth, and maybe because of that we are more sensitive. Now we have more freedom to stand up and do things. I think women should be able to earn as much money as men. This benefits men as well. I'm glad that the women's movement is going this way.

"I work in a blood bank. I've been working there for thirty years, eight hours a day. I don't have a medical background, so my work is not so important; it is just part of something that helps others. And I do love teaching in our Sakya monastery. I received tremendous teachings from lamas in all of the four sects—Kagyu, Nyingma, Sakyapa, and Gelugpa—and now I have my own students on Saturday mornings.

"I was asked to give Green Tara initiations. Tara is very important in Buddhism. She is a deity aspect of a woman who made a promise that she would always appear in female form to help all sentient beings. In Tibet, all lineages worship Tara and pray to her, lamas and monks as well as all the people. Tara is very easy to practice. She is very swift. Whenever you ask her, she is right there to help.

"To me, Tara is not only a Buddhist goddess, but a goddess of all religions, like Mother Mary in Christianity. She is embodied in all women who help beings, like women doctors. Every Tibetan prays to her. I was five years old when I received a teaching of Tara.

"There are lots of deities in Tibetan Buddhism, but Tara is the one that is the easiest because her picture is like any one of us. Some of the Tibetan deities have six arms and four heads, sometimes eight arms, and you have to visualize them when you do practice. But with Tara you can visualize your own mother or your closest woman friend.

"To do her practice, first you have to find a qualified teacher who has a pure lineage. Then you receive the teaching. Then, if you are sincere in wanting to practice, you receive an initiation, an oral transmission.

"As a beginning practitioner, it is good to receive an initiation. That gives you permission to visualize yourself as Tara, recite her mantra, and concentrate on her mind and your mind as inseparable. That's what the whole initiation is—a body, speech, and mind initiation.

"Tara is a very necessary deity in these degenerating times. She helps you to calm down, subdue your mind, to make harmony. There are stories about her—even translated into English—how she saved people from tragedies, from fire, earthquake.

"You see, Tibetans believe that underneath the earth lives a beast or creature. And when we do too many negative things—destroy the environment, nature—it makes the creature angry. So it begins to move.

"But Tara helps whenever you pray. She comes disguised as your friend or your mother, or someone you are close to."

"How did you find time in your day during those years to meditate?"

"As a wife and mother who is doing everything, you don't have time to sit down and practice the dharma. But you can keep the dharma inside, recite mantras, and show compassion and love to others. You can practice the dharma while driving, walking, cleaning. But meditation has to be done in a quiet, isolated place, so I didn't find much time for that in earlier years. But I never gave up, and now I have more time to meditate.

"You know, the Tibetan people had a great struggle. For myself, I lost so much: my country, my home, my mother, the rest of my family, but I got through it all because of the dharma."

GREEN TARA

It had been arranged that I would take Dagmo-la to the airport for her flight back to Seattle. In the car, I mentioned that I would be going to Florida soon to visit my mother, and Dagmo-la, sensing something in my voice, urged me to talk about my troubled relationship with  my mother. I told her about my feeling that my mother and I were ill-suited from the first. It wasn't just that we had conflicting ideas and sensibilities; we were never able to find a single quality to like or admire in each other; a bad cosmic mismatch. Now, with both my father and my brother dead, my mother and I are all that is left of our family. Yet we have no warm storehouse of shared experiences, no fond memories. We are strangers with little to talk about.

"Impossible," Dagmo-la said. We arrived at the airport early enough to continue our conversation. Dagmo-la reached into her tote bag and withdrew a sheaf of papers and a color photograph. "Here are some of the Green Tara teachings. The ten-syllable mantra is there too, and here is her photograph." She pointed to the right foot, which hung over the pillow. "See? She is ready to jump to the assistance of anyone who calls on her. You know, Sandy, I think maybe you owe it to yourself and your mother to ask Green Tara for help—and maybe do some of the practices."

Touched by this gesture, I thanked her and promised to try to teach myself the practices. That same afternoon I was in a bookstore, waiting in line at the cashier's counter, when I noticed a collection of small statues inside a glass case. I went over for a closer look. There, among the various Shivas and Kalis, was a beautifully carved wooden goddess painted emerald green, seated on two lotuses and a moon, her right foot extended. She was ready to spring to action. It was Green Tara. Her left hand was at her heart, her right on her knee in a gesture, the text explained, of granting sublime realizations. In each hand she held the blue utpala flower; jeweled ornaments adorned her hair, her neck, and her arms; and her smiling face radiated love and compassion.

THAT EVENING, text in hand, statue and photograph at eye level on a table in front of me, I began somewhat clumsily my practices. However I was doing them, I found they led me into a more peaceful meditation. I dropped Dagmo-la a note, thanking her and telling her of my progress.

I had also been reading Sogyal Rinpoche's *Tibetan Book of Living and Dying*, which I took with me on the flight to Florida a week later. I am particularly fond of the poem quoted in the book, called "Autobiography in Five Chapters," by Portia Nelson, which I read again and again:

I walk down the street.
There is a deep hole in the sidewalk.

I fall in.
I am lost . . . I am hopeless.
It isn't my fault.

I walk down the same street.
There is a deep hole in the sidewalk.
I pretend I don't see it.
I fall in again.
I can't believe I'm in the same place.
But it isn't my fault.
It still takes a long time to get out.

I walk down the same street.
There is a deep hole in the sidewalk.
I see it is there.
I still fall in . . . it's a habit.
My eyes are open.
I know where I am.
It is my fault.
I get out immediately.

I walk down the same street.
There is a deep hole in the sidewalk
I walk around it.

I walk down another street.

IT WAS LATE when I arrived, but my mother was waiting up for me. She looked amazingly well for her eighty-eight years, and apart from her steadily failing vision, she was in remarkably good health. We are always happy to see each other at first; it is only after a day or so that the old patterns of conflict and resentment begin to surface. I thought about a conversation we once had about my moving from place to place and never settling: "Why can't you plant yourself somewhere?" my mother had asked reasonably in her unreasonable way, and I tried to come up with a suitable answer. Sentences that begin with "Why" always inflamed me. In my childhood they had a belittling effect and made me feel somehow ashamed; in my adolescence they sparked rebellion. Asked now in the same tone of voice, they work as a time machine, turning me into a fourteen-year-old ready for battle.

EARLY THE NEXT MORNING, before my mother was awake, I headed out to the beach for a walk. This was a ritual: I would walk north along the water's edge for a mile or so, swim, then head back in time for breakfast. Except this morning, quite without thinking, I turned right on the beach and headed south. I had never had a reason to walk north. The scenery and the beach are exactly the same in both directions; it was just habit. Now, walking south, I was observing how it feels to change even so small a habit, when suddenly the words "I am walking down a different street" came to mind. I laughed out loud, startling a flock of sandpipers, and broke into a run.

DURING THE WEEK of my visit, there was such a marked change in my mother that I wanted to say, "Look, you're a very nice lady, but where is my mother and what have you done with her?" She expressed interest in my work; she even asked me to tell her something about Tibetan Buddhism. I began to explain karma and rebirths, when the imposter who called herself my mother said in a quiet, wistful voice, "If I thought I might have another reincarnation, I would like to be a nurturing mother next time." The car swerved, and I barely avoided running into a tree.

We were on our way to lunch. Finding the restaurant we planned to go to closed, we drove to another. I spotted a health-food restaurant, new since I was last in Palm Beach, and I asked my mother if she'd like to try it. My mother, who considers "health food" a fad, hesitated. I was about to drive on, when she changed her mind. "Sure, let's try it."

It was crowded; we were given the last available table, one that seats four. Moments later, a woman wearing a name tag, "Rose," appeared with a tray. With a pleasant smile she asked if we'd mind if she took one of the empty chairs. I noticed that several people in the restaurant were wearing name tags. Rose explained there was a seminar on Thai massage, a technique that combines massage with assisted yoga, and that she was one of the teachers. Yoga is a favorite exercise of mine, one I never seem to find time to practice enough. I wanted to know more.

She showed me a pamphlet, and we introduced ourselves. When I told Rose I am a writer, she asked if by any chance I am the author of *The Book of Elders.* Surprised, I told her I am. Rose explained that her artist boyfriend was deeply interested in Native American culture and was reading the book. By the time we finished lunch, we had exchanged telephone numbers, and I had promised to come by the studio to see her boyfriend's work and maybe even treat myself to a yoga/massage.

From my years exploring indigenous cultures, I have learned there are no coincidences: other forces must have been behind that chance meeting. Months later, after my life had taken a sharp turn in an unexpected direction, I could look back with certainty and say, "Yes, it was that moment."

A FEW DAYS later I visited Rose's studio and met her boyfriend; afterward, the three of us went to a small café for coffee, where we met another writer friend of theirs, Joyce. The waiter knew them and greeted them by name. Then he smiled at me and said, "So how's Tenzin Gyatso?"

I looked up at him, puzzled. Tenzin Gyatso is the Dalai Lama's name.

"Your blessing cord," he said, pointing to the red string at my neck. Next I learned that the waiter and Joyce both are members of a Tibetan Buddhist study and meditation center.

"Here? In Palm Beach?" I was incredulous. I had been visiting my parents in Palm Beach since they began wintering there many years before, and had always thought of it as a staid and rather stuffy place, not where one would expect to find classes in Thai yoga/massage or American Indian sweat lodges, not to mention a meditation center.

It is run by two Tibetan abbots, brothers, who came from Saranath, India, in 1980, where they headed the Nyingma department at Varanasi University. Joyce invited me to attend the Tuesday-night meditation session, but I was leaving before then. I promised to come the next time I am in Florida.

I was reminded that it was in Florida where I visited Pete Catches one winter, two years after I had first met the Oglala Sioux medicine man. He had been ill, and his daughter-in-law, who had a house just north of Palm Beach, insisted Pete come stay the winter with them. When I told my mother during my visit with her that I would be spending some time with one of the American Indians I had interviewed, she paused a moment, then said as tactfully as she could, "I don't think we have any Indians in Palm Beach, dear." I could now tell her that not only does Palm Beach have Indians, it has red-robed Tibetan Buddhists too.

THAT EVENING MY MOTHER and I went through some of my father's things still in the drawer where he kept them, and my mother began to talk about their life together. Suddenly we were two women, each with our own stories about our failures, our regrets, the lessons we had learned. Come to think of it, we are quite alike. Before I left, my mother presented me with a string of pearls her mother had given her on her fiftieth birthday. We embraced and promised to see much more of each other.

I had indeed walked down a different street. Om tare tutare tura soha!

DHARMA
IN THE MIDWEST

HIS EMINENCE GELEK RINPOCHE was born in 1939 in Lhasa on the day His Holiness the Fourteenth Dalai Lama was brought to the palace. His father, Demo Rinpoche, was the nephew of the Thirteenth Dalai Lama. Recognized at the age of four and given the title Dagchen Tulku, Gelek Rinpoche was taken to Drepung monastery to begin his studies. His first teacher was Gen Yundung, Denma Locho's Root Lama.

During his years there, Gelek Rinpoche memorized the equivalent of ten thousand Western-style book pages. While visiting Ngagpa Datsang at the monastery, with several other monks, the young tulku's prayer beads flew from his hands while he was praying and landed on the statue of Penden Lhamo. No matter how hard the attendants tried, the mala could not be pried from it.

This turned out to be one of several unusual incidents. In 1959, Rinpoche fled to India in a party of five hundred. They were crossing a vast rocky desert with food enough to last one more day, when three nuns appeared and asked if the son of Demo Rinpoche was among them. When they learned that he was, the nuns offered the group some tea and a night's rest in the nunnery. As the party left, the nuns gave them food to last the rest of the journey, and to Rinpoche twenty-five silver coins.

When the party arrived in India and told others of their good fortune, they were told there was no such nunnery. One monk went back and found no trace of where they had spent the night. Rinpoche believes his father's protectors must have been looking after him.

In 1960, Gelek Rinpoche was selected by His Holiness the Dalai Lama to join a small group of young Tibetan tulkus in Dharamsala to continue his studies and also to learn Western languages. Eventually they would be chosen to teach the dharma to people in the West.

"I WAS NINETEEN or twenty then. I lived in a sort of servant's cottage, where cows would come in at night. In 1964, I went to Cornell in Ithaca, New York, as a student, and learned my ABC's. Through the anthropology department, arrangements were made for eight of us to be taught by graduate students—economics, English, and other subjects.

"After that, I went back to India to the Tibet House in Delhi. By this time the Cultural Revolution was well under way in Tibet, and our sacred objects were being destroyed. We opened a museum for the art, thangkas, handicrafts, and statues; a library to preserve the scriptures; and since we had to make money, we had a handicraft emporium, where we could sell things. I had given back my robes and married Daisy Tsarong.

"Then, when Lobsang Lhalungpa left the Tibetan Broadcast, I took over. In 1977, I went to Arlington, Texas, at the invitation of Dr. Norbu Chen. But just before, while still in India, I went through a sort of teenage rebellion. I rebelled against the religion, the tradition—everything. I wanted to experiment, to smoke, to drink, to see how it felt. And I wanted to have sex, to see how that felt. All the things that were not allowed. But my teenage rebellion had come a little too late. I was looking for something, some kind of very interesting viewpoint or a different kind of feeling, some kind of physical, mental thing that shifts your body and soul, everything. That's what I think I was looking for. I didn't get it."

"Was it a high you were looking for?"

"I don't think I was looking for highs so much as for some kind of an opening, some kind of experience. Or maybe just great sex.

"Then I went back to India, and I couldn't get back to the United States for years. During the eighties I began to teach many more Western students. Then by 1987 I came to Michigan. We have a small society called the Jewel Heart. It is a Tibetan cultural and Buddhist center."

I told Gelek Rinpoche that I had discussed the subject of guru devotion with Sogyal Rinpoche when I interviewed him in France, and asked what his thoughts were.

"Guru devotion is very important, extremely necessary for Buddhist practitioners, yet there is a lot of misunderstanding about that. These misunderstandings are caused by Buddhist practitioners themselves. It doesn't mean doing prostrations, bowing, folding hands—which a lot of Western people do. They think that is guru devotion, but it isn't just this physical gesture. My own personal feeling, confirmed by my experience, is that it doesn't help at all, it doesn't do any good. People have been told to do things that way, and they think that is the Tibetan system, so they do it, half knowing, half not knowing, and then they label it guru devotion, which is absolutely not right."

"I've noticed a hierarchy within the structure around some gurus that I find disturbing. Almost like a cult."

Gelek Rinpoche

"Perhaps devotion becomes distorted because the *namaste* system [greeting the divine within another individual] is not inherent in American culture.

"The gurus come in, so they stand up, fold their hands, bow, but without feeling true devotion for the guru, without real understanding. But true guru devotion is when the guru benefits you, and there is profound love in response. Sometimes it is good to bow down, but not all the time. Individuals are individuals."

"There's an attitude popular among spiritual seekers that you have to be a renunciate to gain enlightenment. Do you think this is true?"

"Absolutely not. That's a total misunderstanding. I think the morality there has a Christian influence rather than Buddhist. In the Christian tradition, you do have this vow of poverty, right?

"Being rich may be the influence of very good karma, and you can make good use of it. Of course, if you have attachment, then it can get in the way. If you don't have desire and attachment surrounding money issues, and if you work hard for your money, then there is nothing wrong with having wealth if you use it to benefit people."

"I've heard that people can change the habitual patterns of their minds. Could you tell me about that?"

"As human beings, we have a beautiful, kind nature, no matter that sometimes, because of the influence of certain things, we behave badly to certain people. Sometimes we do act funny. But we have to acknowledge that by nature we are loving.

"If that beautiful nature could be exposed, made active in the world to interact with others, what a wonderful, kind, loving society we would be. At the moment everybody wants to win something, to win over someone else.

"What we have to remember is that it is not our beautiful nature that we have a problem with, but with the temporary obstacles that obscure this nature. Our problems are impermanent. We can remove them, but we have to see where they come from, what the causes are, and then reverse those causes.

"Karma is cause and effect. The karmic principle is this: You can never work with the result, but you can always work with the cause. When the effects are taking place, you just have to go through it. But at the causal level, you can always work with it.

"We have to work with our delusions—anger, hatred, jealousy—in order to overcome them. It is important to remember that you can't make a deal with delusions. If you make a deal with them, it is like making a deal with the devil. You will lose. So we need to strive to overcome these negative emotions.

"We don't have to learn how to get angry. Anger is part of a strong, engraved, habitual pattern; it comes automatically. But if you do not want to get angry, you have to put forth effort.

"I will tell you one thing: You have to help yourself; nobody else can help you. You can seek help from somebody outside, but the true help comes from yourself. I am responsible to myself, and you are responsible to yourself. But our habitual pattern is to blame others because we are too proud to acknowledge our own faults.

"The true way of helping ourselves is to be aware of our functioning: maintain awareness of our thoughts, awareness of our body, awareness of our speech. Particularly we have to be aware of our mind. If you don't watch your mind it becomes like a monkey let loose inside a museum. The monkey might take a big brush and paint all over a Van Gogh or a Vermeer. Those paintings are really beautiful, rare, and great things.

"Similarly within our mind is the beautiful nature that is as good and as rare as those Vermeer and Van Gogh paintings. You don't want a crazy monkey to go there and smear paint all over it. With jealousy, he paints green; with anger, he puts on red paint; with attachment, blue. Just paints all over. So it is time for us to catch that monkey. You don't want to destroy the monkey—he has a right to be there—but you have to watch it and train it properly. Then it can be very useful. That is awareness. Awareness keeps the monkey from smearing all the different colors on those paintings; it helps you change your habitual patterns.

"Of course, it is easy for me to say all of this. To put it into practice is very hard. Habitual patterns are difficult to change, especially initially. They are embedded in our family backgrounds, individual thoughts, education, whatever. For instance, if you have the habit of getting up at noon, you will not want to get up at nine. You'll resist the very idea. But if you make yourself do it, then you'll find that it is not that bad.

"The first fight, then, is with resistance. Once you break that, then things are a little easier. Then gradually, instead of getting angry, you develop love or compassion; instead of getting jealous, you develop the ability to rejoice in the fortunes of others. If you begin to switch that habitual pattern, go slightly into what is positive, slightly into virtue, slightly away from negativity, it is the biggest contribution you can make to yourself.

"If you keep on watching your own mind, sometimes you might embarrass yourself. When that happens, it is a good sign, it means you are watching yourself. Quite okay. It is not so bad to sometimes put your finger on your own nose. Instead of watching everybody's faults everywhere, it is also good to turn around and watch yourself a little bit.

"The essence of Buddha's teachings is to develop as much virtue as possible, to avoid as much negativity as is possible, and to watch your mind. He had solutions for every problem. For example, the antidote to anger is patience. But when the delusion of anger is at its peak, a person finds it very difficult to remember patience. Buddha's solution is that you should try to acknowledge that you are angry and give yourself a minute or two to watch your own mind. You may feel a little bit embarrassed, a little soft, maybe a little shy. And when that happens, the power of anger has been cut tremendously.

"Some of us get angry with our mothers and keep that anger going for years, right? But once you acknowledge that anger, then you find it lasts for shorter and shorter periods of time. Then maybe you will be able to see the anger coming before you feel it. Then you can avoid it.

"Some people may say that anger is not that bad. Some therapists even recommend it. I'm not a therapist, but I do know one thing: Anger is very expensive. It is more than the fee that you pay to the therapist, much more. For example, say that you've had a good night's sleep; you're happy, relaxed, in a good mood, looking forward to the day. Then you get an irritation. You get upset. Look at your mind once again. Even after the anger is gone, it took away your happy mood with it. That's why it is expensive. Spiritually, it costs a tremendous amount of virtue; mentally, it costs you a clean and clear, lucid mind; and it can even cost you your health. There is a very close link between the mind and the body, so mental difficulties very commonly manifest themselves physically. When the mind is disturbed, we can't sleep, right? When we don't sleep well, we start to get hysterical.

"So it is time to watch and to heal the mind. There are a lot of body healers around, but you also need a mind healer, which can only be yourself. The way to do it is through awareness. Learn a little bit, then think, then meditate, and then acknowledge your thoughts. Through that you can heal yourself. And when your beautiful nature begins to shine, you help not only yourself, you begin to help others. Then you begin to have a wonderful life."

KARMA:

MADE IN AMERICA

HIS EMINENCE CHAGDUD TULKU RINPOCHE was recognized at an early age as a reincarnation of the abbot of Chagdud Gonpa in Tibet, a centuries-old monastery and one of the few to survive the Chinese Communist invasion. Son of Dawa Drolma—one of Tibet's most renowned female lamas—Rinpoche received extensive training from many great lamas.

After years of working for refugee causes in India, he came to the United States in 1979, and in 1983 established the Chagdud Gonpa Foundation, which currently has twelve centers in California, Oregon, Washington, Canada, and Brazil. Now a United States citizen, Chagdud Tulku lives at the Gonpa's main center in Trinity county, northern California. He continues to travel and teach throughout the world.

"I've been hearing a lot about karma. Could you say something about how to purify negative karma?"

"In formal practice we use what we call the Four Powers to purify karma. The first is to visualize an enlightened being present in the space in front of us, or we can visualize this wisdom source above the crown of our head, either way. However we visualize, we confess our negative actions to that wisdom being. The second power is regret. We recognize when we've done something wrong. We really created actions that have accomplished harm, we've misbehaved, and we fully and very sincerely regret that fact and establish the intention to purify that action. Then the third power is to recognize that before, we didn't really understand what had created harm, we didn't know what we were doing. Now that we realize, we won't do it again. We make this commitment: Never again will I repeat that kind of action. Then the fourth power is the power of blessing, where we visualize that from this enlightened being, nectar and light flow down through the crown of our heads through our whole body, completely purifying all sins and obscurations; all negativity is washed away.

"There is real effect in this. It truly purifies karma. It is alive. Something happens when we practice in this way, something very tangible to our own experience. We modify our ordinary dualistic mind with meditation and nondualistic wisdom-mind, with faith and devotion, with wholesome habits, and our experience can blossom into positive wisdom-mind, buddha-nature.

"Through this practice, suffering can be reduced and we can enhance our capacity to deal better with daily things as they arise. The same outer conditions can occur, and yet our response, our perspective, our whole view and feeling will be different."

"How do you integrate practice into daily life?"

"I'll speak a little bit from my own training in Tibet. There, at the age of two, I was recognized as a tulku, one who has directed successive rebirths for the benefit of others. So I was expected to turn out rather special. Even at a very early age I was exposed to profound spiritual teachings. Most to the point of your question about practice in everyday life, I learned through encountering the truths of impermanence—from teachings, yes, but also from directly experiencing the deaths of family and teachers, for example. The point is, the more attached we are to our possessions and relationships in the world, the more important and necessary we find them, the more pain we encounter when they change and cease— as they always do. For this reason alone, it's crucial to start by contemplating impermanence.

"It's also very important to understand that the highest spiritual opportunity lies in having a human birth. Sometimes people won't realize this because their lives are turning out disappointing or very trying, painful, and they lose interest in taking advantage of their human capacities, which is a grave mistake. It's like borrowing a boat to cross a river, and instead of getting right at it, because you know the purpose is to cross over, you take your time or you ignore the chance altogether, forgetting that the vehicle isn't yours indefinitely but only loaned. Then maybe you'll never cross the river. Once the borrowed boat is reclaimed, your opportunity is lost. In this way we think about our human body as a rare vehicle that we need to use well without delay. We have a precious human birth in order to advance spiritually. If we're not able to travel very far, at least we can make some amount of progress. Even better, we can help others. And as a very minimum we can realize profoundly that we mustn't make other people miserable.

"There's a kind of ease that comes when we comprehend the illusory nature of reality, the dreamlike quality of life, this impermanence that pervades everything. Even as it is, it isn't, and someday it won't be at all. This doesn't mean that we deny our involvement with life, but that we approach it with lessened hope and fear. Then we're like adults playing with children on the beach; the adult doesn't suffer when a sand castle washes out to sea, though compassion arises in seeing a child's suffering.

"Compassion is natural to every one of us, but because we have deep, very self-centered habits, we need to cultivate it by contemplating the suffering of those who invest their dream with solidity. We need to develop a sincere, compassionate desire that suffering will cease, that everyone may come to understand the dreamlike quality of life and thus avoid the agony that results from inevitable loss.

"Coming to an understanding of impermanence and having a genuine, good-hearted desire to make others happy are the first steps to true spiritual practice. And effective practice requires a constant reiteration of what we know to be true. This will lead to progress. The great Buddhist scholar Atisha spent his entire life in study and meditation, and he came to the conclusion that everything the Buddha taught comes down to a single point: good-heartedness. That is the essence of the spiritual path, of spiritual maturity. This kind of sincerity catalyzes the transformation of mind and being, and we carry the results into everyday experience.

"Applying spiritual practice in daily life begins when you wake up in the morning and rejoice that you didn't die in the night, in knowing that you have one more useful day—because how can you guarantee you'll have two? You remind yourself of correct motivation. Instead of setting out to become rich and famous or to follow your own selfish interests, you meet the day with an altruistic intention to help others. And you renew this sort of commitment every morning. You tell yourself, 'With this day I'll do the very best that I can. I will do right by other people as much as I am able.'

Chagdud Tulku Rinpoche

"During the day, check your mind thoroughly. How am I behaving? What is my real intention? Reduce negative thoughts, speech, and behavior; increase the positives. When you look back on your day, you may find that you were able to make others happy. Maybe you gave food to a hungry bird or practiced some act of generosity, a key moment of patience. Rather than becoming self-satisfied, resolve to do better tomorrow, to be ever more skillful, more compassionate in your interactions with others. Dedicate the positive energy created by your good actions to all beings, whoever they are, whatever condition they're in, thinking, 'May this virtue relieve the suffering of beings; may it cause them short- and long-term happiness.'

"Whenever you find that you have fallen short, there's no benefit, then, to feeling guilty or blaming yourself. The point is to observe what you have done, because your harmful actions can be purified. When you see your faults and downfalls, in practice you call upon a wisdom being, employ the Four Powers I just mentioned. You don't need to go to a special place, for there is no place where prayer is not heard. It doesn't matter if you consider perfection to be God, Buddha, or a deity, as long as when you objectify perfection, it contains no flaw, no fault, no limitation. From absolute perfection you gain the blessings of purification.

"In daily meditation practice you work with two aspects of the mind: its capacity to reason and conceptualize—the intellect; and the quality that lies beyond thought—the pervasive, nonconceptual nature of mind. Using the rational faculty, you contemplate: the preciousness of human birth, impermanence, karma, the suffering of others. Then you let the mind rest: allow a direct, subtle recognition of that which lies beyond all thought. You think, and then relax; contemplate, then relax. You don't use one or the other exclusively, but both together, like the two wings of a bird.

"This isn't something you do only sitting on a cushion. You pay attention to your spiritual process throughout the day. You meditate this way anywhere—while driving a car, while you're working. That way the mind is always moving toward the ultimate goal of enlightenment. You don't need special props or a special environment. We don't have to shave our heads or wear special robes or leave home or sleep on a bed of stone. Spiritual practice doesn't require austere conditions.

"What meditation produces is a constant refocusing. You have to bring pure intention back again and again; check that your motivation includes helping all sentient beings, not just yourself. Meditation is like the process of stitching and stitching, of reminding ourselves again and again of the deeper truths—impermanence, lovingkindness—until the patch is sewn so strongly it becomes a part of the cloth and strengthens the entire garment.

"When you are out and about in the world, you keep your mind on what you're doing. If you are writing, your mind is on the pen. If you are sewing, you focus your mind on the stitch. Don't get distracted. Don't think of a hundred things at the same time. Don't get going on what happened yesterday or what might happen in the future. It doesn't matter what the work is—focus, stay with what you undertake, hold to it closely, rest comfortably in what you do, and in that way you train the mind as well as with formal practice.

"There's nothing flashy about this kind of progress; it's very measured, steady training, requiring diligence, attentiveness, patience, enthusiastic perseverance.

"If you have the proper perspective, everything you encounter—all the day's experiences and all the night's experiences—everything has something to teach. In fact it is all like a dream, like an illusion, like a movie. It just comes and goes. Now we are happy, next we're sad, or we may even begin to suffer extremely. We have great fortune, then we lose it. Things arise and fall and come and go, as in a dream.

"We simply don't have time to argue with other people, to fight. We don't have time to lose patience. It's like if we were going for a long walk and we stopped to rest on a bench for maybe five minutes, and somebody came to sit next to us. Why should we argue with them? Here we have this short moment that we can rest, why do we spend it arguing? So in the larger sense, we realize that we have such a short time together, why not enjoy the opportunity, use it really well, keep patience, be loving and compassionate? Why would we spoil this precious human opportunity that is so brief?"

CHAGDUD RINPOCHE'S TEACHING reminded me of a teaching I received in Switzerland, from Dagsay Rinpoche, who gives classes on one-pointed meditation, concentration on an object while dropping all thoughts:

"TRADITIONALLY, IN TEACHING Tibetan meditation, we use analytical and one-pointed meditation, concentrating on a meditation object, to explain emptiness. Since not all my students are Buddhists, I ask each to choose an object that they can identify with. If they find it hard to choose one, I usually suggest the letter *I*. I personally quite like this as a meditation object because of the meaning behind it. This very simple letter signifies the famous ego.

"I ask my students to divide this letter into five small parts, each representing the five aggregates that form the human body. Then I ask them to imagine separating the five parts into hundreds of thousands of particles that are constantly changing, never remaining still—like the cells in our body. Next, I tell my students to search for the *I*. Let's find out whether the *I* is in our mind or in our body. If it is in the body, where would you say the *I* resides? Is it in the head? The legs? The heart or liver?

"Or if it is in the mind, in which mind does it reside? In the mind of the past, the present, or the future? The mind does not stand still; it is constantly changing. One moment you are happy and contented, in the next something unexpected occurs and you feel angry and discontented. The more we try to locate the *I*, the more we realize that the *I* does not have an inherent existence, it does not exist on its own. What we usually perceive as something solid and unchangeable is nothing but a projection formed of three factors: cause, condition, and interdependency.

"I teach my students that in realizing this, all negative emotions like greed and hatred lose their targets and slowly dissolve. Likewise, if you feel strong attachment or greed, this practice helps you discover the true nature of the phenomena and to let go."

I then asked Dagsay Rinpoche, "If you cannot find an *I* to hate, can you find an *I* to love?"

"Just the contrary! Love in that way has nothing to do with the *I*. When love is pure, it is neither an attachment nor an aversion; it hasn't to do with specific people or objects. Real love has nothing to do with the ego, which is involved with attachment, but is extended to everyone. If I saw someone hitting my wife, of course I'd be very upset for her, but I'd also be concerned with the person hurting her. If you see children doing something wrong, you need to discipline them, but you don't do it out of hatred, you do it out of love. In Tibetan Buddhism, you have wrathful and peaceful dieties. Sometimes the wrathful faces seem enormously threatening, but their motivation is love, not hatred.

"Love and attachment may seem very similar, but they are very different. Attachment depends upon believing that an object has inherent self-nature, that it is a solid thing you can possess, own. Love means that you are simply happy to be near it. Once we have detached ourselves from the self-oriented and unhealthy love, as well as from negative emotions like ignorance, greed, and hatred, we have neutralized our minds and are in a position to develop genuine love and compassion that truly brings about changes.

"When you learn that this *I* does not exist, that is the first step. When you cannot find the *I*, then you have to look for where you are attached.

"In this meditation on the *I*, you not only analyze yourself, but also you investigate your attachment to your own children and family, and whether this *I* exists in other people. If you can't find an *I* in yourself to be attached to, the same is true of others. If you can't find a person's *I*, then what is it that you hate? Their body? Their spirit? Behavior? When you do this meditation deeply, you can cut down on the three poisons of the

Dagsay Rinpoche

mind: anger, attachment, and ignorance. Hatred can be a form of attachment.

"My students tell me that sometimes when they are meditating, unhappy feelings come up and they find themselves crying. Other times, they become acutely aware of things they don't like about themselves. They find meditation too hard because of what it reveals about themselves.

"When students come to me with these problems, I tell them not to push. Let it go. At the beginning, it is important not to go too deep. Go very slowly. Stay on the surface, looking at the *I*. More and more you'll feel yourself opening to the process. As soon as you get to the point where you're seeing things you don't like about yourself, then drop it. That's a sign that for the moment you've gone too deep.

"It's helpful, of course, to have someone to guide you. First, you have to be interested in finding a teacher, open to the possibility. You find one just like men and women find each other. If the karma is right, the rest takes care of itself. When the teacher tells you something that is helpful, then you know you've found a good teacher.

"My personal message to my students is that by following this path, they actively contribute to peace in themselves, their family, their community, and ultimately to a peace that is universal."

Rinpoche's wife, Yeshe, who works as a nurse in a local hospital, said she observed that meditation helps patients. "If someone has an illness, this is a good time to begin to meditate. You can help the healing process by generating a very deep belief and faith in the goddess or a deity. Of course, when you are working with elderly people who are dying, it is very difficult to teach them how to meditate. Then I just sit there with them and hold their hands, and sometimes people will let go of their fear of dying. Just being present when a person is dying is the most important thing."

PROPHECIES

WHAT HAD SO INTRIGUED me at the beginning of my travels was the striking similarity between the Hopi and Tibetan prophecies. The Hopis warn that the time of purification is upon us, that we will be forced to look into a great mirror and be judged. And when the purification is over, only a handful of people of each nation will survive. When I spoke to Sogyal Rinpoche in France, I asked him if the Tibetan prophecy held such dire predictions.

"I THINK WE are coming to a very crucial time, when we all have to be very careful and aware. Padmasambhava himself said, 'People say the times are bad; but it's not the time, it's the people.' The people make the time. It's up to us; the future is in our hands. If only we can change. Some prophecies can be like warnings. There are certain things that we can do to prevent them, and if we do nothing, they will happen. The choice is up to us. But other things cannot be prevented, because we've done certain things already. The influence is so strong, it's difficult to avoid.

"The difficulty with prophecies, unfortunately, is that sometimes people don't know how to read or interpret them, and it is hard to find people who can. The meanings can be quite hidden. Sometimes, unfortunately, it's only after they've happened that people come to realize what they meant!"

"But is this particular time of the millennium, named by the Hopi and I think also by the Tibetans, a time of acute danger?"

"That's right. In the Indian tradition, in Sanskrit, it's called Kaliyuga; in Tibetan it's Due Ngen Nyigma. It's the dregs of time, when everything degenerates: wrong views abound; emotions are intensified and become more negative; the times are fraught with conflict; life span degenerates; and people's bodies, merit, intellect, memory, and diligence are said to decline. Everything is devalued, drained of nutrition; people become less reliable.

"There's no kind of global awareness. People don't think of the consequences. That's why karma is so important. There are many, many karmas, many, many ripples, which are interdependent, creating a sea of interconnectedness. The state of the world, the state of the environment affects all of us. What happens in France affects Europe, the United States. These interconnections have to do with the collective karma—you are not really completely free of others; what you do has such an influence and effect on you and on the world. So I take the prophecies as warnings, which we must listen to, and if we take these warnings to heart, then we have an opportunity not only to change the circumstances and avert the disasters, but also to turn them into something really good.

"We must become personally responsible and universally responsible; we must have more of a sense of community and establish the principles of love and compassion, understanding and forgiveness. The basic spiritual teachings should be taken deeply to heart and allowed to bring about a change, a revolution of the heart and mind. It always comes back to the practice and to working with ourselves.

"But the Buddhist teachings don't speak of this world coming to an end just yet. There are many epochs, or *kalpas*, and many phases within them still. Anyway, what's important is that our future is very much up to us, finally."

"Why," I asked, "however much people want to practice meditation, do they experience an internal resistance to it? Even when they try to meditate, they end up simply falling asleep, for example. What is it that makes us resist? Is there a tool kit for overcoming that resistance?"

"Generally speaking, when people experience resistance to meditation, it's habit. Ego-habit. And it can be laziness. In the West, this manifests as what I call 'active laziness': we do everything we can to avoid the main issue. I sometimes think that if we put half the energy we invest in not practicing into practicing, we'd end up extraordinary practitioners. Yet at the end of it all, we have to surrender our resistance. There's no other choice. When we come to die, for example, we cannot resist; we have to let go."

"How can our personalities become more true to our nature?"

"That is what the whole Buddhist path is about: the ego aspect of our personality dissolves, and the unique quality of our buddha-manifestation shines. You don't have to worry that when you become egoless you will turn into a vegetable or a robot, end up as nothing, or float around in

Sogyal Rinpoche

outer space. The amazing thing is that when you lose your ego, then you really become 'somebody.' Egolessness too becomes a manifestation of who we are.

"For example, let's talk about the buddhas, which is difficult to do conceptually. The nature of all buddhas is one, yet each of them manifests unique and special qualities. Manjushri is the Buddha of Wisdom; Chenrezig is the Buddha of Compassion; and Vajrapani is the Buddha of Energy. They are the same as all other buddhas, while manifesting their own special qualities. Look also at the great masters, like Dilgo Khyentse Rinpoche and Dudjom Rinpoche. Both are considered to have had the highest realization of the Dzogchen teachings; both come from the same tradition; and yet they were very different.

"One simple thing is that when you discover what meditation can bring you, it seems ridiculous to stop yourself from having such a wonderful opportunity. We need to remember the teachings. With the teachings, we need to hear, then to reflect, and then to apply them. In Buddhism, receiving the teachings educates you and makes you very aware. So then the teachings begin to come back to you. Even though there may be resistance, there's also an inner voice, one which has wisdom and begins to guide you, advise you, and inspire you to overcome your resistance."

THE OTHER OCEAN

SOON AFTER MY RETURN from Europe, during one of our weekly telephone conversations, my mother raised the sticky subject of my future plans. I was still reeling from thinking about the future of the world when she asked me if I would stay in California when this project was finished.

 I paused, held my breath, fearing that her reasonable question would rouse the terrible teenager. "I really don't know," I said. My next project required traveling, but after that I could look forward to staying at home, wherever that might be, with my dogs and my books.

"How would you feel about living down here for a while?" she asked. She went on to say she'd been thinking that it was time I owned my own home, and she would like to help make that possible. "It would be nice to have you near for the next years," she said softly. "Perhaps we can start to get to know each other."

I thought about all the years I had been running from my mother, from the time I got my first bicycle and rode too fast and stayed out past dark. Then fast horses, fast cars; I even learned to fly a plane. Was it really my mother and all I thought she stood for that I ran from? Or from the Me I feared I might see in her? . . .

Now she was inviting me back into her life. The teenager woke up. *It's a trap, dummy. She'd be telling us what to wear and who our friends should be. We'd never write another word.* After such a prolonged silence, my mother checked to see if the line had gone dead. Then, in a gentle voice quite new to me, the most independent woman I have ever known said, "I know you have your work, and you'd have your friends. It would be nice just to spend some time together."

Lobsang Lhalungpa's words echoed in my mind: "Buddhism asks us to accept responsibility. Whatever I do or say or think has an impact—not only on my own life, but on my environment, my family, my friends, my society, everyone whose life I touch. That is the beginning of a responsible life. That is what Buddhism teaches."

So my clearer mind saw this as an opportunity for some badly needed karma repair. A way home—to find a lost part of myself, to "walk down a different street."

EPILOGUE

THE PACKING GOES SLOWLY, but I have learned patience. I will be in Florida in time for Christmas. My sons and stepdaughters, their children and their father, are making plans to be there. We are a fractured family, pieces of a peculiar kind of jigsaw. The pieces can be fitted together to make a whole, yet they are separate, and we each form our own puzzle. Jetsun Kusho had said, "We give our children flesh and blood and all the love and tending we are capable of at the time; their karmas are their own."

On my last trip to Florida I learned there was a sangha there among the palms and sea breezes, and I think: *The Wanla oracle never said* which *great ocean*.

I HAVE MET the people of Shambala and listened to their voices as they spoke of the beauty of simple truths. Moments when I listened carefully and with an open heart, I was almost able to hear strains of the song of Shambala. Moments when my eyes saw clearly, I was able to glimpse—quickly, as from a speeding train—images of that kingdom as it slipped by: flashes of crystal truth; still ponds of knowing under a cloudless, turquoise sky; and flowering trees bearing fruit of pure wisdom planted in the time before time.

To some, Shambala is a mythical place, a movie in black and white called *Lost Horizon* and a stage play set to music called *Shangri-la*. I know better. I know now that Shambala is a very real place, a place a few otherwise ordinary-seeming people know how to find. They walk among us with quiet steps and trusting smiles—and a certain light in their eyes.

I HAVE COME to the end of this particular journey, gathering along the way the gentle wise ones I have met and whose words I have listened to and recorded and taken to heart. Now it seems I am beginning another.

The people of Shambala hold the secrets, secrets we must once have known but somehow have lost sight of, that peace must be found first within ourselves before we can begin to expect peace in the world. Theirs was a civilization that lived peacefully for at least a thousand years, until their borders were invaded. They offer us some practical advice for achieving inner peace, a handbook for saving the world, written by some of the last people alive who have access to the instructions.